First published 2001 by Diva Books, an imprint of Millivres Ltd,
part of the Millivres Prowler Group, Worldwide House,
116-134 Bayham Street, London NW1 0BA.

Illustration credits: pp62-63, Figs 1 & 2 by Suzann Gage, from *A New View of
a Woman's Body – A fully illustrated guide* by the Federation of Feminist Women's
Health Centers (Simon & Schuster, NY, 1981); p66, Figs 4 & 5 by Charmaine Brouard.

The moral right of the author has been asserted.

A CIP catalogue record for this book is available from the British Library.

ISBN 1-873741-62-6

Distributed in Europe by Central Books, 99 Wallis Rd, London E9 5LN
Tel: 020 8986 4854 Fax: 020 8533 5821
Distributed in North America by Consortium Book Sales and Distribution,
1045 Westgate Drive, Saint Paul, MN 55114-1065, USA
Tel: 651 221 9035 / 800 283 3572
Distributed in Australia by Bulldog Books, PO Box 700, Beaconsfield, NSW 2014

Printed and bound in the EU by WS Bookwell, Juva, Finland

IT'S A FAMILY AFFAIR
The Complete Lesbian Parenting Book

LISA SAFFRON

Acknowledgements

This book brings together updated versions of two previous books I wrote, with new material based loosely on my parenting column in *Diva* magazine.

Challenging Conceptions – Planning a family by self-insemination was brought out by Cassell in 1994 (and a later edition was self-published in 1998), based on the original guidebook *Getting Pregnant Our Own Way* published by the Women's Health Information Centre in London in 1986. From these books, I have included the stories of Tim, Theresa, Toni, Sheila, Linda, Kim, Jean, Eunice, Bronwen and Andrea.

What About the Children? Sons and daughters of lesbians and gay men speak about their lives was published by Cassell in 1996. From this book, I reprinted the stories of Rikki, Emily, Callum, Amanda, Alice and Rachel.

Special thanks to:

The forty people I interviewed or who wrote accounts for this book, for their willingness to share their insights and tell the stories of their lives, for their time and for their faith in the power of personal revelation to empower others.

The people who commented on draft chapters and gave me relevant information and ideas: Gill Butler, Helen Cosis Brown, Sue Allen, Margaret Gray, Steve Hicks, Caroline Jones, Tara Kaufmann, Karen Creavin, Lindsey Fowler, Sarah Middleton, Safiyyah Cooper, Savitri Holmstrom.

Helen Sandler of Diva Books, a supportive and encouraging editor; Sarah Thomas for transcribing some of the tapes of the interviews; Maria Kennedy for supporting me with her love and constructive criticism throughout; and Zii for teaching me how to be a good enough parent.

LS, 2001

Contents

Foreword i

Introduction: Celebrating Diversity iii

Part I   Preparing for Parenthood

1   Planning a Baby 1

2   You and the Donor 9

3   Donor Screening 47

Part II   Getting Pregnant

4   When Are You Fertile? 61

5   How to Self-inseminate 73

6   Clinic Inseminations 83

7   When It Doesn't Go as Planned 97

Part III   Adoption and Fostering

8   Adoption 125

9   Fostering 143

Part IV   Family Relationships

10   Leaving a Straight Life 155

11   Coming Out to Children 167

12   We Are Family 173

Part V   Our Children's Point of View

13   What About the Children? 217

14   In Their Own Words 227

Part VI   The Outside World

15   In the Classroom 277

16   Legal Recognition 283

17   Facing Challenges 291

Resources 315

USA Organisations 325

Index 329

Foreword

by Helen Sandler of Diva Books

When Lisa Saffron approached us with the idea of putting her expert knowledge and the personal stories of mothers, donors and kids into one book, we knew it was going to help a lot of women with some of the biggest decisions of their lives.

For many years, Lisa had been running workshops on lesbian parenting; writing for *Diva* magazine about families; campaigning for our rights; explaining how to get pregnant by self-insemination... Most of her previous books had fallen out of print but there was a big need for the information they contained, fully updated for the twenty-first century. If anyone was going to fill the gap in the market for a definitive guide to all this, it was Lisa.

And here it is: a book for lesbians who are planning a family, for those who already have children (perhaps from a straight relationship), for every variety of donor and daddy, and for girlfriends caught up in it all – as co-parents, step-parents or reluctant observers.

Whether you are gearing up to get pregnant, to adopt a child, to bring your girlfriend into your family or to come out to your teenager, you should find the help you need within these pages.

Read on – you're in safe hands.

Introduction

CELEBRATING DIVERSITY

This book is about being or becoming a lesbian mother in Britain. It provides advice on how to tackle the trickier dilemmas we face, and it includes the stories of lesbian mothers in their own words.

My aim is to acknowledge our diversity without judgement and to show that we have something in common. I hope that by getting to know each other, even if only through a book, we can share our successful strategies and learn from our mistakes.

This is not an objective overview. I am too much part of the subject matter to have the kind of distance needed for that. What I can provide is a unique insider perspective based on more than nineteen years' intimate involvement with lesbian parenting in this country. My views are informed as much by my personal circumstances as by my political activities.

Getting involved

In 1975, I left the States as a heterosexual married woman and settled in the south of England with my British husband. By the late 1970s, I had come out as a lesbian. In the early 1980s, I got to know a group of lesbian mothers who had written a self-insemination guidebook and who all had young children by insemination. Having found a donor, I became pregnant with my daughter in 1984. I was a single parent for the first five years and met my current partner in 1990. We moved out of London to a large provincial city in 1995 where we are now living happily ever after (well, as happily as you can when you are raising a teenager).

Since the early 1980s, I have been actively involved in writing, advising, leading self-insemination workshops and organising PinkParents UK. These activities have taken me all over the country but it is through leaving London to live in another city that I encountered the greatest diversity of lesbian mothers. I am sure there are more types I haven't met but I can confidently say that lesbian mothers in Britain are a diverse and unclassifiable group. This book reflects that experience.

When we first left London, my partner and I attended a Parent Network course for lesbian mothers led by a lesbian mother. We had little in common other than lesbian motherhood. Most of us were birth parents, but a few were co-parents and step-parents. Some had children from relationships with men, some by self-insemination. Some were middle class, but most were working class, new-age travellers or hippies. Some were single, others were couples. Fathers were around for most but not all. But these differences were not divisive, thanks largely to the people-affirming philosophy of Parent Network and the skill of the co-ordinator.

A sense of connection

It's not necessary to have the exact same experience to empathise with a mother's struggle to come out to her twelve-year-old daughter, to handle bedwetting in an eight-year-old whose father has let her down, to work out when to be a parent to your partner's birth children, to deal with homophobic name-calling by neighbourhood children or to help children understand the taboo about homosexuality at school. But it made a big difference in the level of solidarity that we were all lesbian mothers.

I found the same sense of connection among the lesbians attending my self-insemination workshops. Since 1994, I have organised one- or two-day workshops for lesbians considering getting pregnant. I have held them in London, Birmingham, Bristol, Brighton, Dorset, Glasgow, Leicester, Manchester and Newcastle – wherever there are lesbians keen on having babies, which is everywhere, including the smallest, most isolated village. The aim of the workshops is to talk through the implications of the various options and to learn about fertility awareness, doing inseminations, finding lesbian-friendly clinics and the legal position of donor and co-parents. As well as sharing information, the workshops provide a chance to meet with other lesbians struggling with the same issues.

It's not necessary to come from the exact same place to feel a sense of solidarity and support for other lesbians pursuing their own dreams. Indeed, the women attending these workshops have very little in common other than the hope of becoming a lesbian mother. They come from a variety of lifestyles and are making very different decisions about how to realise their desire to have a child.

Despite our differences, we have two very important things in common. The first is that we are parenting in a society which does not accept our right to be parents. We all experience homophobia differently. We don't all face physical violence, outright rejection by family and friends, bricks through the window or bullying of children at school, but we do all live in a society that privileges heterosexuality and denigrates same-sex relationships. Our experience of homophobia takes its toll and affects our self-esteem and confidence. We all have to develop strategies for protecting ourselves and our children.

The second thing we have in common is that we are committed to parenting. There is no right way to parent. We make mistakes. But we are each doing the best we can, given our individual circumstances, our upbringing and our mental health. I have never failed to be impressed by the responsibility and care lesbians bring to parenting.

The interviews

I interviewed many people for this book: 23 lesbian mothers (nine single mothers and thirteen in couples); six lesbian couples who tried or are trying to become parents; four men who donated sperm to lesbians, each portraying a different type of donor relationship; and seven children of lesbian mothers, ranging in age from twelve to 34 at the time of the interview. All live in Britain, most in England and a few in Scotland and Wales. Except for three interviews, all names have been changed. (Some of the biographies that preface these accounts will be repeated in the course of the book, so as to help the reader recall exactly who is speaking.) They represent some of the experiences and family types that are found among lesbian mothers and lesbians planning to have children. To include the full range would be impossible, but this is a sample of the diversity that characterises our community.

A lesson for the rest of society

This diversity is our strength. Ultimately, it is the one and only lesson we can share with the rest of society – the lesson that there isn't one best type of family.

This lesson is a hard one to learn and has not yet been taken on board by the wider society. The Government claims that the best type of family consists of a married heterosexual couple living together with their children. But what is important is not the shape of the parcel but what is inside. It's not the sex, sexuality or number of parents that matter but something much more intangible, something that can't be legislated or forced. It's the quality of the relationships within the family and the sense of belonging and connection we get from our families. It's how families manage intimacy and growth under pressure from a changing and often threatening world.

I know that it will take a while before this message gets across, judging by the portrayal of lesbian mothers in the British media. We haven't had a good press. The so-called "quality" papers usually ignore our existence, but the tabloids have a consistent agenda to put across – to portray lesbians as "other", different and deviant. Substitute the word alien for lesbian in these headlines and you can see where lesbian mothers fit in to British society over the last two decades.

DOCTOR STRANGE LOVE

– THE BELGRAVIA MAN WHO HELPS LESBIANS HAVE BABIES

London Evening News, 5 January 1978

CHURCH SLAMS A.I.D. BOOK

– LESBIANS THREAT TO MANHOOD, SAYS CLERIC

The Voice, 29 November 1986

SHOULD VIRGINS BE MUMS?

The Sun, 3 December 1991 [during the Great Virgin Birth Debate, "virgin" was used as a code for lesbian]

IT'S TOO MUCH TO BEAR – FINDING OUT YOUR WIFE'S A LESBIAN IS HARD ENOUGH BUT LOSING KIDS TO HER AND WOMAN LOVER IS MORE THAN A MAN CAN STAND

The Sun, 9 September 1994

JUST LIKE ANY HAPPY FAMILY EXCEPT BOTH HIS PARENTS ARE LESBIANS

Daily Mail, 8 November 1997

FURY AT LESBIAN BABY COURSE

– DIY PREGNANCY WORKSHOP 'SICK AND PERVERTED'

Birmingham Post, 1 June 1998

LESBIANS TOOK MY BABY GIRL

The Sun, 17 August 2000

So when I saw the headline LESBIANS 'CAN MAKE BETTER PARENTS' in the *Sunday Express* on 14 February 1999, I had to put it up on my study wall along with the paper's opinion headlined LESBIAN PARENTS GIVE EVERYONE A VALUABLE LESSON IN EQUALITY. The report was of Gill Dunne's groundbreaking research comparing the division of housework, childcare and paid employment among lesbian couples and married couples with young children.

A few months later, when I'd recovered from the shock of seeing a positive portrayal of lesbian motherhood in the tabloid newspapers, a telephone engineer came in to my study to repair my phone. The job required him to sit by the phone and wait for his mate to ring, so he had plenty of opportunity to examine the contents of my study. After casting his eye over the shelves of books on lesbian motherhood and the lesbian posters on the wall, he finally inquired, "You a lesbian, then?" I admitted this was the case. "That true, then?" he asked, nodding towards the *Sunday Express* headline. I shrugged in a non-committal kind of way, not sure what he might come out with next. He continued studying the newspaper clipping with a thoughtful expression on his face. Then he said, "It don't make no difference, does it? Being a lesbian's got nothing to do with whether you're a good parent or not."

Perhaps the message is getting across.

Part I

Preparing for Parenthood

This part of the book is about making the choice to have children and finding a suitable man to be a sperm donor (and perhaps a father or 'uncle' to the baby). Part II then looks at getting pregnant, including both self-insemination and the option of going to a sperm bank.

Planning a Baby 1   You and the Donor 9   Donor Screening 47

1

PLANNING A BABY

If your main involvement is with women then you're unlikely to find yourself pregnant by accident or on a whim – you'll have to make a definite decision. So this first chapter looks at the reasons for having a baby – and the reasons why it might not be the right choice for you.

Feeling broody

The desire to get pregnant is one of the most powerful urges a woman can have. It may hit you with the force of a tornado, knocking all rational thought out of the way, or it may arrive in a calm and orderly fashion. It may appear when your life is sorted out and you are good and ready for a baby. Or it may come at the most inconvenient time, when your life is a mess and the worst thing you can do for yourself and any baby is to act on that urge.

Who knows where this desire comes from? It may be an innate biological imperative, an unconscious plot by our genes to replicate themselves. Or it may be a result of the conditioning even lesbians cannot escape, dictating that woman's role is to bear children. Wherever it comes from, a lot of lesbians (but not all) get smitten by it at some time in their lives.

At the workshops I facilitate for lesbians who are considering getting pregnant, we explore this desire and the ambivalence that inevitably goes with it. We do an exercise where we write on separate slips of paper five statements completing the sentence, "I want to have a baby because..." and five statements completing the sentence, "I don't want to have a baby because...". The idea is to do it quickly without analysing or censoring the ideas. We then pass the slips around the group and read them out (I learned this from Cheri Pies' book *Considering Parenthood* – see Resources).

This is a useful exercise for getting in touch with the reasons why we want a baby as well as the reasons we don't. We are not judging the reasons or using them to defend our desire to anyone else. By writing them down, we bring to consciousness our hopes and fears about having a baby and we realise a deep connection with other lesbians who are struggling with these same issues.

These are some of the reasons women give for wanting a baby:

- "My heart and soul feels it is the right thing to do."
- "It fulfils a need in me."
- "I feel empty when I see other women pregnant or with their babies."
- "I'm a very family-centred person."
- "We have so much love to give a child."
- "I think I would be an excellent mum."
- "I think I could provide a warm, fun-filled, loving environment for a baby, child, young person to grow up in."
- "To make me feel complete as a family with my partner."
- "I want to be needed and to look after a child that is mine and my partner's."
- "I want to have a baby to feel connected to the future of the planet."
- "I want to join the circle of motherhood."
- "The chance to do it better the second time around."
- "I love being with children and want that close relationship with a child of my own."
- "I'll always feel a failure if I don't have a child."
- "I just do."

At the same time, we all have reasons for not wanting a baby:

- "I feel too young. I've got too much to do with my own life before taking on another."
- "It will alter my lifestyle and maybe not for the better."
- "My partner is unsure – she must be certain too, as I see it as a joint decision."
- "I'm scared of the negative effect of prejudice on a child, afraid that the child will feel stigmatised and unhappy."
- "I'm afraid of not being a good parent. Not sure if I could cope with a child."
- "I'm frightened that if I tried and didn't succeed I'd be more unhappy than if I'd not tried or bothered."
- "I am worried about the pressure it will put on my relationship with my partner."
- "I'm single and maybe I won't be able to manage on my own."
- "I'm too selfish. I'll be alone and isolated."
- "What would happen if my partner left and took the child away?"
- "I'm concerned about their future resentment at being fatherless."
- "I haven't had enough fun yet, just being me."
- "Emotional roller coaster."
- "Loss of individual identity and spontaneity."
- "Scared of commitment."

Making the decision

Once you have acknowledged your desire and all your hopes and fears about having a child, it's time to make a decision. You do have a choice whether or not to act on your desire. You do not have to get pregnant just because you are overwhelmed with baby-craving. Having a baby is an enormous undertaking with no guarantee that everything will turn out as you hope.

It will change your life irrevocably and not always for the good. It is a massive financial responsibility – far too scary to add up all the costs. It exposes your own inner child's unmet needs for mothering.

It brings you face to face with how you accept your own sexuality and it uncovers the homophobia simmering away in the rest of society. Your circumstances may be all wrong – no money, not enough support, the wrong relationship, no partner, chronic illness, a demanding career, absorbing activism, mental health problems, whatever. These are all good reasons to decide not to have a child, even if there is a part of you keen to go ahead. If that's the decision you come to, you can deal with the loss of not having a baby and get on with a child-free life or with a life that includes children you haven't given birth to.

But making a conscious decision is difficult and many lesbians delude themselves into thinking they will decide later, when their life is more sorted out. In fact, if you can't bear thinking about it and keep putting it off, you are unconsciously deciding not to have a baby. Our child-bearing years are shorter than most of us like to believe. Although there are a few exceptions, if you haven't started trying to get pregnant by the time you're 38 or 39, you have made a de facto decision not to get pregnant. Yes, I do know of women who left it until they were in their forties and still got pregnant. One of my best friends conceived by self-insemination at the age of 43 and I am delighted for her. But the exceptions prove the rule. For every successful forty-plus pregnancy carried to term, there must be a hundred failures. (That's my impression from the thousands of enquiries I've had over the years.)

I don't believe that anyone makes rational decisions about something as momentous and as unknowable as having a baby. Decisions emerge from within us and then we rationalise them. The truth is that, like heterosexual people, we don't have that much control over our lives. We don't always know what we want, and when our circumstances change, our desires also change. For some people, the decision to have a child is easily made: it feels right. Others spend months, if not years, trying to decide but paralysed by all the issues.

Whether it's easy or hard, at some point you make your decision. The younger you are, the more leeway you have: you can afford to take the time to think through the implications of the various options. The older you are, the more urgent it is to make a conscious decision. There are no obvious right or wrong decisions but you will have to live with the consequences, so think them through before you start. This is where lesbians are at an advantage over heterosexual couples who have babies by accident: we have the opportunity to plan and prepare. We all know that planned babies are wanted babies and wanted babies are happy babies and happy babies don't grow up into axe murderers. At least that's the theory.

The options

Once you've made up your mind that you do want to get pregnant, you have to sort out your source of sperm. You have three options: sex with a man, self-insemination, or donor insemination at a clinic (sperm bank).

i. Sex with a man

The first option has been tried and tested. It is a proven method of getting pregnant. Some lesbians feel that the other options are too clinical and impersonal. They prefer to have sex with the donor in order to get pregnant even though they are not having an ongoing sexual relationship with him. The issues about screening, timing of intercourse, legal position of the man etc. are the same as for self-insemination. (See Kat's story, p44.)

ii. Self-insemination

Self-insemination is the simple act of placing a man's sperm in a woman's vagina without intimate contact. It is a non-medical, low-tech way of making a baby without having sex with a man. It has a good track record. Sometime in the 1970s, lesbians figured out how to do it. They found men willing to donate their sperm or Harley Street doctors willing to provide them with fresh sperm. They inseminated themselves at home using kitchen implements. And we've been doing it ever since.

In this book, Bronwen, Sheila, Tara, Justine, Jude, Eunice, Lou, Andrea, Angela, and Jean have all done self-insemination, and the next few chapters tell you how.

iii. Clinic inseminations

Donor insemination at a clinic is a variation of self-insemination but tarted up to appear like a reproductive technology. The differences are superficial. At a clinic, sperm is frozen rather than fresh. It is placed in your vagina by a nurse using a long thin straw. You lie on a table with a speculum inside your vagina. You pay a lot of money. But fundamentally it is the same as self-insemination. It is not a fertility treatment. If you have fertility problems, donor insemination will not increase your chances of getting pregnant. In fact, the freezing of the sperm means that you are less likely to conceive at a clinic than you would be using fresh sperm.

Of the women in this book, Theresa, Linda, Amy, Casey and Andrea have been to these clinics. For more information, read Chapter 6.

Conditions for success

None of these methods allows you to overcome the limitations of your biology. To maximise your chances of getting pregnant, take account of these five factors:

i. Fertility

Both you and the donor should be fertile. Some fertility problems can be treated. Women with blocked Fallopian tubes cannot have them unblocked but may be able to conceive by IVF (in vitro fertilisation) instead of donor insemination. There may not be a treatment for men with low sperm counts.

ii. Age

Getting pregnant is something to do in your twenties or early thirties. For women in their late thirties and early forties, it is often unsuccessful. It is harder to conceive as you get older and the chance of miscarriage is higher. Above the age of forty, half of all pregnancies end in miscarriage. Women in heterosexual relationships having unprotected sex over many years do occasionally get pregnant in their forties, but the circumstances are very different.

The drop in fertility is due to ageing of the eggs, which causes their gradual loss and inability to fertilise. This happens even if you continue to ovulate and have regular menstrual cycles. There is not the same drop in fertility for men, although an upper age limit of 55 is recommended for men donating sperm to clinics. Pregnancy is somewhat less likely to occur with the sperm of older men.

iii. Timing of inseminations
You should be able to recognise the days in your menstrual cycle when you are fertile. (See below.)

iv. Frequency of inseminations
You need to inseminate at least twice during your fertile days, and preferably three or four times. The more inseminations you do, the more likely you are to conceive.

v. Realistic expectations
It may take a year even if you are under thirty and meeting all the conditions for success. As you get older, it may take several years before you conceive.

What next?

Assuming you have taken account of all the conditions for success, the rest of this part of the book looks at the arrangements you will need to make with a sperm donor or 'daddy' before trying to get pregnant. Part II then describes how to go about getting pregnant, whether with a donor or at a clinic.

2

YOU AND THE DONOR

If you have chosen self-insemination by donor then you will also need to choose a man! This chapter looks at finding a suitable donor and sorting out what kind of arrangement will be right for you. It includes several stories from women and men about their own arrangements – what worked out well, and what caused problems.

Finding a donor

There are various ways of finding someone suitable. Some women have a friend who seems an obvious choice or has raised the topic himself – often a gay man. Others cast the net wider, perhaps asking around until they find a friend of a friend, or advertising in the gay press for someone they don't know. Before and after finding someone who seems suitable, you will need to think about what kind of relationship you will have with each other and how involved he will be with the child (see "The relationship" below).

Whatever you do, it will be cheaper and less medicalised than using a clinic (explored in Chapter 6) but, unlike the anonymity a clinic provides, there will be a connection of some sort with the man. Even if he is not going to be involved with the child – and many donors aren't – he will be around for a while as you try to get pregnant; and both you and your child will think about him in the future.

In other words, whether or not the donor is in it for the long term, you are entering a relationship, with all the uncertainty inherent in any kind of relationship. So, how you can you possibly know if it's going to work out? It is very tempting in your initial meetings to seek what you have in common and to focus on building a harmonious relationship. You are on your best behaviour and eager for it to work out; and you may have to force yourself to talk about how you would cope with differences and conflict.

It seems sensible to learn from each other's experiences and not repeat mistakes, so based on my own and numerous other stories I've heard over the years, I've drawn up a few guidelines. They will not provide any guarantee though, and you should not go ahead until you feel comfortable with the degree of risk that remains. The guidelines are listed below under two rules: "Check" and "Talk".

Rule 1: Check

If a complete stranger offers to be a donor, check him out before you start inseminating, even if he is not going to be very involved in the child's life. Here are some guidelines:

- Talk on the phone or correspond a few times before meeting in person.
- Don't give out your address until you've corresponded.
- The first time you meet, go to a public place. Bring a chaperone.
- Take references from someone who can vouch for him.
- Ask to see some ID.
- Get to know him over a period of time – weeks or months rather than hours. You cannot tell what someone is like after talking to him for half an hour in the pub.
- If your gut feeling is uneasy, trust it. Break off the relationship at this stage while you can. Don't leave it until you've got a baby and you're stuck with him for the next 18 years.

- If he asks you to marry him in exchange for donating, do not even consider it. (If you marry the donor, he has automatic parental responsibility, the same as that of the birth mother.)
- If he won't agree to get tested for sexually transmitted diseases, find another donor.
- If he says, "What's the matter? Don't you trust me?" or refuses to answer your questions openly and honestly, find another donor.
- Explain what self-insemination is. He may genuinely not realise that it doesn't involve sex.
- If he insists on doing it the natural way, find another donor.
- Explain that you need him to be available whenever you are fertile and that it may take six months or more.
- Agree to reconsider after a set length of time.

Rule 2: Talk

When you know a man well enough to go ahead with inseminating and you're planning anything more than a traceable donor arrangement (see below), talk with him about the expectations you both bring to the arrangement. Don't assume anything – we don't have the language to communicate effectively with each other about different kinds of parenting arrangements. You may want him to be a "distant uncle" donor but he may be thinking "close uncle" (see the categories below). You may want him to be a "daddy" when he's thinking "uncle". Spell out what you mean, preferably in writing. Clarify your own bottom line before you talk about it with him. Don't be so flexible that you'll do whatever he says he wants. It's not honest. Here are the main themes to discuss:

- Parental responsibility – what kind of parenting role do you want from him? Who are the primary parents going to be? Who makes the main decisions? Do you want him to have a parental responsibility order?
- Relationship to your partner – if you are in a couple, how does he relate to her? Does he understand and respect her position as parent?

- Amount of contact – of course, you can't know yet but if regular contact means twice a year to you and twice a week to him, then you need to know that sooner rather than later.
- Money – is he going to make a financial contribution to you to help raise the child? Is he going to set up a fund for the child's future? Are you going to accept gifts? What are you going to say to the Child Support Agency if you ever need to claim benefits?
- Birth certificate – you can only put his name on if he agrees.
- Wills – who are you planning to name as guardian if the birth mother were to die?
- Last name – whose last name will the child have?
- Support – are you expecting him to be part of your family support network? Do you want him to babysit or take the children on holiday? If you have to go into hospital for a few months, will he look after the children?

The relationship

There are five main types of donor relationship you can arrange via self-insemination and they can be labelled as follows:

i.   *Anonymous:* You and the donor do not know each other's identity.
ii. *Traceable:* The donor is not involved in the child's life but is willing to be contacted.
iii. *"Uncle":* He is involved but does not have parental responsibility.
iv. *Daddy:* He shares parental responsibility.

i. Anonymous donor

When I went looking for a donor back in 1983, the lesbians I knew who were into having babies were all into having anonymous donors. They were mistrustful of men and for good reason: at the time, fathers were getting the better end of the deal in custody disputes with lesbian mothers. I put the word out to my friends and within weeks, I'd got an offer. It was a rather complicated and, as it turned out, unworkable offer, but it was an offer.

Someone knew of a heterosexual men's group who were willing to donate on condition that their anonymity be protected. The men were worried about a mother appearing out of the blue to pursue them for child support. I was worried about them showing up out of the blue to claim their paternal rights and take my baby away. It was an agreement based on mutual mistrust. Unfortunately, it was also an arrangement based on mutual disorganisation and poor communication involving conspiratorial intermediaries, reckless car trips, mistimed donations, and sperm left in front of a gas fire to cook. I put up with this for three months before taking up the offer of a traceable donor.

There are other ways to assure anonymity. You could go to a clinic, in which case the donor will not be the legal father of your child: under the Human Fertilisation and Embryology Act, he abdicates parental responsibility by signing a consent form. You don't have to go to a clinic if you want an anonymous donor but when you do it by self-insemination, you don't have the same guarantees. You have to put your trust in the intermediary rather than the donor. It's the intermediary who will keep your identities a secret from each other and will reassure you that the donor is not posing any risk of sexually transmitted diseases. If you don't have confidence in the intermediary, this option could cause a lot of anxiety.

Men who are willing to donate anonymously are often prepared to donate to many different women. That means your child is likely to have siblings around whom they may well meet at some point, not knowing that they are related. They deserve to know that they have brothers and sisters around.

It is also fairly inevitable that children will ask where they came from. They usually become intensely interested around the ages of three to five, especially after they have been told the biological facts of life and have met a few children with fathers. They ask questions like, "Who is my daddy? Why don't I have a daddy? Why can't I meet my daddy? Why doesn't my daddy come to see me?" If you have used an anonymous donor, be prepared with answers to these questions.

Without revealing his identity, an anonymous donor could write a letter addressed to the child, explaining why he agreed to donate and what he's like as a person, including a photo. That may be all a child needs to satisfy their curiosity about where they come from. It seems a small thing to ask and would mean a lot to the child.

In this chapter, Sheila talks about using an anonymous donor, and Mark talks about being one. Sheila's son, Tim, gives his perspective later in the book (p227).

ii. Traceable donor

A traceable donor is a man who is not involved in the child's life but who is willing to be traced and contacted. He may be anonymous but prepared to keep an intermediary posted of his current address. Or he may be known but have little to do with the family once the child is born. As with anonymous donors, the least a traceable donor can do is provide a photo and write a letter for the child to read when they're old enough.

If the child traces the donor when they are grown, then whatever comes of that relationship is up to them. Hopefully it will be rewarding for both. More problematic is what to do if the child wants to trace the donor while they're still a child. Presumably you discussed this eventuality with the donor before you went ahead. If the deal was no tracing before age sixteen and you've got a persistent ten-year-old, you can try to persuade either the donor or the ten-year-old to change their minds. If neither will budge, you know who your child inherited their stubbornness from.

If you didn't discuss this eventuality, it's still worth a try. But it could potentially be a big change for all of you. You may decide to upgrade your donor from "traceable" to "close uncle" or even to "daddy". Everyone in the family may have different desires about the donor's future involvement. Don't be surprised if you and your partner feel threatened by the possibility of greater involvement with the donor: it can destabilise a couple's co-parenting arrangement. And don't be surprised by how much even a child as young as three years has internalised the concept of Daddy. When I introduced my daughter to her donor, she was three and a half and had never met him before. Within an hour of their first meeting, she was calling him Daddy, looking at him adoringly, telling him she loved him and trying to get him to hold hands with me. We converted him into a "close uncle" and fortunately that worked for all of us.

If you haven't already got to know him before you got pregnant, I would advise you to spend some time getting to know him before you introduce your young child to him and before you decide what new role you want him to play in the family. Try to determine, if at all possible, what kind of influence he'll have on your child. If he's racist or homophobic or unreliable or violent, do you want him in your child's life? As the parent, you are responsible for your child's welfare. You don't have to introduce them even if the child wants to meet him.

Read Tara's account for a story of a change from "traceable" to "close uncle".

iii. Uncle donor – distant or close

The uncle donor role is an attempt to change the rules of the game and to establish new types of parenting relationships. The idea is that the donor is known and involved but does not have full parental responsibility. Parental responsibility is a legal concept defined in the Children Act as "all the rights, duties, powers, responsibilities and authority which by law a parent has in relation to the child and his property." When you ask a man to be an uncle donor, you and he are picking and choosing from these rights and duties. It can work, but he could later invoke the law if you had a disagreement about his involvement.

In law, a father is a father regardless of whether he made the child by sex or by self-insemination and regardless of how much contact he has had with his child. (There is no legal recognition of the uncle donor role.) A donor is considered an unmarried father and does not automatically have parental responsibility but could acquire it if he applied to court for a parental responsibility order. The court could grant it even if you objected and even if he had signed a donor agreement contract saying he would never apply.

When deciding applications for parental responsibility, the court has to heed the Children Act, which is based on the presumption that a child needs a father, not that a father has rights to the child. The court will look at the commitment the father has shown to the child, the attachment between them and his reasons for applying. Although there is homophobia in the courts, you should assume that a gay donor would be granted parental responsibility, especially if he has established a relationship with the child. But the court wants to be satisfied that giving parental responsibility will positively add to the child's welfare, not just meet the father's needs.

Contrary to what many lesbians believe, it is contact with the child, not payment of money, which the courts are interested in. If the known donor had never paid a penny towards the child's living expenses nor given any gifts but had had regular contact, the court could still grant him a parental responsibility order.

Should you put his name on the birth certificate? You can only do so if he agrees. But since you asked him to be a known donor and he has agreed to be known, it doesn't make much sense to keep it a secret especially from the child. What message does it give to the child to grow up knowing their birth father and then see a blank space on their birth certificate where the father's name should be? A birth certificate is an important document of identity. Currently, an unmarried father whose name is on the birth certificate does not automatically have parental responsibility, but the Government have debated the possibility.

In practice, a parental responsibility order does not necessarily mean any change to your child's day-to-day life. However, if the donor applies for and is granted a residence order, it would have implications for who the child lives with.

Andrew and Alan share their experiences as known "uncle" donors. For the mothers' perspectives, see the stories of Tara, Bronwen and Angela.

iv. Daddy donor

A daddy donor is a birth father who shares parental responsibility with the birth mother. As an unmarried father, he has no automatic legal rights but may acquire them in one of two ways:

- By applying for a court order for parental responsibility under Section 4 of the Children Act.

- By entering into a parental responsibility agreement with the birth mother. This must be properly witnessed and registered with the court.

If he acquires parental responsibility by either of these means, he will share this with the birth mother and anyone else who has it. His responsibilities will be equal to those of the birth mother. In practical terms, the possession of a parental responsibility order has little effect on a father's role unless the relationship with the mother breaks down or she becomes unable to exercise her parental responsibility.

You can get a form for a parental responsibility agreement from Oyez Law Stationers (telephone 0870 737 7370). Having been signed by you both, it must be sent with two copies to the Principal Registry of the Family Division of the High Court, Somerset House, Strand, London WC2R 1LP.

If you're going for the "daddy" or "close uncle" options, get to know each other inside out. Talk about your values, your childhood experiences of family life, how you were parented, your fantasies about having a child, your politics and life plans. Have dinner together. Visit each other's homes. Meet the parents and important people. Ask close friends what he's like on a bad day. Find out his failings and weaknesses. Spend some intensive time together – go off for a weekend or a week-long holiday. Plan a project together so you can see how you resolve conflicts. Show each other your true selves, warts and all. Take your time. For accounts of this type of getting-to-know-you process, see Justine's and Simon's stories later in the chapter.

Another thing to be aware of is that when you make a baby with a man, you can develop intense feelings for him. If you fall in love with him, neither your partner nor the man is likely to be pleased by this new development, especially if the man is gay.

Child support

If you want financial support from the donor, you are entitled to apply to the Child Support Agency for him to pay maintenance as an absent parent. If you ever need to claim income support, the Child Support Act requires you to name the father. This act came into force in April 1993 and is part of the Government's attempts to make fathers face up to their financial responsibilities. The Act is enforced by the Child Support Agency.

The Agency has issued guidelines saying that where a woman has "made her own private arrangements for artificial insemination, the man concerned is the child's father and should be named". The Agency will not accept the validity of any arrangements you might have made with the donor releasing him from parenting responsibilities. You are only exempt from naming the donor if you can show that "there are reasons why harm or undue distress would result" or that you genuinely do not know who he is. The rule is retrospective, meaning it also applies to women who did self-insemination years ago. If you refuse to name the donor, you could have your benefit cut by twenty per cent for the first six months and by a lesser amount for another twelve months.

The Child Support Act has worried potential donors and may have deterred some men from agreeing to donate. In fact, most lesbians do not want financial support from the donor – if this includes you, tell him. If you are claiming income support, there is no advantage to you in naming the donor – you will still get the same amount of benefits from the Agency regardless of how much he is asked to pay. In any case, he is not required to pay you; his payment goes to the Agency.

These guidelines do not apply to women who have had donor insemination with an anonymous donor at a clinic. In that situation, the child is considered to have no legal father. However, you will be asked for evidence that you did go to a clinic.

A family lawyer's perspective

I spoke to Gill Butler, a family law solicitor who has been working with lesbian mother cases since the early 1980s and is on the Board of Directors of Stonewall. She has seen disputes where the donor has gone to court to push for more rights, against the wishes of the mother.

If it does come to court, the court won't look at what money's been paid, only at what kind of contact there's been. There could have been three years of regular contact between the donor and the child and no money from him whatsoever – the court will only consider the contact as important. ... Lesbians can't have it both ways – if you get men involved in these relationships, you can't wheel them in and out when it suits you. You're stuck with them. No one can ever say that you won't end up with more than you bargained for. So unless you're prepared to take that risk and to accept that you can't control what that father is going to be like, you shouldn't get into a known donor relationship.

You can't sign a binding contract determining in advance how much contact the donor will have or that he doesn't have to pay any money. A written donor agreement is not binding. It is not enforceable. The most you can say about a donor agreement is that it could be useful in court depending on what weight a judge gave to it. I think they are worth doing from a psychological point of view rather than a legal point of view. It helps to concentrate people's minds on the issues that they need to think about and the ones that they can't resolve now but which could become an issue later.

It's not always easy to sit down and consider the things that might go wrong. The fact is that a man's emotions may change when he sees his child. He may say he won't do this, that, or the other but as soon as the child is born, he may want to be more involved. To give them the benefit of the doubt, some of the men didn't know that was how they would feel once the child was born. Once you start to build a relationship with a child, it's very hard not to want much more than was agreed at the beginning. Unless you have contact with small children, you don't realise how often you have to see them in order to get them to know who you are.

I think that we don't respect the child enough in all this. The contract should be between the child and the parent rather than between the donor and the mother-to-be. There could be several separate contracts – one between the child and the donor, one between the child and the birth mother, one between the child and the other mother. That would get people to think seriously about what they're getting into.

Donor by self-insemination – Summary

Legal position
Considered an unmarried father. Has no legal rights but may acquire parental responsibility by court order (Section 4 Children Act). This gives him status as a parent but the amount of contact and who the child lives with will have to be decided by a court, if it can't be reached by mutual agreement.

Birth certificate
Not named unless both mother and donor agree.

Inheritance
Child has the right to make a claim to inherit from donor's estate if the donor dies when the child is in need of financial support. The donor can make a will stating why he should not make financial provision for this child.

Financial considerations
Donor may negotiate expenses with mother/s for inseminations and for child support.

If mother is claiming benefits, donor could be named to Child Support Agency. If mother refuses to name donor, she risks having benefits reduced.

An anonymous donor – Sheila's story

Sheila became pregnant by self-insemination with an anonymous donor and gave birth to her son Tim in 1979. She gave this account in 1993.

As soon as I learned that it was a possibility, I decided I wanted to have an anonymous donor rather than pick up a strange man and sleep with him. There were a number of reasons. I knew that sleeping with a man could never be a neutral experience for me. If I did get a baby out of it, then I might have ended up with lovely feelings about the man or I might have wanted to have more contact with him. If it turned out to be a horrible experience, I wouldn't want that to be the start of my child. I always felt that I didn't want to make a long-term commitment to someone for all those years, whether to a man or to a woman. It seemed to me that that's what I would be doing if I knew the man. Tying us to someone else was just not what I had in mind for me and my child. I felt that it was better not to have a father than to have a vague shadowy figure, some hazy memory. Doing it by an anonymous donor was more neutral.

In 1978, there was a big shock-horror scandal in the papers because the *Evening News* had exposed the fact that lesbians were going to a doctor in Harley Street and getting sperm from him.

DOCTOR STRANGE LOVE – THE BELGRAVIA MAN WHO HELPS LESBIANS HAVE BABIES,
London Evening News, 5 January 1978

At that point I was definitely thinking about having a baby, but I only knew how to get pregnant by the traditional method. So the *Evening News* opened up another possibility. I actually went to that doctor once and did it. I got his name from Sappho [a lesbian organisation]. He gave me a five-minute interview during which he told me to work out for myself when I ovulate and come along when I was ready. When I did go along, I was given the sperm in a little plastic vial inside a brown envelope. I don't even remember being given any advice about keeping it warm or having to hurry home. We went in a pub and I put it down my bra to keep it warm and then went home and did the insemination.

Having done that once, I realised that it was crazy going to a doctor.

All I needed was to find a man and do it myself. Just when I was thinking that, I saw an ad in the *London Women's Liberation Newsletter* advertising a group for lesbians who were thinking about getting pregnant. I answered the ad and six of us started meeting and talking about it. Most of us had already tried some way or other. Very soon after we started meeting, we began thinking about ways of finding men. The obvious way at the time was to think about gay men. Through a friend of a friend, we heard of a gay men's consciousness raising group. We asked them to talk in their group about being donors for us; and the answer came back that they would do it. We set up a dinner for some of the women and some of the men to talk about the practicalities and what we wanted from the arrangement – to make sure there were no misunderstandings.

We set it up so that whenever we needed the sperm, we rang up a man who took responsibility for that task for a couple of months, until someone else took over. That man would phone round all the blokes, sort out who would do it for us, then ring us back to tell us where to go and when to pick it up. The first few times I did it, I arranged for somebody to go and pick it up for me. We were really careful about keeping it all anonymous. By about the third month, it didn't seem important anymore not to know where the donor's house was. We started to go to their houses and do the inseminations there. That was much nicer than having to drag all the way back again, especially as I couldn't always find someone to go and get it for me. It seemed easier to just go there, do it in the room, lie down for a few minutes, and then go away. I did get a glimpse of the men but it was a different man on each occasion so I only have vague memories of what they looked like. I couldn't distinguish which one it was that gave me the sperm to get pregnant.

Fourteen years later and with a twelve-year-old son, I feel confirmed that the decision to use an anonymous donor was right for me and Tim. The way Tim and I always talk about it is that he doesn't have a father. We talk about the story quite often. He knows the exact details. I don't want to say that I haven't questioned it but I don't think anything has ever led me to feel that I wish I had done it differently.

An anonymous donor – Mark's story

Mark is a 39-year-old gay man who has donated anonymously to two lesbian couples. He was motivated by an urge to pass on his genes, which first arose after he was bereaved. He was interviewed in 2001.

I'd always mocked the idea you sometimes hear of obtaining immortality through your children or that there's a basic male urge to leave children behind [when you die]. I'd always assumed it was a social construct. But the way it came up for me [after my lover was killed] made me wonder if perhaps there is something instinctive there – that I had such an urge on an unconscious level. I can't say there was any rationality to it. Facing the certainty of death made me want to at least leave my genes behind.

Although I liked the idea of knowing that I had a child out there somewhere, I didn't really want to be involved in any way or committed emotionally or financially. Since any child that knows you're its father is likely to expect some involvement, that would require that he or she didn't know the identity of the genetic father. That is the way that I grew up. I was adopted when I was a few months old. I am very happy with the parents I've got and have no interest in finding anything out about my genetic parents. Certainly, there are people who don't get on with their parents who fantasise about having 'real' parents somewhere else. Those are the ones who cause the media reports giving the impression that all adopted children want to trace their birth parents. My guess would be that my sister and I are more typical than the ones who get in the media.

I was aware that there are lesbians who self-inseminate, and that they tend to go for gay donors, for convenience or ideological reasons. I was well aware of this from talking to my landlord who had brokered such an agreement about thirty years ago. More recently I had seen quite regular ads in the *Pink Paper*.

… Then I saw an advert for a 'Donor or Daddy' course for gay men. I thought that if I learned one useful thing, it might be worth it! So I did it and found it very valuable. I was the only one there who said I would prefer to be completely uninvolved. There were men who wanted only occasional involvement and some who were interested in the godfather/uncle style of donor. But I was the only person who was quite happy to deposit my sperm and walk away.

I would feel unhappy about donating to a single woman. Without wanting to sound like a *Daily Express* reader, I do think children are much better brought up by at least two parents – children need to observe a successful loving partnership at close quarters, if they're going to be good at doing that sort of thing when they grow up themselves.

I wouldn't mind how old the prospective mothers are from the point of view of parenting ability. I don't think age makes a difference there – my mother was pushing forty when I was adopted. But I guess one has to take into account the reduction in fertility – until I went on the 'Donor or Daddy' course, I didn't realise how that works. We all hear about women's biological clock, but I guess I tended to think of the menopause shutting it off, that the clock suddenly stops. Of course, after my first success, I thought I could get anyone pregnant!

I was happy to donate to lesbian couples but didn't realise until I met the first couple how important it was to me that they be good parents. The woman who led the course got in contact with me a few months later and asked if I was interested in donating to a lesbian couple in this area. Out of the blue, I started feeling terribly responsible for the potential baby. I had visions of a genetic child of mine coming back in twenty years' time complaining that the couple hadn't been perfect parents, or indeed that they had been seriously inadequate parents. I was unhappy about donating without feeling confident that they would be really good parents. I met them with their existing child and spent about two hours grilling them. When I got back home, I felt I'd really gone over the top. They knew what they were getting themselves into as they already had one child who seemed to be a sweet, happy little thing. They seemed good common-sensical people. But I was still affected by long-term depression, and my obsessive carefulness was probably part of that. They very sensibly took the donation from somebody else they'd met.

It was my own silly fault they went elsewhere but I knew there would be other opportunities. Which there were, thanks to PinkParents. A year later, I was contacted about another lesbian couple. By then I was much better, and I took a much more sensible view. I didn't ask to see any dark secrets there may have been in their cupboard. Let's face it, heterosexuals have children without anyone expecting them to give any proof of qualifications!

They asked me to have a sperm test – which I did, thinking there'd be no problem. I got a decidedly unfavourable report back. What surprised me was how unpleasant it was getting the letter telling me that my sperm count was low and I would be unlikely to be a father. It wasn't one of the great disappointments of my life – it certainly was nothing compared to my lover's death, but it hit me hard below the belt. The instincts are stronger than I'd given them credit for.

I phoned the PinkParents helpline and told them the results. I was asked if I'd taken antibiotics in the previous three months which I had. I was told that the antibiotics could have affected my sperm production. I hadn't known anything about that and the doctor at the GUM clinic – who wasn't an expert in fertility – also didn't know about antibiotics affecting sperm production. So I don't know if it was that.

The couple decided that low-rated sperm was better than none. We tried and it worked first time round! I was delighted. I couldn't believe how much I was like the stereotypical male. I was not only pleased that I'd got what I wanted and pleased for the couple, but compared to those heterosexual so-called men, I was on top form. How many of them get a woman pregnant the first time? I had thought this male hang-up about fertility was a culturally determined thing, to estimate your masculinity and worth by your ability to produce children, but it was a real boost to my ego.

When the baby was born, they left a message on my answerphone saying, 'Since we don't have your address, we can only send you a photo, if you'd like it, through PinkParents.' I left a reply message on their answerphone, saying unclearly, 'I'll pass on the photo, thanks.' I think they heard it as, 'Pass on the photo.' So I got a photo. He looked like any baby. It didn't matter to me at all to see him – just knowing he was there was what mattered. The masculine urges that I thought I hadn't got were extremely delighted that he was a son. Seeing the photo did not change my views about being involved.

In a sense, once was enough. Certainly after the baby's birth, I thought 'Right, that's done. I've achieved it.' But another two or three would be fine. Basically, what it does come down to, and this is at a level I am just about conscious of, is wanting to be sure there is going to be someone there. This baby could die of cot death or in a motorcycle crash in fifteen years' time or he may not leave descendants himself. Increasingly, people nowadays don't. Even heterosexuals decide they can't be bothered. And so when PinkParents asked if I would consider another lesbian couple, I was happy to try and oblige.

Both of the women tried to get pregnant. One of them might not be too fertile herself, whereas the other had fallen pregnant the first time she tried with another donor. We carried on trying for about ten months without success. The last time we spoke, they were going on holiday, and they said 'Let's take a break and come back to it again afterwards'. I've been meaning to call them and ask how things are going. Maybe they've found another donor and are hoping that that'll be more successful with someone else. In which case, I've no problems with that and wish them the best of luck.

It is discouraging that they're still not pregnant. It's a big effort for them. They live about an hour and a half drive away and they come to where I live. It interferes with the rest of my life to a certain extent. I'm not able to go out on a certain night. I have to fit things round and take a bit of time. It's certainly an inconvenience. And yes, it is disappointing carrying on doing this and nothing happening. I didn't say I wanted to call a halt or anything, when they were obviously putting in so much more effort than I was.

It's useful to have an intermediary with the kind of arrangement where the donor is anonymous. I've wanted to feel confident that I am providing sperm to women who will be good future parents. Having been over the top about it the first time, I thought it through and came to the conclusion that you have to trust people in life, and I know the woman at PinkParents well enough to trust her on this.

On the identity question, I feel more comfortable with the women knowing only my phone number and alias. None of the women seemed in the least offended. One even said they preferred that, too. That way, if any of their friends did ask what the donor's name was or where he lived, they could honestly say they didn't know. I never knew the names of the first couple. They had an intermediary phone me to arrange collection of the sperm. I do know the names of the second couple and what town they live in and I'm sure I could track them down easily enough. They must have known that when they gave me their names and phone number. Obviously they were happy to trust PinkParents' assessment of me that I wouldn't be demanding parental rights. They took it on trust that if I'm arranging all this to remain anonymous, I'm not likely to change my mind and want access to the baby.

I'm very happy being an anonymous donor. I don't regret anything I've done. I have made two lesbians very happy. I hope I've contributed towards creating someone who will enjoy life. You can't be sure what somebody's life is going to be like and whether they're going to end up feeling glad to have been born, but at least he's got the chance.

From traceable to uncle donor – Tara's story

Tara's experience is of starting off with a traceable donor agreement and ending up with an uncle-type donor – Pierre, who has sadly died. She got pregnant in 1984 and has a sixteen-year-old daughter, Tyger. She first wrote this account in 1993 before Pierre died, and updated it in 2001.

My girlfriend had asked Pierre, a gay friend of hers, if he would donate. Being a generous person, he agreed. But being a thoughtful person, it wasn't an easy decision for him to make. He wondered what kind of world the child would come into, what kind of mother I would turn out to be and how he would feel not having any involvement with the child. In the end, he did it partly as an act of solidarity between gay men and lesbians but mostly because he came to like me and to respect my wish to be a mother.

We met once or twice, talked it over and agreed that he would have nothing to do with the baby but was willing to meet the child whenever the child wanted. He seemed nice enough, but I didn't get to know him very well. Since he wasn't going to be involved, I didn't think it mattered what he was like as a person. I asked him a few questions about his risk of sexually transmitted diseases and probed no further. Although I went to his house to inseminate, I didn't have the time to get to know him any better because I was pregnant by the third month. During that time, Pierre always made himself available when I needed him, even cancelling other arrangements.

As agreed, that was the end of his involvement with me. He was pleased to have helped me out and I was over the moon to be pregnant. I felt immense gratitude and affection towards him but no desire to have anything more to do with him.

When Tyger was born, I held in my arms a miracle of life that he had made possible. Pierre had given me the most wonderful gift I'll ever have in my life and for that, I'll be forever grateful to him. In 1991, just before he became ill, he told me that he had no regrets and believed it was one of the most valuable things he had done. I was struck by how much she looked like him, how I could see him in her eyes and face. I felt a connection to him that I might not have felt if I hadn't met him at all.

I sent him a photo of her, inviting him to come and see us, and was very disappointed not to hear from him. I assumed that it was of no interest to him and let it drop. He told me later that the photo stirred up a whole heap of emotions that he didn't think he could handle. But he did think about us over the next few years and there were times when he thought of making contact. Being a considerate person, he worried about scaring me with a letter out of the blue and was sensitive to the effect of stories about child custody cases on lesbian mothers.

In 1988 after he'd tested HIV-positive, I heard in a roundabout way that Pierre wished he had visited us when he'd had the opportunity. Becoming HIV-positive had influenced his feelings about seeing Tyger. He told me that he had always had a fantasy that Tyger might contact him when she was sixteen or so and wanted to meet her daddy. Since the test, he was aware that he might not be alive when she became old enough to look for him.

When Tyger was just three, she had begun to ask about her daddy. In fact, 'Where is my daddy?' were nearly her first words, after she had perfected the word 'no'. I gave her my prepared line that her daddy was a very nice man named Pierre who had generously given me sperm so that I could have a baby and she was that very much-wanted baby. I had decided not to describe him to her as a donor because I can't relate to that term. He was a real person, not just a source of sperm. In my mind it didn't seem very real to make a distinction between the donor and the daddy.

She bought this story for about a week. Then, out of the blue, came the next logical question. 'I want to see my daddy. Where is he?' Again, I was ready with the line about different kinds of families with different kinds of daddies. We have the kind of family where the daddy does not live with us. Some families have two mummies and no daddy. Some have one mummy and one daddy where they all live together. In other families there is one mummy or only one daddy. Then again, there are daddies that live with their children all of the time, some of the time or hardly ever. I was able to provide examples from people she knew for most of these variants of family life. I was quite pleased with myself. At the end of this recital, she said very firmly, 'Why can't I see my daddy?'

If I had never known Pierre, I suppose Tyger's curiosity could have gone no further. But I did know him and I was happy about them meeting. Since he had only agreed to be a donor, I didn't feel I had the right to change the conditions we had set years before. Unknown to me, Pierre was thinking along the same lines. He too wanted to meet Tyger but felt he couldn't invade my territory or presume that he had a right to see the child he had made possible. I wrote to him and he and I met without Tyger to discuss what we were getting into. I didn't think that a one-off meeting would be enough for her nor did it feel very satisfying to me. We agreed on regular contact but that he wouldn't take on any parental responsibility. He saw his role as more like that of an uncle. He respected our original arrangement and the kind of family I had created and never had any desire to subvert that.

We knew that we were embarking on relationships for which we had no role models. Most other donors that I knew of were anonymous. I was aware of hostility from other lesbians who disapproved or felt threatened by my choice to let Tyger know Pierre as her daddy. Pierre and I were both willing to take the risk and see where it ended up.

At first, it was clear that I was responding to a strong desire on Tyger's part to meet her daddy. After several years of asking to see him, she was intensely interested in him when they did meet. But within a few months, the novelty wore off or she was satisfied with what she knew of him. She stopped asking to visit him and didn't seem bothered when I suggested it.

Then I became aware that I was organising visits with Pierre because I wanted to make Pierre happy. It was obvious that he was thrilled to meet his daughter and I wanted him to have a good time with her. She didn't always co-operate and would sometimes ignore him when he came around. I became anxious for his sake that he was pushing her to like him.

Every time he came, he brought her presents. I could see that it would backfire and was worried that she would reject him because he was so obviously trying to buy her love. I finally told him not to give her so many presents. I was doing this to protect him but I did wonder how much I should interfere in their relationship.

I became aware of my own needs in this complicated set of inter-relationships. Was I trying to make him the kind of father I never had? I found myself caught up in my own unmet childhood needs, projecting them on to Pierre and Tyger.

In 1991, Pierre became seriously ill with lymphoma, cancer of the lymph system. This was his first AIDS-related illness, only three years after becoming HIV-positive. I felt shocked. I had not expected it so soon. More than that, I realised that my grief was not just because Tyger might lose a daddy but because I might lose a very good friend. Somehow, without my knowing it, I had become very fond of Pierre. Over the months of hospital visits and chemotherapy sessions and concern over what kind of support everyone needs, I came to feel very close to Pierre. I stopped focusing on his relationship to Tyger. Maybe he did, too. Perhaps as a consequence, Tyger's basically loving nature was given space to surface.

It would have been a great loss to Tyger never to have known Pierre. Until he became ill, he gradually increased the time he spent with Tyger, until we were seeing him about once a week. He was generous with her, giving her presents and his time. With Tyger, he was gentle and patient and calm. My favourite memories are of the two of them sitting on the floor playing Lego together. It's very painful to think that Pierre won't have the chance to see Tyger growing up and that Tyger won't have Pierre around as she gets older.

The tragedy of AIDS is that it made him cut off just when our relationship with him had begun to flower. Like an injured fox, he went off by himself to die. For the last year of his life, he saw no one but his mother. He was depressed and angry about dying so young. He was only 35 when he died. He could not bear to be around people who were full of life and promise and hope. I tried to understand what he was going through and had no choice but to stay away. But I felt desperately hurt by his rejection of us. I explained to Tyger that he was too ill to see anyone and tried to accept that there was nothing we could do.

Tyger was nine when Pierre died. She cried at his funeral and then didn't mention him again for another three years. She tried to tell herself that he was gone and that was that. When she started talking about him, she was very confused and had convinced herself that she had no right to grieve because he was only a donor, not a real daddy. She couldn't remember what he was like and had forgotten all the time she had spent with him. She was racked with guilt for having abandoned him when he needed us most.

I have never regretted introducing Tyger to Pierre but I do feel angry at Pierre for leaving without saying goodbye. By agreeing to become a known and involved uncle donor, I felt that Pierre had agreed to take emotional responsibility for his daughter. He hadn't agreed to take on full parental responsibility in the sense of financial commitment or decision making. But he had agreed to have an ongoing relationship with her. In my mind, you don't end a relationship with a child by cutting off. Before you leave, you say the truth in your heart. I know that in Pierre's heart, beneath all the distraction of his illness and dying, there was deep love for Tyger. I know that he cared about her with an intensity greater than mere affection. The bond between them was special and treasured by him. I wish he had been able to say that to her or write it in a letter.

His dying was so absorbing and debilitating that he couldn't do anything but withdraw. But he made up for it later. He never knew how to express his love in words but he was good at giving gifts. Three years after he died, in keeping with his generous nature, his spirit sent Tyger a gift of money, relayed by his grandmother. Neither Tyger nor I are in any doubt what was in Pierre's heart.

An unsuccessful search – Sally and Joan's story

After several years of searching for a known donor, Sally and Joan finally decided to go to a clinic. They wrote this letter in 2001.

We have perhaps a half-dozen close gay male friends, three of whom we have approached regarding donating. All said no eventually, usually because they were concerned about emotional commitment. I think they were worried that they would become too involved or alternatively would feel guilty if not involved, although we felt that we could be flexible in either respect. We have other friends whom we have not asked because it takes a lot of courage to risk embarrassing a friendship. It's difficult to have self-insight into personal issues but if I am to be honest, I would never have imagined that we would have had such difficulty in finding a donor, as we are an easy-going, attractive professional couple. We have tried not to make this a focus of our lives but to remain cool and just pursue it quietly, but time marches on and we are now 34 and 32 and panicking a little bit.

We have advertised intermittently for a donor in the local events guide. Most of the guys who replied were heterosexual although the magazine has a large gay readership. We met regularly with two guys, the first a couple of years ago and the second currently. Although we explained the details of insemination, when we came to agreeing to go ahead, it emerged that both of their motives were sexual. Perhaps we are just unlucky to meet two such men. Obviously we must be making some mistakes in the way we present lesbian relationships and insemination to potential donors. We have now decided to attend a clinic privately, because we feel we have wasted so much time in the recruitment of dishonest donors.

An uncle donor – Andrew's story

Andrew Berg is a documentary producer for a major cable television network. He lives in New York City with his partner Dominic. Andy's second biological child with the same mothers was born in the autumn of 1999. (Reprinted with Andrew's permission, originally published in Alternative Family Magazine, *Jan/Feb 2000, Vol. 3, No.1, pp31-32.)*

She is a part of me in so many ways. I can see it in her smile and the funny curls in her hair. I can hear it in her voice as she sings the ABCs. I can feel it as she sits in my lap gazing sleepily into my eyes. And I can sense it in the little things she does that make me laugh. Pictures of her brighten both my home and office. Her beautiful little face sits framed on my dresser. She is the first thing I see in the morning and the last thing at night.

But she doesn't call me daddy or uncle or grandpa. I am not her parent and I am more than just a close friend. I am her biological father. And in the lingo of today's alternative family, I am also a 'known donor.'

In the fall of 1995 my cousin introduced me to a lesbian couple who were interested in starting a family. They had decided that a sperm bank was too anonymous yet none of their friends seemed right as a donor. So they set out looking for the right candidate. They didn't want a third parent but rather a father figure whom the baby would know and love. They stumbled upon me.

I was 25 years old and this seemed like the perfect opportunity; a way for me to experience the wonderful bond between a father and child while at the same time retaining what I considered at that time to be my freedom – the ability to pursue my career, to date and to travel, to be selfish with my time and money.

It was an experience I knew I had always wanted, but the hardest decision I would ever have to make. There was very little literature addressing the issue of 'known donors'. I talked to friends and family with mixed results. Many of my gay friends didn't quite understand what I was doing or why. My family, although supportive, was worried that I wouldn't be able to handle the emotions that would come with having a child who really wasn't mine. I had conflicting advice from almost everyone. Even the potential mothers wondered if I had ulterior motives. Why would I want to do this knowing full well that the child would be theirs and not mine?

To make sure I really understood the ramifications of this decision, the potential moms decided to spell everything out in black and white. They presented me with a contract – and had I been trained in either law or business, I surely would have backed out. They wanted to safeguard themselves against me becoming too involved. So the contract explained that I would have 'no expectation of a relationship with the child'. It denied me decision-making ability on every level when it came to the life of the baby. I would have no say in his or her name. No say in how the child would be raised. No say in his or her education or religious upbringing. The contract made it clear that for my protection I had no financial obligations to them, ever, and finally, that the child would one day know I was his or her father. They would control the scope of that relationship as well.

There is no question that they had the upper hand in this agreement.

The soul searching I endured over the next few months was incredibly difficult. Probably more so than I let on to friends and family.

There was no way to know what the future would hold. I wondered if they would keep their verbal agreement to involve me in their child's life. On the other hand I wondered if this child would come to hate me for creating a life I wasn't really a part of. I questioned whether or not I would be able to achieve the fulfilling relationship I had hoped for. And it dawned on me that I would not be able to guarantee my family and friends any relationship with this child.

On paper the cons surely outweighed the pros. But when it came down to the basics, I liked the idea of helping two people who loved one another create a family. And ultimately, it just seemed like the right thing to do. I thought it out carefully, consulted the limited resources available to me, and then – I leaped.

She was born in October of 1997 – but I wasn't invited to her birth. It was the first test of my emotional strength. I had anticipated this event for over a year – envisioning myself in the hospital waiting room, jumping up with tears in my eyes as the doctor came out to tell me if it was a boy or a girl. And now my giddy excitement had quickly turned to quiet disappointment.

In time I would come to understand that I had entered into a special relationship where the dynamics are constantly changing. New issues and challenges arrive. Some are obvious – others harder for me to anticipate.

For the new moms the birth of their child and the start of their family was something they wanted to share only with each other. They were concerned that my presence at the hospital might result in some awkward moments; perhaps a doctor referring to me as the father and ignoring the fact that this baby had two mothers. These are the issues that arise when one creates an alternative family in a heterosexual world.

A compromise was reached and I was asked to visit them in the hospital the day after the birth. There is a lot I could say about that day, but one thing sticks with me the most. Leaving that hospital was one of the hardest things I have ever had to do. I sat alone with the baby for about five minutes – telling her that I loved her and that I always would. I stared down into that bassinet and marvelled at how amazing the creation of a child actually is. Wiping the tears from my eyes, I got back into my car and started the three-hour drive back to my home.

Two years have passed and the road has been fairly smooth. I visit them almost every five weeks. We talk on the phone. We exchange photos and emails. I've developed a very loving and warm relationship with all three of them. I sometimes tell people that my experience being a known donor is much like being married to two people and a baby. We have built a relationship based on trust, caring and most importantly, honesty. But there will always be awkward moments and times when I wish things were a little different.

I've done my best to give them space, to let them be a family when I'm not around. I make sure I refer to both of them equally as her mother. I'm careful about the questions I ask and the things I say. I take their feelings into consideration and I think about how my actions will affect them. I accept the decisions they make about how to raise their daughter. And because of that I have learned that a different way of doing things may not always be a bad way or a wrong way.

They have graciously accepted presents from my friends and family even though it sometimes makes them uncomfortable. They've kindly allowed time for my family to get to know their daughter – even though she already has two sets of grandparents and many aunts and uncles. They have spent holidays at my parents' house even though seeing pictures of their daughter on the refrigerator makes them feel a little funny.

Those awkward little moments continue to arise even today. Right now we're discussing whether or not I'll be referred to as 'dad' – and how to explain that relationship to a two-year-old who is quickly figuring out that not all kids have two moms.

But whether or not she calls me dad isn't really important. I've slowly come to understand that there won't be a call or a card on Father's Day. That I will miss her first step and her first word; her first piece of birthday cake and her first time down the slide by herself. I know that my relationship to her is sometimes difficult to explain to strangers. That my parents can't treat her like their other grandchildren. And that I won't always be able to see her when I want.

But sometimes the seconds are just as good as the firsts. And everything I don't get to share with her makes the time I do have that much more special. I do my best to look at the big picture. And when I do,

I see that the only thing that is important is that I continue to have a loving relationship with this special child. That I have the chance to watch her change and grow, discover and learn. That is my reward for all of the things that I miss.

A distant uncle – Bronwen's story

Bronwen asked a straight friend to be her donor. She told her story in 1993.

The donor I used was the only one available. His partner had suggested it. It was there on offer and, since I felt that it was very urgent to get pregnant, I saw it as the only option. All other options had failed. I had tried to get pregnant by heterosex. I had also asked my best friend, who agreed to donate and then changed his mind. I had advertised for donors, but they all seemed dodgy.

It's not like me not to have everything all worked out, but it is most organic how our [Bronwen and her son Rhys's] relationship with the donor and his family has developed. Because I trust the donor and his partner and we share a lot in common, I feel we can handle just about everything. I'm very, very fond of his partner and trust their values and love their parenting and would even consider asking them to have Rhys if anything happened to me, and if my friend David couldn't have him. This is not because he's the donor but because they are the family whose parenting is closest to mine. At one point a long time ago before I had Rhys, they talked about me having their son if anything happened to them.

I'm lucky in retrospect that they are such a great couple and great parents, though I do worry occasionally. He could always go odd, go haywire. If his partner left him and took his children away from him, then you've got somebody in a distressed state likely to do odd things, like try to get parental responsibility for Rhys.

A distant uncle – Alan's story

Alan is a 46-year-old heterosexual man who has donated anonymously at a fertility clinic and as a known donor to lesbian couples throughout the country. I interviewed him in 2001.

What I get out of donating is the success at making babies and the contact with the children over the years. I got into it because I finished my first family too early. I was married at sixteen and had four children so by the time I was thirty, I had completed my family. All four children are now grown up. As I finished my family, my peers were just starting theirs. I felt left out. I would have liked more children but after the last child, my wife got herself sterilised. Since then we've divorced.

I got a bit broody, in a man's kind of way. Rather than getting into a full-time relationship with a woman and having children that way, it seems ideal to me that I can help other women become mothers of my children but I don't have the full responsibility of being a husband. I don't think it is irresponsible not to take parental responsibility for the children I father this way. All of the women know what the situation is from the start. If I went into a normal relationship and had children and walked away, then I would be irresponsible; but what I'm doing is helping women to be mothers. That is understood from the beginning. It's also understood that I won't have financial involvement because I literally can't afford to bring up several more families. It would be irresponsible to help a woman have a baby when she doesn't have the means to bring it up.

The reason I like helping lesbian women is because my aunt was a lesbian, so I have no problems about that. Also I have a thing about other men bringing up my children. I'm not homophobic towards lesbian women, although I don't like gay men. I see nothing wrong with gay women having children. As long as the woman and her partner are loving, I think it's fine. My only worry would be if the other partner takes a male role, tries to be the dad. As long as they're both honest about their own relationship to the child, there's no problem.

My GP suggested I donate anonymously at a fertility clinic, which I did for three years. I gave it up because the clinic was taken over by an

American organisation and one of their rules was not to use donors above the age of 35. We parted company.

I was surfing the internet and looked up sperm donation. I found Surrogate Mothers Online which had a section for donors to advertise on. So I put an advert on there. Within 24 hours, I got a reply from a lesbian couple in the north of England. They were both professional women. Within 36 hours, I'd actually met them and donated to them. After three cycles, she conceived. We keep in touch, not regularly but every other month. That was a good experience.

It just went on from there. I also advertised in the *Pink Paper* and on one or two other internet sites. I got involved with an American woman living in London. I said I wanted to keep in contact. She conceived after four months, but then broke contact. I had an email that a baby girl was born and that she'd gone back to the States. I won't pursue her. The third reply was from a university lecturer. After I donated to her, she broke contact. Seven months later, after quite a few emails from me, she emailed back saying she had had a baby. I'm waiting for her to confirm what the situation is.

I helped a heterosexual couple once. The husband was infertile and the wife had been through the mill with the clinic system. After several failed IVF treatments and a miscarriage, they were desperate. She said I was her last chance. I found it difficult to say no. I donated to her and she caught on the third month. They want to bring the child up as their own. I assume the husband's name will be on the birth certificate. The agreement with them is that I'm kept informed throughout the pregnancy, that I'll see the baby when it's born but that is it. It was a one-off. I won't get anything out of it but I feel great for them.

So far, that's four babies born. At the moment I'm helping two other lesbian couples and I'm on standby for several women who are having fertility treatment.

There are no set rules. We make it up as we go along. There are two basics: my donation is free of charge (I don't even ask for travel expenses), and I'm a known donor. I prefer donating to couples. I haven't been approached by a single lesbian but I wouldn't turn her down as long as I was happy that she was able to support the child and that she'd thought it out properly.

The main thing is that I am kept informed and that I'm allowed to see the baby. Otherwise, what's the point in me doing it? I've had a bittersweet experience – some women keep in touch with me, others don't. Now I'm a damn sight more careful who I choose. I would like contact and would like to know what's happening through the pregnancy, when the baby's born, what it is, how the child is growing up.

I disagree with keeping the child's biological origins a secret. I think every child has got the right to know who its proper father is. I would not donate to a woman who didn't want the donor to have any contact with the child during their childhood. The amount of contact I leave up to the mother. The first baby is now one year old and the mothers think she doesn't get enough contact with men. They want her to have a male role model and for me to come visit more often. That's fine with me.

I want as much contact as possible. The best times of my life have been when I've had my children around. I want to be known as their father but I would not dictate what schools they went to or what clothes they wore. The children know they've got a dad somewhere that they might see at Christmas, on their birthdays, at their first school concert but they would have to know that I won't be there every single day. Their dad's not living with them but they can always pick the phone up or send an email. I don't think that a lesbian can act the role of father but as long as the child has got a dad, they will know they're not different from other kids.

For DIY insemination, the woman's got to have perfect fertility. Otherwise it won't work and it's a waste of my time. I've decided that from now on, 35 is going to be the maximum age of the women I donate to. I've been involved with some women in their forties but with these older women, it's one thing after another – polycystic ovaries, fibroids, hormonal problems. The women who got pregnant have been younger – 28, 32, 38 – except for the heterosexual woman who was 40, so it shows it's not impossible. To be fair to me, they should get checked out if they're over 35. I have to decide whether to put myself out.

When I meet a couple, I make it very clear what I want out of it. We don't proceed unless we can trust each other. I don't think writing down on paper that you want this to happen or that to happen is going to work. I've gone into the legal side of it – a contract is not worth the paper it's written on. I make sure I know where the women live. Any time that I want, I can trace the woman concerned, but there's no point in getting heavy about things. If they break contact, they must have their reasons. I've just got to let sleeping dogs lie. I would not donate to anybody unless I know where they live, what kind of house they've got, where they work. I check things out in a lot more detail. It's a learning curve. When I went into it, freelance, I was a bit naïve. After a few bad experiences, I now know what to do.

I'll meet with the women a few times before I even begin donating. We have lengthy conversations. I can usually suss out whether they will be good mothers. You can never be 100% sure. Being a father for the best part of thirty years, I can tell if they've got their heads in the clouds or not. You can see it in their eyes and by their mannerisms. If the women are prepared to let me into their house, then I think that they're pretty genuine.

Straight from the start, I can give them whatever information they want about me. Most have been to my house, so they know my background and something about my family. They can't be 100% sure that I'm not a child-beater or a madman. But after a chat with me, they know I'm pretty well genuine. If they want to talk to any of the other women I've donated to, I'm happy that the women know of each other. At least if anything does go wrong, they know who I am and where I work. That's about as much as I can do.

Women do need to be careful. I put a warning at the end of my advert on Surrogate Mothers Online saying that women should check out the guys before they go ahead. The first women I donated to, I donated within a week of meeting them. I don't think they would do that again. Some women are that desperate.

The worst possible thing for a man is if the woman has to claim benefits and the guy is liable for maintenance. I make sure that the women concerned are able to support the child. I look for women who are professionals. I ask them to give me an undertaking that they will not involve me with the Child Support Agency. That's the best I can do.

The thing about being a donor is that you need success. I went through a time period where the women were not catching on, as they had fertility problems. For one woman, it's been about a year now. That means me doing a lot of travelling after work. For one couple, I did a 450-mile round trip three nights a week to donate. If it hasn't worked in six months, then I give them the opportunity to try somebody else and it gives me the opportunity to pull out.

A daddy donor – Justine and Simon's story

Justine was single when she decided to get pregnant. She wanted to share parenting with the father of her children but didn't know any men who she could ask. Undaunted, she advertised in the Pink Paper *and met Simon, a single gay man. She conceived by self-insemination and they had two sons: Connor, who sadly died just before birth, and Declan, born a year later. For the past five years, they have been co-parenting together. Justine gave this story in 2001; Simon's follows it.*

Justine

For a long time, I thought you couldn't have children if you were a lesbian. Then I met a lesbian who was pregnant by self-insemination and I realised that I didn't have to be in a relationship with a man. Within a few months I got it together to open my closet door and come out. I haven't looked back since.

Before I started, I was clear about what I was looking for. I placed an ad in the mixed personals in the *Pink Paper*. I had a little questionnaire. If a man had a problem with my questionnaire, then obviously he wasn't the right co-parenting partner for me. One man called it my exam paper. I corresponded with several men, spoke to a few on the phone and got as far as meeting one. Most backed off because it brought up huge issues in their relationships with their partners. It's a difficult thing to take to a relationship. Your child would obviously be the most important person in your life and that's a heavy number to lay on your partner. You would both have to be equally committed.

Simon advertised in the *Pink Paper* about the same time I did. We corresponded and phoned and then met shortly after Christmas in 1994. We decided we'd give it a try. We agreed to break off negotiations with other potential parenting partners and to spend six months to see if we could work it out. It turned out that we were looking for something similar in a parenting arrangement. He wanted to be a father, not just a donor. His family is very family-focused and our children would have a huge extended family.

Effectively Simon and I are two single parents with a joint parental agreement. We don't live together. We live about an hour from each other, I don't think it would work if it was longer than that. I have Declan during the week. We do some ordinary family things most weekends, then the boys go off together.

As parenting partners, we're doing pretty well. When it comes to the bit that counts, Simon and I are 100% together. If you're involved in a heterosexual relationship, you have a personal relationship that bonds you, but that can get in the way of being an effective parent. Simon and I are very different people and have very different interests, but we have similar values and we get on well. We're fairly consistent about our parenting style. If it's going to work, we both have to be doing the same thing. And you have to work on relationships if they're going to succeed.

When Declan was about eighteen months, he began hitting and kicking. We weren't sure how to cope with that but we talked it through and worked out a common approach. Declan is basically a very bright, well-behaved, secure, confident and happy little boy.

I haven't been in a relationship since I decided that being a parent was more important to me than anything else. I split up with my last girlfriend – who is still a close friend – shortly before I met Simon. The thing that finally split us up, though there was lots of other stuff too, was that she didn't want parental responsibility. Ironically, recently she's been looking for a similar kind of parenting relationship to the one I have with Simon. I think you have to be really single minded. That's what makes it work for me and Simon. We're both clear that parenting is more important to us than other relationships. It is important to keep a roof over your head, to have friends and companions, but if anybody were to get involved with either of us on a long-term basis, they would have to realise that Declan is our primary responsibility and that Simon and I are his parents.

Simon

I was always sure that I wanted to be a dad. I was not quite sure when or how, but I was sure. When I started to write to Justine, I had already met a few women and none of them seemed right. For a start they seemed to want a husband without the sex. At least one discussed marriage at a very early stage. Whilst I understood where they were coming from, I was looking for a family life that was practical, honest and open. Pretending to be a married couple was not what I was looking for.

Justine and I agreed right up front what the bottom line was: a mum and a dad bringing up children together. We were flexible on the details, but to agree our bottom line was most important. We got on well partly because we were from the same part of the country, but also because we were prepared to listen. Justine is committed to the vegetarian lifestyle, whereas my own politics are sceptical of some of this. We found common ground, which recognised a respect for each other's views.

Seeking and finding common ground is a practical way through difficulties on personal issues. When we have rowed about bringing up Declan, the solution has been found in working out what we agree on and taking it from there. For us, Declan's interests come first and we need to be willing to give way at times. This is not as easy as it sounds, but I think it is the key to our success.

We have been a great success in many ways. We survived the stillbirth of our first child, Connor, by drawing on our friends and family, sharing our grief but respecting that we were each a parent separately, not just jointly. Our Declan is a very happy, well-adjusted little boy – a nursery star pupil – and although he may try to play us off against each other, we form an iron front on good manners, no temper tantrums and bedtimes.

Practically, even if I don't share Justine's style in relationships, I support her without question in front of Declan. In dealing with 'the authorities' we insist that they deal with both of us, having a parental responsibility agreement registered with the court early on. Schools and doctors see us as joint parents, and we have to make sure that is very clear to them from the start.

We build on each other's strengths. Justine says I don't do sympathy very well, but I do make Declan laugh a great deal and we do lots of robust father–son things. Justine respects my role as a man in Declan's life and understands that there are things he and I will share as males that she may not. The same would be true if we were a father and daughter. Conversely, I will never be his mother and I need to accept that. We both agree that to be a [good person] is to respect other people, listen to them and to take their feelings on board. How we put this philosophy into practice varies between us.

My role in the pregnancies has been to support Justine and to prepare for fatherhood. I helped to decorate Justine's new home and we shared the setting-up expenses of a home for a new baby. I attended all the scans, several antenatal appointments, classes and both deliveries. I made sure that Justine's views were heard in the delivery room and I knew what to do if things went wrong. No one ever doubted that Justine and I were parents of the coming child.

Sex with a donor – Kat's story

Kat is a single mother with an eight-year-old daughter. She wrote this in 2001.

My lover and I were in a committed lesbian relationship when we started talking about having a baby together in 1988. My partner felt she had reached a stage in her life where she wanted to realise her desire to have a child. I had co-parented the children of a previous lover, and felt able to take on the commitment of full-time parenting, and was delighted at the notion that we would be having this child together. This feeling was very much connected with our closeness and love, a deep bond which made sense of our lives, a 'raison d'être'.

Unfortunately, life had other plans for us, and we never reached a stage where we actively engaged in the conception process. However, we did discuss the fact that my lover would carry the child (I was not too keen on being pregnant myself at the time), and that she would conceive by having sex with a male friend. In retrospect, I can see that problems may have arisen from this approach. However, my lover radiated integrity, maturity and pride; she commanded respect, and I feel that the chosen birth father would have responded with appropriate maturity, having been selected on the basis of similar personal qualities.

To us, the important thing was for my partner to get pregnant. The notion of sex with a man did not feel threatening, as its purpose was to procreate and the love we felt for each other transcended this level.

We never particularly considered the possibility of insemination – if we had, it would have been a 'jam-jar job'. That option would certainly have been very special as well as fun, but it didn't feel quite right to us in the initial considerations. Sex with a man felt like the most straightforward way to get pregnant. Furthermore, the fiery passion of sex felt like an important ingredient of conception, fertilisation, creating a new life... as opposed to the more clinical, sterile artificial process. Maybe I'm wrong, but I can't imagine being able to inseminate a lover from a jam-jar in a state of sexual exaltation!

My lover never got to realise her dream of having her own child. She passed on at the young age of 33. ... I feel it is important to honour her spirit by stating quite definitely that she was one of the most lesbian-identified, woman-loving women I have ever known, and that this identity shaped her life, which she in many ways dedicated to ensuring that the women around her were enjoying theirs. ...

Just over a year after her death, I conceived a child by having sex with a man. [My child's] story flows on from that of my lover in a way that I cannot explain here. In some way, she is the daughter of our love, and has one real live mum and a spirit mum (one of her Guardian Angels, and whose name is reflected in hers). She is aware of her rich and varied heritage – in its many facets, comprising ethnic, cultural, social, linguistic, spiritual and sexual variations from the majority 'norm' – and is growing up with pride in and awareness of this reality.

I am quite an impetuous person and do things very much following my gut feeling – but I knew what I was doing when I became pregnant. Heterosexual conception is not necessarily an easy option. I think it is most likely to work if you have a healthy mature friendship with mutual respect and clear communication, and ground rules are clearly set out and agreed by all concerned parties prior to conception – so finding an appropriate donor to plant a seed may not be easy. Furthermore, this option is only viable if you feel you can enjoy it, as whatever way the seed is planted, I feel it needs to be blessed with positive energy from the start – so if having sex with a man is a totally repulsive notion to you, it's best avoided!

... Since my daughter's birth I have had sexual relationships with both women and men, none of which have proved easy, and the only viable trend for now seems to be celibate single parenthood.

3

DONOR SCREENING

Given that you are consciously planning to get pregnant, you have the opportunity to choose a fertile donor and to protect your baby and yourself from a number of illnesses and conditions. You can ask potential donors to be tested for HIV and other sexually transmitted diseases, as well as asking about inherited conditions.

This chapter looks at some of these issues, mainly with regard to self-insemination. You may also want to consult other books on how an expectant mother can look after her own health and that of the baby.

The risks

There are always some risks with any pregnancy, but the chances of miscarriage or birth defects from donor insemination through clinics are no greater than normal, and there is no reason to think it will be any different for self-insemination.

Screening is necessary but no matter how thorough your screening is of the donor nor how careful you are of your health, you still cannot prevent many of the diseases or accidents that could affect you or your baby. Again, this is no different from trying to get pregnant by sexual intercourse.

Asking difficult questions

Any man who is genuine about donating will understand why he is being asked and should be happy to answer your questions. There are a number of ways to do it. If the donor is anonymous, get a friend to ask the questions or be the intermediary. If you know other women looking for donors, you can get together as a group and advertise together for prospective donors, produce a leaflet for them and interview them on behalf of other women in the group. Most women sit down with the man and have a chat. A sample leaflet is included at the end of Chapter 5 for you to photocopy (Advice for Donors, page 79).

The questionnaire at the end of *this* chapter is meant as a guide to help you decide if you want this man to be your donor. You may find it useful to take a fuller medical history of the donor in case doctors ask for a family history if your child becomes ill. You may also want to draw up your own questionnaire or add questions of your own.

Male fertility

When choosing a donor, first try to find out that he is fertile. There is no way to guarantee this but you can get a good idea by asking the following three questions.

i. Has he fathered children already?
This is the surest test of a man's fertility and worth asking him when you first interview him.

ii. Does he have a sperm count?
Ideally, have a semen analysis done before you start inseminating. If the first test is abnormal, have the test repeated. A donor can arrange this with his GP or he can go to a private clinic. The sperm should be plentiful, active and normal in shape. Specifically, there should be:
- more than 50 million sperm per ml (average is 60 million per ml)
- at least 2 ml of semen

- more than 50% should have progressive motility (able to move forward) after one hour.
- less than 50% abnormally shaped sperm
- 75% or more alive

(Values given in the *WHO Manual for Standardized Investigation, Diagnosis and Management of the Infertile Male*, Cambridge University Press, 2000)

iii. How old is he?

Conception is somewhat less likely to occur with the semen of older men, although there is not the same drop in fertility that women experience. In 1997, the Human Fertilisation and Embryology Authority reviewed the evidence on the risk of an increase in serious birth defects due to the father's age but found no compelling reasons to lower the upper age limit below 55 years.

Sexually transmitted diseases

You and your baby could be at risk if the donor has a sexually transmitted disease such as HIV, gonorrhoea, syphilis, hepatitis B (serum hepatitis), hepatitis C, mycoplasma, chlamydia, herpes, cytomegalovirus (CMV) or Trichomonas. These diseases can be spread by semen, through insemination as well as through sexual contact.

HIV

HIV is one of the most important health risks to ask your donor about, whether he is gay or straight. It is not enough to ask a man if he has HIV because he could carry the virus without any signs of illness for many years – or be ill without knowing it's HIV-related. You can only know that someone is infected if they have a positive HIV test result.

To accept someone as a donor, the man must have had a recent negative HIV test result and must be able to satisfy you that he has not been and is not involved in any current activities that would put him at risk of HIV since the last test.

Be aware that there is a three-month "window period", when the test could be negative even though the person is infected with HIV. This is because the test looks for antibodies to HIV, and these may not appear straight away.

At a donor insemination clinic, this is not a problem. When he first donates to a clinic, the man is given an HIV test and his semen is frozen and stored until he returns six months later for another test. Only if both tests are negative will his stored semen be used for inseminations.

Self-insemination, however, involves the use of fresh sperm, and you cannot store the semen for three months to be used after the man's second HIV test. Therefore, you have to find out whether he could have been infected in the three months before he took the test – or since then. HIV can only be spread in bodily fluids – blood, semen, or vaginal secretions – from an infected person. So you must find out if the donor has taken certain risks:

- **During sex:** Risky sexual activities are anal sex or vaginal intercourse without a condom and with an infected person.

- **By sharing anything that can pierce the skin:** This means sharing drug-injecting equipment, razors or blades with people who are infected. It also means having tattoos, piercings (ears and otherwise) or acupuncture at a place that does not use disposable or re-sterilised needles. There is no risk from licensed piercing clinics.

- **Through infected blood and blood products:** Blood and blood products have been screened for HIV since 1985 in the UK. In some developing countries, the blood supply for transfusion is not yet safe.

It can be embarrassing, but you and the donor have to talk openly and honestly about sexual practices and drug use. If he has been engaging in risky activities, he should practise safer sex or stop the risky activity for at least three months before taking the HIV test. At the end of that period, he can donate sperm if the test is negative.

Testing

Men who agree to be donors are generally willing to have the HIV test and to reassure you about their sexual practices. But not all men are prepared to take the test: they may be confident that they are not at risk or they may be (understandably) frightened of a positive result. However, no matter how good his reasons, there is a baby to protect and you should not accept sperm from him unless he takes the test.

HIV testing and tests for other sexually transmitted diseases are available from any NHS Sexually Transmitted Diseases Clinic (also called genitourinary medicine or GUM Clinic). They are better at safeguarding confidentiality than your GP. Call the clinic first to see how long it takes for the results to come back. At most clinics, the result takes one or two days but some clinics can provide the result the same day. Also check that they offer counselling before and after taking the test.

To get the address of the nearest clinic or of a recommended one, you can call the National AIDS Helpline on 0800 567123 (24 hours, free support, information and referrals) or look in the Yellow Pages under "Clinics – NHS". You can also get the test done privately. If you are concerned about confidentiality, give a false name.

Blood groups

It is useful but not crucial to know the blood group, both ABO and rhesus factor, of both yourself and the donor. One in eight people are rhesus negative, the rest rhesus positive. If the mother is rhesus negative and the donor rhesus positive, the baby is at risk from jaundice or even death if the mother produces antibodies to the rhesus factor. Sensitisation usually occurs at birth, so a first baby is rarely at risk, unless the mother became sensitised through an earlier abortion or miscarriage.

There are about fifty foetal deaths a year from rhesus sensitisation, but it can be prevented by giving immunoglobulin to rhesus negative women after delivery of a rhesus positive baby. It is useful for a rhesus negative woman to know the donor's blood group so that she can be monitored for this as part of her antenatal care.

A rhesus positive mother is not at risk, so it does not matter if her donor is rhesus positive or negative.

Genetic conditions

Through questioning the donor, you can find out if he or any of his close relatives have suffered from a genetic disorder. There are thousands of genetic conditions which could be passed on to your child by the donor or by you or by the combination of the two of you. Most of the conditions are very rare.

Some of the conditions such as sickle cell anaemia, thalassaemia, cystic fibrosis and Tay Sachs have a simple pattern of inheritance and it is possible to calculate the odds of passing it on. If both parents are carriers of the gene, there is a one in four chance that the child will inherit the condition. As long as only one parent is a carrier, the children will not be affected though they may themselves be carriers.

Certain population groups are more likely to carry these genes. For example, Tay Sachs is only found among people of Ashkenazi Jewish background. Sickle cell anaemia is most common in people with an Afro-Caribbean background and thalassaemia is found in descendants of people from the Mediterranean and Middle East. Cystic fibrosis is most commonly found in northern Europeans. Carriers have no illness themselves and will not know about it unless they have been tested. Your GP can arrange for simple blood tests. (The one for cystic fibrosis carriers only detects about 85% of them.)

If you have been tested and shown not to carry the gene in question, then you can decide whether to question the donor about that particular condition. You may decide that you don't want your child to have the chance of being a carrier, in which case, make sure the donor is not a carrier. If you are a carrier, then only accept a donor who is not also a carrier.

With many other kinds of inherited conditions, the patterns are very complex and involve many genes, so the odds cannot be calculated precisely. If it runs in either your family or the donor's, your child could have a greater risk. For example, your child would have an increased risk of having a heart attack if a relative had a first attack before the age of fifty. If a relative had adult onset diabetes (the kind where the person doesn't need insulin), the child would have an increased risk of developing diabetes, especially if overweight. Hyperlipidaemia (a condition where there are abnormally high levels of fats such as cholesterol in the blood), also runs in families and carries an increased risk of having a heart attack, stroke or circulation problem. Glaucoma, which can lead to blindness if untreated, is another condition which tends to run in families, as do allergies such as eczema, asthma and hayfever.

If you know that the donor has a family history of one of these conditions, you can decide whether to go ahead with him or find another donor. If you do accept his sperm, you can do what is necessary to prevent or monitor the condition in the child. For example, with a family history of glaucoma, the child would need an eye test every two years. If there is a family history of allergies, you can protect your baby by breastfeeding rather than bottle feeding and by reducing your baby's exposure to substances that cause allergies, such as the house-dust mite and various foods.

Aside from any conditions which run in the donor's family, there may be risks from factors in his own life. The chromosomes which carry the genes can be damaged by exposure to radiation, certain chemicals, alcohol or drug abuse, by age or just by chance. Men are just as vulnerable to reproductive hazards at work or in the environment as are women. It is worth asking a donor if his occupation involves an increased risk of radiation or chemical exposure.

Questionnaire for donors

Personal details

Name _____

D/O/B _____ Height _____ Weight _____

Hair colour _____ Eye colour _____

Race _____ Ethnic origin _____

Fertility

1. Have you fathered any children? If so, how many? _____

2. Have you had a recent semen analysis? If so, when and what was the result?

Sperm count _____ Motility _____ Abnormally shaped sperm _____

The following could also affect how fertile you are:

3. Have you been in an occupation involving a risk of radiation or chemical exposure or had an accident involving radiation or chemical exposure?

4. Are you a heavy user of:

alcohol _____ drugs (which ones?) _____ cigarettes _____

5. Are you taking chronic medication? What kind and what for?

Medical history

Blood group

A ____ B ____ O ____ Rhesus positive _____ Rhesus negative _____

Sexually transmitted diseases
Have you tested negative for:

gonorrhoea _____ hepatitis C_____ syphilis _____

hepatitis B (serum hepatitis) _____ herpes _____

non-specific urethritis (NSU) _____

HIV

Date of last negative test? _____

Even if your HIV test was negative, you could still be infected with HIV in the three months before the test or since the test. For this reason, it is important that you answer the following questions about 'high risk' activities.

Since your last HIV test, have your sexual partner/s all been HIV-negative? _____

How do you know? _____

Do you have anal or vaginal sex without a condom? _____

Do you share sex toys that could get blood on them?_____

Do you inject drugs and share injecting equipment?_____

Do you share razors or blades?_____

Inherited conditions

1. Have you or anyone in your family had any of the following conditions? *Consider your family to be brothers, sisters, father, mother, maternal and paternal aunts and uncles and grandparents, including those who have or did have any of the following conditions.*

allergies (e.g. eczema, asthma, hayfever)	
cirrhosis of the liver (juvenile)	
cleft palate or lip	
clubfoot	
congenital heart disease	
cystic fibrosis	
deafness before age 50	
diabetes (adult onset)	
glaucoma	
heart attack before age 50	
Huntington's chorea	
hydrocephalus	
hyperlipidaemia	
kidney disease – early progressive	
neurofibromatosis	
restricted growth	
spina bifida	
stroke before age 50	

2. If yes to any, please tell which specific relation had which condition.

_____

_____

_____

_____

3. Are you a carrier of:

Thalassaemia_____ Sickle cell disease_____ Tay Sachs disease_____ Cystic fibrosis_____

Being a donor

1. Over how long a period would you be committed to donating sperm?

_____

2. Can you be available when needed, two to four times per month?

_____

Part II

Getting Pregnant

If you're ready to get pregnant, you will want to know how and when to go about it. This part of the book is about working out when you're fertile – and then inseminating.

When Are You Fertile? 61   How to Self-inseminate 73
Clinic Inseminations 83   When It Doesn't Go as Planned 97

4

WHEN ARE YOU FERTILE?

There are only a few days in each menstrual cycle when you are fertile, that is, when you have a chance of getting pregnant. They are easy to identify, as explained later in this chapter: you don't need any expensive equipment; you just need to recognise fertile mucus and inseminate when it's present. First though, it is helpful to understand what is going on in your body during your "fertile days".

Fertile days

You are fertile at ovulation (when a mature egg is released from the ovary) and for a while before it. The number of these fertile days varies for different women, from two to seven days in each cycle.

In the days before ovulation, while the egg is ripening, the egg sac (or follicle) makes oestrogen. This hormone causes the cervix to produce thin, clear, slippery mucus – the "fertile mucus" (see Figure 1 overleaf). The entrance to the cervix (the os) is open. When sperm arrive in your vagina during this time, the fertile mucus protects and feeds them and directs them up into side pockets in the cervix. From here they are gradually released over a period of days and swim up through the uterus to the fallopian tubes to meet the egg (or eggs, if two are released).

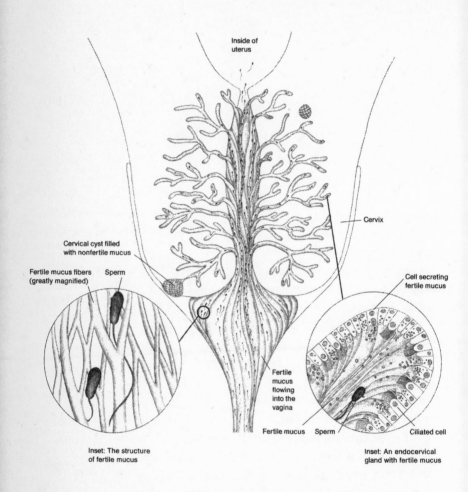

Inside of
uterus

Cervix

Cervical cyst filled
with nonfertile mucus

Cell secreting
fertile mucus

Fertile mucus fibers
(greatly magnified)   Sperm

Fertile
mucus
flowing
into the
vagina

Fertile mucus   Sperm   Ciliated cell

Inset: The structure
of fertile mucus

Inset: An endocervical
gland with fertile mucus

Figure 1: A cross-section of the cervix with fertile mucus

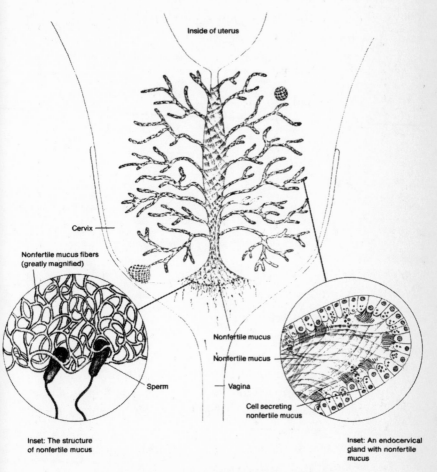

Figure 2: A cross-section of the cervix with non-fertile mucus

Inside of uterus

Cervix

Nonfertile mucus fibers
(greatly magnified)

Nonfertile mucus

Nonfertile mucus

Sperm

Vagina

Cell secreting
nonfertile mucus

Inset: The structure
of nonfertile mucus

Inset: An endocervical
gland with nonfertile
mucus

The egg is only actually available to the sperm for 24 hours; and only one of the millions of sperm (if any) will bore through the jelly-like coating to fertilise the egg, which then proceeds to the uterus.

Immediately after ovulation and at all other times of the menstrual cycle, your cervix produces no mucus or a thick white tacky mucus (see Figure 2) and the os remains tightly shut. This type of mucus acts as a barrier to the sperm: they cannot swim through it and they die within a few hours. So for the majority of each cycle, you are not fertile.

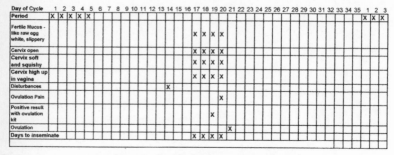

Day of Cycle	1	2	3	4	5	6	7	8	9	10	11	12	13	14	15	16	17	18	19	20	21	22	23	24	25	26	27	28	29	30	31	32	33	34	35	1	2	3
Period	X	X	X	X	X																															X	X	X
Fertile Mucus - like raw egg white, slippery																	X	X	X	X																		
Cervix open																	X	X	X	X																		
Cervix soft and squishy																	X	X	X	X																		
Cervix high up in vagina																	X	X	X	X																		
Disturbances														X																								
Ovulation Pain																			X																			
Positive result with ovulation kit																		X																				
Ovulation																				X																		
Days to inseminate																	X	X	X	X																		

Figure 3: Sample fertility awareness chart

Signs of fertility

Everyone's menstrual cycle is different. What is important here is not whether you fit into some idealised pattern but whether you can tell what is going on in your cycle. This requires direct observation of your body. It is useful to keep some records, at least at first. You can use a fertility awareness chart to record whatever signs you find useful (see Figure 3). Blank charts are included in the self-insemination kit from PinkParents UK (see Resources).

The following pages describe four ways to identify your fertile days so you can know when to inseminate:

i. Recognising fertile mucus.

ii. Recognising changes in the position and firmness of your cervix.

iii. Using an ovulation kit.

iv. Keeping a basal body temperature chart (this method is useful to confirm whether you did ovulate in that cycle, but no help in timing inseminations).

i. Fertile mucus

Vaginal secretions change in consistency and amount during the menstrual cycle. The secretions consist of mucus produced by the cervix, plus cells sloughed off the vaginal walls. You can tell when you are fertile by becoming familiar with these changes, which is quite easy after a bit of practice. You simply need to get familiar with the feel of the mucus inside your vagina and to take some out on your finger to examine for stretchiness, tackiness, smell, look and even taste, if you want.

The mucus is produced in the cervix but falls to the outside and can be felt at the opening of your vagina. A convenient time to feel for mucus is after you have gone to the toilet when you have been pushing and the mucus is more likely to have fallen to the opening. You can push the mucus down the vagina by squeezing and relaxing the muscles around the vagina. (Imagine that you are trying to stop yourself urinating.) This brings the mucus down where it is easier for you to reach.

On your non-fertile days, as mentioned, the cervix produces nothing or a white tacky mucus that can look like thick icing (see Figure 4 overleaf). When you reach into your vagina and bring some out, you will find that you cannot stretch it between your fingers. It feels dry. It is usually thick and sticky. It smells sharp and somewhat vinegary. The amount of mucus will vary from woman to woman and some days no mucus can be seen. The opening of the cervix (the os) is tightly closed. The vagina feels dry.

On your fertile days, the cervix produces a thin, clear mucus very much like raw egg white (see Figure 5). It feels wet and slippery. If there is enough, you can pull it out of your vagina and stretch it between your fingers. Fertile mucus stretches, sometimes up to several centimetres. If you can't pull it out, you can often see the mucus on toilet paper when you wipe yourself after going to the toilet. The smell and taste of fertile mucus is sweeter and less acidic than that of the non-fertile mucus. You can use a speculum, as described below, to see the clear, transparent mucus on your cervix. With the speculum, you can also see the os open before ovulation and close afterwards.

The only way you can tell how many days you have this fertile mucus is by looking for it. Some women might produce it for two days,

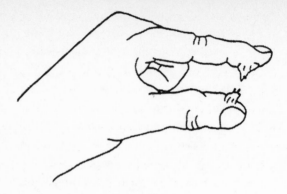

Figure 4: Tacky mucus between the fingers

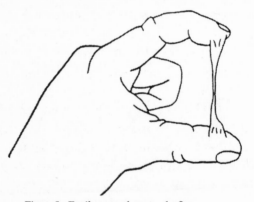

Figure 5: Fertile mucus between the fingers

some for six. The amount of mucus varies from woman to woman. You might find fertile mucus pouring out of your vagina. Or you may have to search to find it. The amount of fertile mucus is not important, unless there is hardly any present. *As long as fertile mucus is present, it is worth doing the insemination.*

Your mucus observations can be disrupted by vaginal infections which produce a discharge, by some drugs and by anything which affects your menstrual cycle such as exhaustion, stress, or travel. If you have no fertile mucus at all, it is unlikely that you have ovulated in that cycle.

Feeling and looking at the cervix itself gives you even more information. You can find your cervix by reaching deep into your vagina until you feel something smooth and firm like the tip of your nose. It is easier to do if you stand with one leg on a chair and reach in. The opening of the cervix, called the os, feels like a dimple in the cervix. You can see your cervix yourself by using a speculum, a light and a mirror (speculum and leaflets explaining its use are available from Women's Health, see Resources).

It may take several cycles before you feel confident that you can recognise the changes in your secretions and that you can tell the difference between fertile mucus and the secretions you produce when you are sexually excited. It is worth getting familiar with your cycle before you want to start trying to get pregnant.

ii. Position of cervix

Another way to find your fertile days is by observing the changes in the position of your cervix inside the vagina and its texture or condition. These changes come about because of the same menstrual cycle hormones that influence the production of the cervical mucus. You can add this information to your fertility awareness chart.

On your fertile days, your cervix "ripens" and is drawn up towards the abdomen. It feels soft, spongy or rubbery, similar to the way your lips feel to the touch. The sensation is of slipperiness because of the fertile mucus. The os opens wide. This can be felt as a dimple or a gap in the centre of the cervix and can be seen clearly using a speculum. The cervix may be harder to reach as it moves farther away from the opening of the vagina by as much as a few centimetres during the cycle.

On the days when you are not fertile, the cervix is lower, closer to the opening of the vagina and it feels firmer, more like the way the tip of your nose feels. The sensation is drier. The os is closed. If you use a speculum, you can see that the os looks like a tiny dot or a thin line.

To feel for these changes, start checking during the days when you are not fertile as the cervix is easier to reach then. Check it once a day at the same time of day, preferably the evening, as the position of the cervix varies slightly during the day – it is generally further from the vaginal opening in the morning than in the evening. Use the same posture each time, whether it's squatting or putting one leg up on a chair, as posture also affects the cervix's position. Reach in with one or two fingers. If you can't reach your cervix, try to bear down first or press lightly on your abdomen.

These signs of fertility require you to remember subtle changes in position and texture and it may take a few cycles before you feel confident to recognise them. Not all women notice all the signs mentioned. Just record what you do notice.

iii. Ovulation kits

There are several ovulation kits available from chemists – Clear Plan One Step, First Response, Persona and Discretest. Using a kit gives you a bit of advance warning, at most a day, to organise inseminations. The tests are simple and fun to do. Tests detect luteinising hormone (LH), which is sent by the pituitary gland in the brain to the ovaries to trigger ovulation. LH appears in the urine 24 to 36 hours before you ovulate. The kit contains a chemical which changes colour in the presence of LH in the urine. The test is a good confirmation that you are ovulating, although it isn't proof: you can produce LH and still not ovulate and you can have high background levels of LH giving false positive results. Many women use ovulation kits together with observing their fertile signs directly and find them very useful. You may want to use a kit for one cycle to give you confidence that you are able to recognise your fertile days.

However, it is not essential to use a kit and they do have disadvantages, the main one being the cost. Another major disadvantage is that the kit focuses too much on pinpointing ovulation. It can add to the stress of self-insemination and the risk that you inseminate too late.

iv. Basal body temperature charts

The basal body temperature is the temperature taken as soon as you wake up, after you have been asleep for at least three hours. If you keep a chart for several cycles, you may notice a distinct pattern (see Figure 6). In menstrual cycles in which you ovulate, your temperature rises very slightly (a few tenths of a degree) a day or two after ovulation, and stays at this higher temperature until your next period.

To see if there has been a temperature shift, record your basal body temperature every day for the entire menstrual cycle, counting the first day of bleeding as Day 1. With a ruler, connect the dots. Then draw a horizontal line across the chart so that most of the readings at the beginning of the cycle are below the line and most of the readings towards the end of the cycle are above the line.

Most charts seem to have so many ups and downs that it is quite hard to interpret them; and their only purpose is to prove to yourself that you did ovulate in previous cycles and roughly when that ovulation occurred so that you can estimate when you might ovulate in future

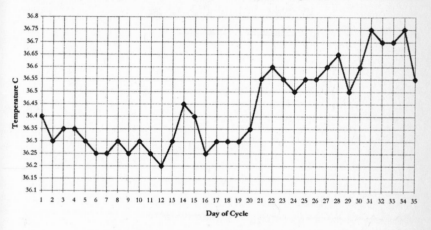

Figure 6: Sample basal body temperature chart

cycles of the same length. It will not help you determine when you are going to be fertile. Some women look for a drop in temperature before the rise but this is not the important sign: it is the rise in temperature after ovulation that is important. If you try to use temperature charts to time your inseminations, you will invariably be too late.

Emotionally, taking your temperature every day might feel like a sign of commitment to getting pregnant – a statement that you have really begun the process. Or it might become oppressive – you might feel you're never allowed to forget that you are trying to become pregnant.

The two-week wait

Once you've got your sperm, you have a two-week wait to see if it met up with an egg. There are many signs of early pregnancy. Not all women experience them and none by itself is a sure sign. Some women notice changes a week to ten days after conception. Others feel nothing different until weeks after they have missed a period. Common signs are breast swelling and tenderness, nausea, more frequent urination, tiredness, more vaginal secretions, and constipation. A missed period is somewhat more conclusive but you could have a bleed when the fertilised egg implants into the uterine wall. If you have been recording your basal body temperature and it is still high twenty to twenty-two days after the temperature rise following ovulation, you can be fairly sure that an egg has been fertilised.

There are several home pregnancy testing kits available from chemists. All pick up the hormone human chorionic gonado-trophin (HCG) which is produced by the placenta and appears in your urine or blood. The kits will be accurate as early as one day after your period should have started.

You can also get a similar test done by your GP which is reliable 41 days after your last menstrual period. It has the advantage of costing nothing and will confirm what you may already know by this time.

The birth – Jude's story

Jude and Lori had been together for three years when Jude got pregnant by an anonymous donor and gave birth to her son in 1984. Three years later, Lori gave birth to their second son. I interviewed Jude in 2001.

Having children was very enriching for our relationship. Both the babies were wanted, planned and welcomed into our little set-up. The sharing of that was magic. Neither of us was put out at all by the arrival of either the first or second child. But we had thought about it for a long time. We had enough money, a nice house and jobs where we could work part-time.

And we had lots of lesbian friends also having children at the same time. It was a happy time. It felt right and quite groundbreaking at the time.

Because I'd done self-insemination, I knew the date when my baby was supposed to be born and that was the date I went into labour. He was born at four o'clock in the morning. I had hordes of people at my birthing. This was at home with a midwife there. The pain was so bad that I just gave up and said to Lori, 'I'm going now. You take over.' But apart from that, I remember thinking what a miracle it was. It was the same with Lori's baby. Lori had to be snipped which was a bit shocking but once snipped, the baby came flying out. He had lots of curly hair and was just gorgeous. My son had stayed overnight at a friend's house and came round first thing in the morning – then it was love at first sight.

My GP didn't want me to have a home birth because I was thirty. I asked him what was the worst thing that could happen and he said that I'd get tired. I asked how I could stop that happening and he said by eating. Eating little and often will stop your blood sugar levels going down and enable you to be in control for longer. Usually people give in to going to hospital, having pain-killers, whatever, just because they're so exhausted. So I conscientiously ate throughout the 36 hours of labour.

It is incredible to grow a child and to give birth. It's been underrated like anything else women do. I think lesbian couples are in a wonderful position to worship the child that you both want that's growing in your partner. It's amazing.

5

HOW TO SELF-INSEMINATE

Now that you have found your donor and checked when you're fertile, this chapter tells you how to carry out the insemination. All you need is a jar for the semen, and any implement which can move it from the jar to the vagina – a plastic needleless syringe is the most convenient but even a spoon will do. You can order a self-insemination kit from PinkParents UK (see Resources).

Getting the sperm

Sperm are carried in a small quantity of fluid called semen. Ask the man to masturbate and ejaculate into a clean jar, preferably plastic or porcelain. Plastic food containers, particularly yoghurt pots, are ideal. The jar does not have to be sterile but should be well washed and rinsed of all traces of detergent. Metal and styrofoam may harm the sperm. The use of a condom is not a good idea, especially condoms impregnated with spermicide.

The amount of semen should be somewhere between two and six millilitres (a teaspoonful is about 5 ml). Semen should be milky white or grey white with a characteristic odour. If it is green or brown in colour and/or has an extremely unpleasant pungent odour, it is likely that the man has an infection or is bleeding somewhere in his genito-urinary tract. It may still be fertile but should not be used. Semen which is very clear (like saliva) usually contains very low numbers of sperm and should not be relied on for self-insemination.

Donors should *not* be advised to abstain before each insemination, as it will not improve the sperm count or strengthen the sperm in any way. Sexual activity in general increases sperm production. The man should have ejaculated three to four days before the insemination; if he has not ejaculated for ten days, his sperm count goes down. The use of broad-spectrum antibiotics within the seventy days before ejaculation may also decrease his sperm count.

Immediately after ejaculation, the semen clots, but within twenty minutes, it liquefies. It is then easier to suck it up into a syringe.

Sperm are fairly robust, but need special care once they are outside the body. They live longer (at least six hours and probably more) if they are not allowed to dry out and if they have little contact with air. If there will be a long time between ejaculation and insemination, put the semen in a tall thin pot rather than a short wide one. Or suck it up into the syringe as soon as it has liquefied, secure the plunger and wrap the syringe in clingfilm. Never mix semen with water as the sperm will explode.

You can carry the semen around at room temperature or body temperature, but certainly not any warmer. It is safer to keep it too cool rather than too hot. You can keep the jar next to your skin while in transit but this is not an obligatory part of the process. Heating the sperm by placing the jar in front of a fire or in direct sunlight will kill them.

Some women mix the semen from more than one man at each insemination in order to make it more difficult to identify the father. There are two problems with this: the sperm may block each other and, with the availability of genetic fingerprinting tests, it would still be possible to determine which donor was the biological father, if the man was determined to pursue this.

Inseminating

The easiest implement for inserting the semen into your vagina is a plastic *needleless* syringe. This is included in the self-insemination kit from PinkParents UK (see Resources). You can practise sucking up yoghurt into the syringe before you do your inseminations to get the hang of the technique.

With the plunger of the syringe all the way in, put the tip of the syringe in the pool of semen. Slowly pull out the plunger, drawing the semen up into the syringe. You may need to wait until the semen liquefies before you do this. Try to avoid sucking up air bubbles.

To inseminate, lie on your back and insert the syringe into your vagina as far as it will go, as if you were putting in a tampon. You want the tip of the syringe to be as close to your cervix as possible, for the fertile mucus which protects and directs the sperm through the os. If you cannot reach your cervix with your finger, you probably need to attach an extending tube (from the self-insemination kit) to the syringe before inserting it in your vagina. Once the syringe is in place, push the plunger all the way in.

There are several ways to keep the semen in your vagina long enough for most of the sperm to end up in the right place. The simplest is to lie down for fifteen to thirty minutes with your buttocks raised – a pillow will do. If your uterus is in the most common position, that is, tilted forward towards your front or lying straight, it is best to lie on your back. But if your uterus is tilted backwards, you may be more successful lying on your stomach. (You only know the position of your uterus after a pelvic exam by an experienced person.) The semen will drip out when you eventually stand up but enough of the sperm will stay inside. Thin sanitary pads are handy for catching leaks.

When and how often

The man's sperm count and motility may be higher if he ejaculates in the afternoon rather than in the morning.

It is possible to conceive after only one insemination, but you will maximise your chances by doing at least two and preferably three or more inseminations in each cycle during your fertile days.

The more inseminations you do within the fertile part of the cycle, the more quickly you will become pregnant. However, there is no advantage in inseminating more than once a day.

Try and try again – Eunice's story

Stella got pregnant with her son after inseminating with two donors. Her partner, Eunice, told this story in 1992.

The first donor Stella and I found was a work colleague of a friend and although he never met Stella, I interviewed him with one of the other women from our SI (self-insemination) group. He was quite young with a good head of hair – an important criteria for us when selecting a donor! – and was initially very co-operative. He agreed to all the health checks that we asked for, so there was only the delay of waiting for the test results. This was really nerve-racking, as we kept thinking that having more time to think about it, he'd change his mind, or that there would be a problem with the test results – in fact, we pretty much covered everything that could go wrong. Nothing did go wrong, and this donor remained with us for six months.

We were working on getting a 'back-up' donor in case the present one dropped out. We'd had an idea that this might happen when despite all the information we'd given him, he expressed surprise that Stella hadn't got pregnant on the first attempt. We eventually advertised and met with some of the potential donors but this didn't really work out, until another group member put us in touch with someone who had replied to their advert and whom they had interviewed. This time Stella met him by herself as I'd managed to convince myself – after several unsuccessful meetings with potential donors – that together we were probably rather overwhelming. This time we were lucky and the donor turned out to be the sort of person we were looking for. He was prepared to donate without wanting anything further in terms of contact with a child and his requests were reasonable. After successful medical checks, we started inseminating and Stella fell pregnant on the seventh attempt.

We read so much about pin-pointing the fertile period – temperature charts, mucus tests, chemical thingies in test tubes – but Clearplan launched their ovulation detection kit just around the time that we were due to start inseminating. We had already had a run-up period using the less expensive methods and thought that we had cracked it, but the idea of just weeing on a stick and looking for a colour change seemed so much easier. It worked well for us, although other people haven't found them so useful. They are also expensive and I remember going to as many branches as possible of a well-known chemist to collect money-off vouchers which were part of the launch promotion. We were also lucky with co-operative donors. We would give approximate dates from one month to the next and then confirm nearer the time. I also think that the fact that this tended to fall towards the end of the week and usually at weekends also made arrangements easier.

It took eighteen months for Stella to get pregnant. I think that we always did something slightly different, each time thinking that we must have found the reason why it hadn't worked the time before. Initially friends did collections for us and Stella would inseminate at home, but we ended up collecting it ourselves and just doing it in the back of the car. This was much easier than it sounds and actually lightened things up, as we ended up laughing at the ridiculous traffic situations we got into. This was the method that worked in the end. It could just be that our time had come and it would have worked anyway – who knows?

Second time lucky – Bronwen's story

Bronwen got pregnant by self-insemination using a known donor. She gave birth to her son Rhys in 1984 and told her story in 1986.

I had so much fun arranging my late night self-insemination assignations. I would get my room all ready so that when I got into bed I wouldn't have to get up again all night to fetch a book or a glass of water. The whole situation appealed to my sense of farce and often I would laugh out loud at my fumbling attempts to not spill the jar of sperm as I tried to draw it up into the syringe. The first month I tried I had bought a 10 ml syringe – very optimistic. Most of the sperm remained in the nozzle. And so the second month I went to the other extreme with a 1 ml one and that time was filling it time and time again, most anxious not to get air bubbles in, as I had heard that was a bad idea. Well, bad idea or not, it worked fine and 39 weeks later I stood up and gave birth to Rhys in triumph.

SELF-INSEMINATION LEAFLET : ADVICE FOR DONORS

Self-insemination – Advice for donors

Self-insemination is a way for a woman to get pregnant without having sex. This leaflet tells you how to do it and is for men who have agreed to donate sperm for this purpose. Don't agree to be a donor unless you understand the legal and practical implications of becoming an "unmarried father."

Screening for health
Test results from the STD/GUM clinic will tell you whether you are free of most sexually transmitted diseases. But with HIV, there can be a three-month gap between exposure to the virus and a positive test. During that time, the HIV test will be negative but the virus can be passed on in the semen. Because of this possibility, you should be able to reassure the woman that you have not been doing anything which puts you at risk of HIV infection in the six months before donating. Make sure you know what is considered safe sex. Do you know about the sexual practices of all your partners?

Are you fertile?
Unless you have fathered a child within the last few years, it's worth having your sperm tested. You can arrange this with your GP or you can go to a private clinic. A good result is:

- Count – at least 50 million sperm per millilitre.
- Motility – more than 50% motile.
- Abnormal shapes – less than 50%.

Smoking, heavy alcohol consumption, poor nutrition, certain medications such as antibiotics, anything that heats up your testicles (daily long hot baths, wearing tight underpants, trousers, or polyester jockstraps, driving more than three hours a day), exposure to radiation and toxins can affect men's fertility. Three months prior to donating, start following healthy living guidelines.

An upper age limit of 55 is recommended for men donating sperm to clinics. Pregnancy is somewhat less likely to occur with the semen of older men, although there is not the same drop in fertility that women experience.

Donating

Masturbate and ejaculate into a clean plastic container, such as a yoghurt pot. Avoid using styrofoam containers or condoms. The pot does not need to be sterile but should be well washed and rinsed of all traces of detergent.

Your sperm count and motility will be higher in the afternoon than in the morning. It will also be higher if this is not the first time in the last few days that you have ejaculated. You certainly do not need to abstain from sexual activity – including masturbation – before inseminations, as it increases sperm production, as long as you do not ejaculate more than once or twice a day.

The woman needs to inseminate within two hours of ejaculation. If there is a delay before you can deliver the semen, keep it at room temperature.

Being available

A woman is fertile for only a few days (two to seven) during her menstrual cycle. It is not usually possible to predict much in advance when these fertile days will be. She can give you a rough idea when she might be fertile but will have to contact you nearer the time to arrange the best days. This means you must be flexible and easy to contact.

How long will it take?

It is possible to conceive after only one insemination, but don't count on it. Be prepared to donate for several months to a year. You will maximise the woman's chances of getting pregnant by doing at least two and preferably three to four inseminations in each cycle. The more often you do the inseminations within the fertile part of her cycle, the more likely she is to become pregnant.

6

CLINIC INSEMINATIONS

If you want to get pregnant, you need to find some sperm. As discussed in Chapter 2, some women ask a friend for sperm; others advertise for a donor. There is also the option of donor insemination at a clinic or "sperm bank", which is the focus of this chapter.

Pros and cons

If you go for donor insemination at a clinic, you don't have to find a donor or get involved in any kind of a relationship with the man who provides the sperm. If you've had a bad experience with finding donors, going to a clinic could be a relief.

But there are also problems with clinics. They are not set up to help lesbians to get pregnant and many discriminate against lesbians and single women. And as they run on a medical model, they may want to use unnecessary medical procedures.

There are pros and cons, so before you decide on this option, ask yourself the following questions:

Are you worried about health risks?
Clinics do a thorough job of screening their donors for sexually transmitted diseases, particularly HIV infection. At clinics, the sperm is frozen. It is only used for inseminations after it has been stored for six

months and the donor has tested negative for HIV at the beginning and end of that period. If you cannot be sure that a known donor is free of sexually transmitted diseases (as discussed in Chapter 3), you are better off with a clinic.

Do you mind that your child won't know its birth father?

As a society, we attach great significance to genes. It is widely believed that the transmission of genes is important to an individual's sense of identity, that an individual will not feel complete unless they know who it was that provided their genes, even if the donor has no involvement or influence on their life past conception.

Many lesbians also share these beliefs and do not even consider going to a clinic. But it's not always easy to find a donor. If you don't have a close friend willing to donate, you are faced with the daunting task of finding, assessing and involving a stranger in your family life. Some lesbians weigh up the pros and cons of advertising for a donor and reluctantly decide to approach a clinic for an anonymous donor. Many would prefer an anonymous donor whose identity could be traced when the child grows up. A few have arranged for semen to be imported to a UK clinic from those California clinics which offer the option of so-called "yes" donors or "identity-release" donors, willing to have their identity made known when the children reach the age of eighteen. Another option for men not willing to be known is to prepare a video tape to give to the child at the age of eighteen. In the 1997 catalogue of the Pacific Reproductive Services, only four of the twenty-eight donors listed were not willing to be known.

However, in terms of the research evidence, children conceived by anonymous donation are not only functioning well but have more devoted and actively involved parents than children who have been naturally conceived. The conclusion from the evidence is that a genetic link appears to be less important for positive family functioning than a strong commitment to parenthood.

What information do you want about the donor?

You won't be given his name, but ask for as much information as possible. It's important for your child to know not only his physical features and medical history but his personality, interests, job, hobbies and reason for donating. Ask the clinic how they recruit donors.

Can you afford to go to a clinic?

Most of the donor insemination clinics in the UK are private, but even NHS clinics charge fees. The service is expensive, especially if it takes more than a few months to get pregnant. After paying for an initial consultation and a series of tests (which can also be done on the NHS by your GP), you pay a fee for the sperm (about £100) and an additional fee for the insemination (ranging from £250 to £600 per cycle). If you have to travel to the clinic, your expenses mount up. In 2001, you could easily pay more than £2,500 for six months of inseminations.

Is there a clinic nearby which will accept lesbians?

There are more than 100 private and NHS clinics throughout the UK licensed to provide donor insemination. Clinics are regulated by the HFEA, the Human Fertilisation and Embryology Authority. Although the HFEA's Code of Practice specifically says that "centres should avoid adopting any policy or criteria which may appear arbitrary or discriminatory", they can get away with discriminating against lesbians by referring to the "child's need for a father" clause in the law. One condition of the licence is that, "A woman shall not be provided with treatment services unless account has been taken of the welfare of any child born as a result of treatment, including the need of that child for a father."

I know of only 25 donor insemination clinics which do not discriminate on grounds of sexuality. This is based on reports from lesbians who have been to these clinics and on a postal survey carried out in 2000 (K Saira's dissertation, see Resources). Nearly all of these are private clinics and it is rare for an NHS clinic to accept lesbians. Lesbian-friendly clinics are mainly in London and Manchester; those who live in Scotland, Wales, the southwest of England, many parts of the Midlands and parts of the north of England either have to travel long distances or find a known donor.

To find a donor insemination clinic that will accept you, phone the one nearest to you. The HFEA has a list of all the clinics licensed for donor insemination and other assisted conception techniques in the UK; to find out which are known to be lesbian friendly, contact PinkParents (see Resources for both addresses).

Are you prepared to travel to a clinic that will accept lesbians?

Bear in mind that travelling to a clinic is inevitably stressful. You may have to do it for months before you conceive. You have to take time off work to get to the clinic during opening hours. Travelling to another city is not only expensive but often disruptive.

Are you prepared to appeal?

If you are turned down by a clinic, you do not have to give up. Just because the receptionist says forget it, that doesn't mean you have to accept the situation. Write to the director of the clinic, explaining that you are a lesbian and as deserving of access to the service as any heterosexual woman. Perhaps the director has never been contacted by a lesbian before and hasn't thought about the issues. Your letter may be just what's needed to bring about a change of heart.

If your letter does not open any doors, the next step is to appeal through their complaints system. The clinic is required to put in writing the reasons for their refusal to provide a service to you. They cannot refuse to hear your appeal and to do so in an open and fair way.

There is a precedent for appealing. A woman was refused donor insemination because her partner was a female-to-male transsexual. The couple wrote a persuasive and well-argued letter. Their case was referred to the hospital ethics committee who reversed the clinic's original decision. They went on to have two children at the clinic. (If you want help and advice on drafting an appeal letter, contact PinkParents UK.)

If after all that, the clinic won't budge, you can take them to court, arguing that they are in violation of your human rights. There has been no test case yet under the Human Rights Act, so it is impossible to say what would happen if a case were brought to court. The civil rights organisation, Liberty, is looking for a lesbian refused access to a donor insemination service who would be willing to bring a test case.

In the meantime, they asked a barrister to speculate about the outcome of such a case.

In the barrister's opinion, lesbian couples who have been refused NHS fertility services on grounds of sexuality have a good chance of proving in court that such treatment is unlawful. There are two articles in the Human Rights Act which are relevant – Article 8, the right to respect for private and family life and Article 14, the prohibition of discrimination on the basis of sex, race, religion, etc. and any other status. The court has to decide whether section 13(5) of the Human Fertilisation and Embryology Act is compatible with these two rights. This is the section of the Act requiring that the clinic "take account of the welfare of any child born as a result of treatment, including the need of that child for a father".

Not all discrimination is unlawful but the barrister believes that a court would find it hard to justify treating lesbian couples differently from heterosexual couples. The court would have to take into account the precedents set in other UK court decisions, namely:

Adoption: courts have been willing to grant adoption orders to lesbians.

Family: in custody disputes between lesbian mothers and ex-husbands and in applications for joint residence order by lesbian couples, courts are no longer accepting that sexuality is grounds for refusing to make an order.

Tenancy: a court case went to the House of Lords involving succession to a tenancy. The House of Lords accepted the fact that same-sex relationships are to be treated as equivalent to heterosexual relationships.

If you're up for a good fight and willing to bring a test case, contact PinkParents (who are working with Liberty on this).

Do you have fertility problems?

For some fertility problems, you're better off with fresh sperm than the frozen sperm used at the clinic. Frozen sperm is less effective so it may actually take longer to get pregnant.

If your fertility problem is caused by your age (if you're over forty), your chances of conceiving are lower at a clinic. If you've had investigations and there's no obvious explanation for not conceiving, you may as well keep trying with fresh sperm.

For other fertility problems, though, you're better off at a clinic. If you're not getting pregnant because your donor has a low sperm count, then it's worthwhile going to a clinic, where you will get help. Similarly, if you have blocked Fallopian tubes, polycystic ovary disease, hormonal problems, lack of ovulation, incompatibility between the donor's sperm and your cervical mucus – all of these can be diagnosed and dealt with at a clinic. You may need an assisted conception technique such as in vitro fertilisation or intrauterine insemination.

Can you avoid being turned into a patient?

The main problem with clinics in this country is the medicalisation of the procedure. You are considered a patient, rather than a consumer of their service. Donor insemination is licensed as a medical procedure for the "treatment" of infertility, giving the medical profession total control of the way the service is provided and who has access to it. By approaching a clinic for donor insemination, lesbians are trying to get pregnant, which is a natural and non-medical activity. We are seeking a source of sperm, not medical treatment. Medicalisation disempowers women by turning them into patients. It has resulted in a profitable business for the clinics and, I believe, an inappropriate, exploitative, unjustifiably expensive service for the users.

To justify its status as a medical procedure, the clinics offer a full medicalisation package, including high-tech checks on the woman's fertility, high-tech ways to detect ovulation and high-tech methods to place the semen inside. Some of these procedures are invasive and uncomfortable. Drugs such as Clomid have short and long-term side effects. All high-tech medical procedures add to the cost, the time and the stress of getting pregnant.

It is up to you whether you agree to have any of these tests (see next question). You do not have to go along with IVF (in vitro fertilisation) or IUI (intrauterine insemination) instead of donor insemination. You can make your own decision whether to have a hysterosalpingogram or an ultrasound. But if you do not accept what they offer, they will put you under enormous pressure. The tactics used in some clinics are outrageous – some have been known to tell outright lies. One woman was nearly persuaded to go ahead with IVF because she was told by the clinic that her chance of getting pregnant with IVF was 25%. This was a lie. The success rate they gave her was for women in their twenties – she was 42. Above the age of forty, the pregnancy rate with IVF is less than 5% (per cycle of treatment) and the live birth rate is even lower.

The trouble is that clinics have a different perspective from the client. At worst, they are out to make money – and some private clinics will do anything to cash in. But that is not the main problem. Doctors and nurses want job satisfaction and they need to justify their professional status. You don't need a medical degree to insert semen in a woman's vagina and let nature take its course: women can do it themselves and in the 1980s quite a few clinics gave women the semen to inseminate themselves at home. But it's much more satisfying for the medics to play with high-tech equipment and to think they're improving on nature. In fact, the legal requirement to freeze semen to exclude HIV risk means that their donor insemination service is actually *less* effective than self-insemination using fresh sperm. So when clinic staff tell you that their techniques improve your chances of getting pregnant, take it with a pinch of salt.

Which extra procedures do you want?

There are several factors to consider when you decide which extra procedures to take advantage of:

Effectiveness – If it improves your chances of conceiving then yes, do it. But the most common reason among lesbians for not getting pregnant is age. None of these procedures affects the quality of your eggs, which decline with age. If you are having trouble conceiving because you are over 35, there is no technique which improves your chances other than donor insemination, time and patience.

However, if you have fertility problems, these techniques make all the difference. For polycystic ovaries, the drug Clomid does help. If your

Fallopian tubes are blocked, you can only find out by a hysterosalpingogram and IVF would be the most effective course of action. A hysterosalpingogram is a test where dye is inserted into your reproductive tract and then an X-ray is taken. Unless you have a history of pelvic infection or ectopic pregnancy, the chances of your Fallopian tubes being blocked are remote. The trouble is that you may not know that you have had pelvic inflammatory disease as there are often no outward signs. You could decide to try inseminating for six to twelve months before having a hysterosalpingogram, or you might feel it's better to have the test than to inseminate without knowing whether your tubes are blocked, even though it is unlikely. If you are over 35, the chance is slightly higher, so you might come to a different decision. If your tubes are not blocked, IVF is no better than donor insemination (DI).

If your fertile mucus interferes with the donor sperm, then IUI is more effective than DI. If there is no problem with your fertile mucus, I am not convinced that IUI is worth the extra cost. I have read a systematic review comparing IUI with DI and thought the conclusions were ambiguous and uncertain. It's very hard to draw conclusions even from properly conducted studies, let alone from statistics presented by the clinic. Even if there is a definite increase in effectiveness, it is not a large increase – it won't double your chance of conceiving, but you will pay nearly double the cost.

Cost – IUI costs about £350, compared with about £200 for DI. At the Bridge Fertility Centre in London, IVF costs £1,950 for one cycle. A hysterosalpingogram costs about £185. I know of women who could not afford to continue with these expensive procedures and had to stop after a few months without conceiving. If you didn't have to pay for unnecessary interventions and you didn't have to travel to a clinic, you could afford (both emotionally and financially) to inseminate at home for one or two years, if it takes that long.

Discomfort – IUI involves inserting a thin tube right through the cervix. IVF is an invasive medical procedure involving drug treatment, monitoring by ultrasound scanning, egg collection under local anaesthetic, fertilisation in the lab and transvaginal transfer of the embryos.

It's your decision. You are not a patient, but a woman trying to get pregnant. Make your own decision based on all the factors that are important to you. The following stories of Linda, Amy and Theresa's experiences may help.

Say the right thing – Linda's story

Linda is a black woman who went to a clinic for donor insemination, where she conceived her daughter Marcy. Although I interviewed Linda in 1986, I thought it was relevant to include her story, as her experience is not that different from the experiences of lesbians at clinics in 2001.

I got pregnant with Marcy through a clinic in London. I wouldn't mind a father being involved with Marcy, if only because my older son Dean has got a father somewhere. I wouldn't want to have a relationship with a man to get her. But I would rather have known who Marcy's father was. All I know about him is that he was supposed to be a dark West Indian and that he was probably a medical student.

After being turned down by a black gay men's group, I thought of other ways to find black donors. A friend of mine said that she knew a lesbian who worked for a clinic, and maybe she could ask her. I had thought that only heterosexual women could go there. I didn't think that lesbians could go. She got me an interview. They said it would have to go through a 'board' with a couple of doctors on it to see if they'd accept me.

The first interview was quite OK. They just asked what I wanted and how they could help me, if at all, and why I had come to them. I said that I chose a clinic because I wanted a black donor. However, there were hardly any at the clinic and there were women in line for them anyway. They said there were three women and three donors, plus me.

After that, it got quite difficult because I had to go for an interview along with the woman I had been having a relationship with for a few years. I had to force her to go at the time. It took her ages to say that she'd go with me. She went because she knew how much I wanted the baby. I said to her, 'Don't you dare get anything wrong!' She said, 'I won't. I won't.' It was terrible once we were there, because we were both trying to say the same thing. Halfway through the interview, they sent me outside and kept my lover there. Then they asked her, 'Do you really want this baby?', and she had to sit there and say, 'Yes, we've thought about it for years now, and we've decided we really, really want to have a baby.' And then she had to go out and I came back in and they asked me the same question.

We had to be like a husband and wife, and have a home together. They asked me how many 'straight' friends I had, to balance it out I think, and how many men friends I had. We told a lot of lies! We didn't like that at all. But we felt we had to do that to get what we wanted in the end. ... It was my last hope, especially wanting a black donor, so I thought if I have to lie my way through, I will. But they were actually really, really nice, especially my counsellor. They don't discriminate against lesbians at all. Maybe they wouldn't have failed me [if we hadn't lied].

After that interview was over, it was very easy. They wrote to me saying they had accepted me. Then I had to go and be examined by the doctor. During all this time I was doing a temperature chart, so I knew when I was ovulating. I would just ring up in the morning when I needed to go up.

It's a lot of money. You have to answer questions you know aren't their business and you have to be a file, a case. But they're really friendly and nice and it's good that they don't discriminate against lesbians. Because it's an organisation, you can understand them and you tend to trust in them. I did totally. I just assumed that it was totally tested and that it was strong semen and that it was probably the best. It wasn't just somebody I knew as a friend or I didn't know anything about at all.

Pushing for what you want – Amy's story

Amy and her partner came to a workshop I led for lesbians considering getting pregnant. They had been thinking and talking about having a baby for about four years before coming to the workshop. Her story is taken from a letter she wrote in 2000.

What had made it complicated for us was how to do it and whether my partner was into it as well. When we came away from the workshop, it was almost like we were on honeymoon. It really helped to just get some practical information. It was one of the best experiences of my life to be able to talk about wanting to have a baby by insemination without having to go through all the usual shit of having to explain the process. 'No, someone doesn't just wank into a jar and then you get pregnant. There's usually a bit more to it than that.' When we came away, it felt like we had been able to make a decision together about what we were going to do. We decided to try our damnedest to have a baby. I'll carry it. We'll go to a clinic.

Since the workshop, I contacted the HFEA (the Human Fertilisation and Embryology Authority) and wrote to all the clinics that offered donor insemination to lesbians in London. I have more or less decided which one we will go to. I have spoken to them a couple of times and they always seem quite nice. One of my big problems is that I hate doctors and medical things. The story I want to tell is about how 'medical' and heterosexual clinics are. It made me so angry at the time and also made me realise how vulnerable the whole process already makes me feel!

I went to my GP to say that I was gay and I wanted to be referred to a clinic for donor insemination. I wanted to have some blood taken to check I am ovulating. I knew I would have to pay, but wanted him to write a letter of referral. The doctor said, yes, fine, no trouble. When I got home, there was a message on the answerphone asking me to go and see the head of the practice the next day. Perhaps there was a problem after all.

When I saw him the next day, he said that the practice was not prepared to do any tests for me on the National Health. He said that my sexuality was not a problem but the private clinic should do all the tests. He didn't think private doctors should try and get the NHS to do their donkey work for free. He had a point, but as I didn't have any choice in this instance but to seek private treatment, I felt the least he could do was a few blood tests. He agreed to write the letter and dictated it in front of me.

Four weeks later, I decided to chase up the clinic, as I had not heard anything. They had never got the letter so I rang the practice. The receptionist said that the letter had been erased from the computer by mistake and they had been meaning to contact me. I was furious. Were they going to tell me? When? What about any other letters that might have got rubbed off by accident? Thank god, it wasn't a referral letter about anything life-threatening.

I had to go back to try again to get the letter. This time I saw a different GP who had never heard of a lesbian who wanted a baby. It was as though he didn't know such things existed. But he wrote the letter there and then and gave it to me to post. I also told him that the last doctor had said that there was no way they could do any tests for me. He fell hook, line and sinker and agreed to do the blood test and to give me the results himself. Nice one, it saved us £145.

I guess the moral of this story is to push a little bit harder every time and don't get too complacent.

No place like home – Theresa's story

Theresa was 43 when she finally decided to try to get pregnant. She had always wanted children, but was afraid to act on her desire out of fear of the disapproval and censure directed towards lesbians who have children. After years of wavering, she finally recognised her right to live her life as she determined, regardless of what her mother, the Catholic Church or the bigots in society think. Sadly, she left it too late and didn't conceive either by donor insemination at a clinic or by self-insemination with a known donor. Theresa wrote this in 1999.

When I decided to try and get pregnant in 1997, my first choice was to find a known donor so that I would be able to tell my child who the biological father was. My attempts to find a donor were not successful for various reasons and I realised that what was the most important issue for me was to have a child by whatever method was possible. I knew that a lesbian friend had become pregnant and subsequently had a baby through the Bridge Fertility Centre in London. She assured me that the clinic did not discriminate against lesbians, especially those who could afford to pay the very high fees!

My partner and I made an appointment to see one of the medical directors at the Centre. This appointment was relatively straightforward. Dr S asked some questions about my health and menstrual cycle. I was surprised at how little probing there was about our motivation or suitability for parenthood during the appointment. She then did a short internal examination and asked permission to write to my doctor. This letter did request my doctor's views about whether she was aware of any contra-indicators that would make treatment by the Centre inadvisable. It was then suggested that I ask my local health centre to do a series of tests to identify any possible loss of fertility, due to my age. This stage took quite a long time, approximately two months, which was difficult to cope with.

The next step was a visit to see a nurse at the Bridge Centre to discuss what sort of donor I would like. She was very friendly and dealt with the issue in a practical way. She did assume that I wanted a Caucasian donor but was quite accommodating when I explained that this category was not specific enough. I actually wanted an Irish donor to match my own ethnic origin. The nurse then asked for further information about my menstrual cycle so that she could work out when I was likely to ovulate. It was explained to me that I would have to bring in urine samples from a certain day of my cycle to test for an LH [luteinising hormone] surge. Once the surge was detected I would have to attend the Centre the next day to have the insemination, which would be intrauterine. The first cycle was very stressful – mainly because I live one hundred miles outside of London and it was a strain travelling first to London and then 'across town'. [Theresa had to travel to the London clinic because none of the clinics in her home town would accept lesbians.]

Almost in passing, the nurse told me that there was another clinic in Reading which provided the same service. This was a much better experience. The Berkshire Fertility Centre [since closed down] is located in a health centre, a short bus ride away from the train station. It is staffed by two nurses and unlike the Bridge Centre, which is rather clinical, is smaller and more intimate. The nurse who did the inseminations was very warm and reassuring. I experienced some pain and discomfort because I was unable to relax completely and she did her best to support me during the procedure. I eventually had four inseminations (one per cycle) without becoming pregnant. I stopped using the clinic because purely by chance I met a gay Irishman who agreed to be my donor.

To conclude, I have mixed feelings about using a fertility clinic. It is good that there are some clinics who will see lesbians and all the testing and screening of donors is taken care of. On the negative side it was very expensive (£431 per insemination without any extras), there is no possibility of finding out who the donor is and the procedure is medicalised. Self-insemination in my own home has been so much better by comparison.

7

WHEN IT DOESN'T GO AS PLANNED

This chapter looks at the reasons why insemination may not be successful (including age and fertility problems), at miscarriage, and at strategies for coping in difficult circumstances.

Unpredictability

Conception is not a mechanical process which must automatically work if all conditions are right. It is true that some women get pregnant the first time they try. But it may take many months or even years of trying before success, or it may not work at all. It is sometimes possible to identify the reasons for not conceiving and occasionally to do something about them, but there is a great deal of unpredictability around conception. It is a process that is not within our control. The irony of the situation is that self-insemination is essentially a means of taking control of your life and choosing to become a parent against opposition, yet you cannot choose to conceive – you can only provide the conditions for conception to happen. This is hard for most of us to come to terms with.

How long should it take?

As far as I know, there are no statistics for the success rate of self-insemination (compared to donor insemination from a clinic). There is no reason to assume it will be any quicker or take any longer than for women trying to conceive with male partners by sexual intercourse. Among young heterosexual couples who try to get pregnant, one in ten are unable to conceive after one year of regular trying. In clinics using frozen sperm (which leads to lower pregnancy rates than fresh sperm), about one fifth of the women who do conceive, do so in the first month, and three quarters in the first six months. The remaining quarter conceive between six months and twelve months. Although it is frustrating, there is no reason to worry about your fertility or the donor's until you have tried for at least twelve menstrual cycles.

Getting pregnant over forty

For one good reason or another, there are many lesbians who do not try to get pregnant during their fertile years. When they reach their forties and become aware of the imminent approach of the menopause, whatever circumstances that stopped them before – fear of prejudice, insufficient money, lack of support, the wrong relationship or no relationship, illness, demands of work and political activity – are no longer obstacles. They go all out for a baby. What these women don't do is review their decision in light of their now-advanced age.

The harsh and unfair biological reality is that women are most fertile in their early twenties. After that age, fertility drops steadily until the menopause when it ceases altogether, sometime between the ages of 45 and 55. Between the ages of 20 and 24, the chance of getting pregnant during a year of determined effort is very high – nearly 90%. By determined effort, I mean inseminating more than once (from two to four times) every month for a year with a fertile donor during the fertile days. From 25 to 29 years, the pregnancy rate is still high but has slipped to just below 80%. For 30 to 34-year-olds, it is just above 60%.

For women aged 35 to 39, it is 50%. From 40 to 44 years, your chance is slightly better than a third. Only 5% of 45 to 49-year-olds conceive.

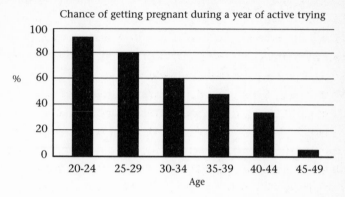

Chance of getting pregnant during a year of active trying

There is no medical treatment for this natural end to fertility. The cause is the ageing of the eggs. They've been in our ovaries since before we were born and, after hanging around for forty years, they are much less capable of being fertilised by sperm. An egg may be released in each menstrual cycle and you may still have regular periods. But the fertile mucus, the basal body temperature rise and a positive result in the ovulation detection kit do not necessarily mean that the egg is capable of fertilisation.

At a donor insemination clinic, a woman over 40 has only a 2% chance of having a baby (per cycle of treatment). Drugs such as Clomid which induce ovulation do not improve the fertilisation potential of the egg. However, Clomid often induces ovulation of more than one egg, increasing the chance of at least one being viable. IVF (in vitro fertilisation) is less successful in older women – for women under age 30, the chance of conceiving per cycle of treatment is 25%, from age 40 to 45, it is 5%. The birth rate from IVF is even lower. Egg donation from a younger woman followed by IVF is the only medical treatment with a higher chance of success.

A few of the eggs *are* fertile and some women do conceive in their forties. A friend's grandmother conceived her fourth child at 41 and her fifth child when she was 49. But this last pregnancy was the result of nine years of unprotected heterosexual sex. Translate her circumstances to today's forty-plus lesbian planning a child by donor insemination. Imagine having two to three inseminations per month for nine years – that's at least 216 inseminations.

The circumstances of insemination mean that your chances of having a child by this route are low after the age of 40. I realise that many women don't want to hear this, but I think it's better to have realistic expectations before you begin than to be devastated because of false hopes. Donor insemination does not often work for women over 40 because you would have to inseminate for years before you happen upon the few good eggs still left in your ovaries.

The cost of long-term insemination is high for a number of reasons:

- It's a rare man who is willing to donate for years, especially if he won't benefit in any way. Most donors give up after a few months. It's reasonable to expect that the man will be disappointed and frustrated if his donation does not lead to pregnancy within a year. Some men will not donate to women over forty, knowing that their chances of success are low.

- Many clinics have upper age limits or will not let you inseminate for years. It's bad for their success rates but, in any case, they should not be offering a service with such a low success rate.

- Inseminating has enormous emotional costs. You have to put your life on hold and delay making any major commitments that would have to be dropped if you did get pregnant. The stress of waiting for your period to come and the disappointment when it does is hard to bear for long.

- Years of inseminating do not improve relationships. Rarely are both partners equally committed to having a baby. If the non-inseminating partner has had bad experiences with her own children, she may be unenthusiastic and may become more so over the years. Few couples can survive the single-minded self-absorption required to sustain years of inseminating. No matter how much of a joint effort it starts off as, the non-inseminating partner has little role in the process. Eventually she may feel excluded and rejected, fearing that her partner has a closer relationship with the donor than with her.

So, if you are over forty, think hard about the costs to yourself, your partner and the donor. If you try for one or two or three years and don't have a baby, you will still always regret that you didn't do it when you were younger.

If you are under forty, don't delay making your decision. You won't regret having a baby in less than ideal circumstances, but you may well regret having waited until it's too late.

Success factors

Before you begin to worry about your fertility, first of all, satisfy yourself about three crucial success factors:

i. Is the donor fertile?

It is much easier to investigate infertility in a man than in a woman. Ask him to have a semen analysis if he hasn't done so already.

ii. Are you sure you're inseminating during your fertile days?

It is not necessary to focus on finding the day of ovulation, as this tends to cause too much anxiety – which you certainly don't need if you are having trouble already getting pregnant. But do you feel confident that you know roughly when you are fertile – by one of the signs previously discussed (Chapter 4)? This may be a time to use an ovulation kit for one or two cycles.

iii. Are you having enough inseminations?

Do not be surprised that you are not pregnant after a year of trying, if you have only had one insemination each cycle.

Infertility investigations

If you are inseminating frequently, are reasonably confident of the timing of the inseminations and of your donor's fertility, you may begin to question your own fertility.

You should consider seeking infertility investigations
in one of these circumstances:

- When you have inseminated during your fertile days with a fertile donor for more than 12-18 cycles without conceiving.
- When you do not menstruate.
- When you have no fertile mucus at all.
- When there are less than 10 days between your temperature rise and your next period.
- When you have no temperature rise during the cycle, or very irregular cycles.
- When you have miscarried more than three times.
- When you have a history of anorexia.
- When you have a history of endometriosis, pelvic surgery, polycystic ovaries, fibroids, pelvic inflammatory disease, or infection as a result of childbirth, abortion, or use of the coil (IUD).
- When you have had gonorrhoea.
- When you have a history of excessive exercise at the level done by women athletes in training.
- If you recently used the contraceptive pill or the injectable contraceptive Depo Provera.
- If you had a ruptured appendix.

If any of these apply to you, don't jump to the conclusion that you are infertile. But if you are concerned about your fertility, your GP can carry out some investigations or can refer you to a fertility clinic. Fertility services are patchy on the NHS, with great inconsistencies between health authorities, long waits (up to five years), and different definitions of who is eligible. Some fertility clinics will see lesbians but others won't. If you have a donor and he is willing, consider taking him along as your "partner". You might not be seen until you have been trying without success for at least a year, while some say two or more years. At least 90% of people seeking fertility treatment go privately.

Trying to get pregnant – The feelings

If you have been inseminating for a long time, don't underestimate the effect this can have on you. It is inevitable that the longer it takes to conceive, the more stressful it becomes. No matter how hard you may try to be relaxed and patient, you are likely to suffer extreme disappointment every time another period starts. It is a very emotional time and feelings of anger, frustration, jealousy, despair and inadequacy are not uncommon.

Bereavement

The feelings women experience when not conceiving are those of bereavement. They go through the same stages of grief felt by those grieving over the death of an adult or a child. These stages are denial, numbness, anger and acceptance. The grief is for the loss of potential – the potential child, as well as your image of yourself as a mother. The bereavement is especially difficult because it is unfocused. There is no object to fix on – no memories, no clothes, no photographs. Until you stop inseminating, the grief is complicated by the hope that next month it will work. Only when you decide to stop inseminating can you work through the process of bereavement.

Waiting

Waiting is a constant feature of the process of trying to get pregnant. There is the waiting while finding a donor, the "two-week wait" between the inseminations and the next period, the wait for fertile days and the next inseminations, the wait for referral to a fertility clinic, the wait for test results, the wait while you try some new method or drug suggested by the fertility clinic. Waiting can feel interminable and unbearable. It is usually thought of as time wasted doing nothing, yet at the same time, you may feel unable to do anything else. The waiting fills the time.

Jealousy and alienation

As soon as you want to be pregnant, you tend to notice pregnant women and women with children more than you ever had before. At first this is exciting and you wonder what your child will be like when it reaches the age of the child you see. Eventually it becomes too painful. You may find yourself feeling alienated from your friends who already have children. It can seem as if everyone else is getting pregnant except you and that people you know are caught up in family life while you are left on the outside. Intense feelings of jealousy and wanting to withdraw are not unusual. Those friends with children who are sensitive to what you are going through often do not know what is best to do. They might try to protect you by keeping their children out of your sight, but this might result in greater feelings of isolation and alienation as you share less and less with them. Or they might bring their children with them and risk intensifying your distress. Many people are so caught up in their own lives that they are unable to be aware of what you might be feeling. Trying to get pregnant is an invisible activity.

Preoccupation

The desire to be pregnant and the trying can dominate your life. You can become preoccupied by your bodily processes and think of nothing else. You may feel betrayed by your body and angry that it is not doing what you want it to do. Just wanting to be pregnant can change how you view yourself and may exacerbate your desire for a baby. You might start out feeling enthusiastic but fairly detached and yet find as the months or years go by that you become almost driven. Some people may label you as obsessive if you pursue infertility investigations or carry on for many years.

Anxiety

Years of unsuccessful insemination inevitably create anxiety, especially if the wish for pregnancy becomes overwhelmingly important. You may worry about the method itself, the fertility of the donor, your own fertility, even whether you have a right to be a mother. You may be anxious about having sex after inseminating, even though sex does not cause miscarriage. You are likely to feel anxious about being turned down for fertility investigations because of not having a male partner. Women doing self-insemination often feel that they have to renew the decision to get pregnant every month. This in itself can be stressful.

Coping strategies

There is probably no way that months and years of unsuccessful inseminations can be made enjoyable, but there are strategies you can develop to protect your mental health while you are in the midst of it. From discussions with women inseminating, I have compiled a list of suggestions.

Acknowledge your feelings

Start by recognising whatever feelings you are experiencing, even those "unacceptable" feelings of anger, jealousy and despair. It is not necessary to do anything about these feelings but accept that you have them. Acceptance is not the same as abandoning yourself to them, which can only lead to bitterness. Acceptance is about noticing what you feel in each moment, seeing it for what it is, and letting it go. Above all, be gentle and loving with yourself.

Avoid blaming yourself

There is controversy about whether stress causes infertility and you will probably hear this expounded as fact from one source or another. It is possible that stress does play some part, though it is difficult to prove such a statement. Unfortunately you may interpret this to mean that somehow it is your fault you are not conceiving. This kind of thinking will not help. Whether or not stress causes infertility, it is definitely true that not getting pregnant causes stress. The advice to relax and avoid stress can be infuriating. It is not so easy just to forget about getting pregnant when you have to go to such lengths to organise the inseminations in the first place.

Support

Long-term insemination is very stressful and the women I talked to felt they needed as much support as they could get. It is usually helpful to know someone else who is doing insemination at the same time as you. There are a few support groups in existence but if there isn't one near you, you can try to set one up. If you are the partner of the woman inseminating, think about your own support network. Your needs are somewhat different and you may find the best support from other partners.

Involve a partner or friend

Suggestions that worked for some women were to keep your fertility awareness chart in a prominent place for both of you to consult; and to delegate responsibility for making arrangements and picking up the semen.

Friends

Consider which friends you feel too vulnerable to expose yourself to. Protect yourself by not telling everyone. You don't have to tell people who are likely to be judgemental or dismissive. Make sure your friends know that you will tell them when you *are* pregnant. Although you know that they are well meaning when they ask, it can be too discouraging to be constantly reminded of your lack of success. Some women commented on the importance of keeping up friendships with women who are not involved with children so you can get away from it all.

Take breaks

If it is getting too much for you, miss a few cycles. You don't have to inseminate every month.

Keep it all in balance!

Don't worry about having the odd drink or cigarette. Stay in touch with your reasons for wanting a child in the first place. You can forget that the goal isn't to get pregnant but to have a child. Weigh up the effect of the stress of not getting pregnant on your mental well-being against your desire to be pregnant.

Miscarriage

About one in five of recognised pregnancies end in miscarriage and some estimates give a figure of one in two of all pregnancies, most of which occur so early the woman may not even be aware she was pregnant. The majority of miscarriages occur in the first three months of pregnancy. As you get older, your chance of miscarriage increases – about half the pregnancies end in miscarriage in women over forty.

Miscarriages are a real bereavement. A miscarriage may bring up intense feelings of grief, anger, jealousy, guilt and anxiety. The grief may be as great when the pregnancy is eight weeks as at eight months, though is usually deeper the further along in pregnancy you are. You will need plenty of time to mourn. Some women find that their sense of loss increases after the miscarriage until the due date and comes back on anniversaries in later years.

Women are usually advised to wait until they have come to terms with the miscarriage before attempting another pregnancy. This seems sensible for psychological as well as for physical reasons, but may not be the right advice for all women. It is not uncommon to feel anxiety about the next pregnancy and if or when you do conceive again, to hold yourself back from getting excited.

Many women do not tell anyone they are pregnant until the time of the greatest risk of miscarriage is past (at the end of the first three months). The danger with this strategy is that you risk isolating yourself with your grief and you could lose the support you might otherwise have had if friends had been sharing your excitement and the reality of your pregnancy all along. However, people are not always as sympathetic as you might like. They often make insensitive remarks along the lines of, "It's all for the best. There was probably something wrong with the baby anyway" or "Never mind, you can have another". People do not always know how to react to a miscarriage, because it isn't as real to them as to you, even if you have told them.

With a first miscarriage, satisfaction that you are able to conceive may accompany the grief. It is clear evidence that you can conceive and have a chance of conceiving again and carrying the baby to term.

A long wait – Kim's story

Kim and Wendy now have three children by self-insemination. Kim gave me this story in 1986.

Wendy and I decided that we would like to have children. As I am the older of us, we decided that I would bear the first child and we'd see what we wanted to do after that. Once the decision was made, I began trying to become pregnant. That was mid-1978, and I gave birth to our daughter at the end of 1983. There is many a tale to tell of those intervening years, but what is relevant here is that it took a long time.

Like most women I was brought up thinking that I would bear children. If I wanted children, then I would have them. I assumed fertility, and easy fertility at that. The emphasis in our lives was to prevent conception and heterosexual women have to spend a lot of time and energy doing this and have to place their health at risk in the process. It [the initial fertilisation process] was disappointing and disheartening. Others in the self-insemination group were pregnant, so it seemed that I was the failure. I was so in tune with my body during these months of taking daily temperatures, checking mucus and feeling every minute ache and pain, yet I could not control it. I had no control.

It seemed I could not choose to become pregnant. It was frustrating not being able to make pregnancy happen, but more than frustration, my body was causing me to feel a deep sense of failure in a way that I had not felt before.

After twelve months it was found, by chance, that I had a double uterus and that this might affect my fertility but not to any great extent. There seem to be more reasons which cannot be explained by medical science for my not becoming pregnant during those months. Over the last few years, medical science has provided some answers to why women don't conceive, but of course, they don't know it all. And besides, lesbians do not have easy access to medical science! With self-insemination you feel you have a time limit; you can't just 'keep trying'. Self-insemination is often difficult to organise, it involves you with men and it takes over your life for a while. So it in itself can feel like a pressure.

This is not to be a tale of woe. It has the ending we wanted. We now have two children. We each have given birth to a child and they are lovely. But I want to help other women not to assume fertility. And also, when we think about having children, we should think about the possibility of having a disabled child. Hopefully, if our lives aren't built on myths, we will have more control over them.

A lost dream – Casey's story

In March 1998, Lesley and Casey came to a workshop I held in their town for lesbians considering getting pregnant. Two years down the line, their dream of having a baby has not come true. This is a story of what can happen when you go past the age barrier of forty. Their experience illustrates how long and how difficult the process can be – months were spent searching for a donor and inseminating at a clinic with inconvenient opening hours. Most cruel of all, Casey conceived easily but miscarried just as readily. She wrote this letter at 2.30am one morning in 1999, having been woken by cramps. I thought the letter would be helpful to others.

I did the second pregnancy test last night – again negative. I shared the pain with Lesley, took painkillers and cuddled in, but I'm still awake an hour later. I got up to make a cuppa, cried and wrote this letter.

We came away from the self-insemination workshop filled with hope. Two years later, we've been through three inseminations, two pregnancies, two miscarriages, lots of love, heartache, learning, and turmoil. It's been an emotional roller coaster and believe it or not, there is nothing I regret. I don't wish I'd never started, even if it ends here. However, I'm not ready to give in yet. We want to keep trying but I'm aware now that if it doesn't work, I'm more truly ready to accept a life without a child than I was a year ago. My biggest fear was that if I opened myself up to wanting a child, it would be worse than not trying. The answer is clearly no. Lesley and I have been through this process together. It has strengthened our relationship. I have experienced early pregnancy at least and know that I can conceive. We have weathered the storms and know how much we mean to each other. It seems to have taken our relationship on to a deeper, surer foundation.

The workshop opened up the debate we'd been having with each other and got the self-insemination support group going. We had regular meetings every six weeks. Everyone was at a different stage. Although some dropped out, we met and discussed and shared ideas. We planned to contact donors, meet parents, support each other through pregnancies and meet at family barbecues. In the end, the group fell apart. However, the contacts remain. This weekend we're meeting one couple who I'm sure will support us through this current grief.

Lesley asked her brother to be a donor. We waited, procrastinated, went through other male friends and never got round to contacting the very few we felt could possibly be donors. We initially wanted a known donor who could have a limited role as an uncle or at least be known to the child. Like with so many things, we had to compromise. Our fantasies of us performing the inseminations ourselves at home with love had to be lost to the reality of time running out.

One year later, I was 41 and we still had no donor. We felt we had to drive the process forward and open up opportunities ourselves. We decided to go to a clinic. I went off to my GP who I've known since I was a child. Poor man! I was embarrassed but at least I got a good response. He said, 'You probably know much more than me. What do you want?' He referred me to a consultant who did hormone tests. More embarrassment, as he hadn't seen any lesbian couples before, but he handled it well. We felt like pioneers and ambassadors of the lesbian community.

Evidently I had the hormone levels of a woman younger than forty years old. The consultant referred us to the local fertility clinic, where the consultant in charge of the clinic gave us a bit of a grilling. He said to us, 'We don't normally take lesbians or single women. We don't want any publicity. Why do you want to do it? Have you thought it through?' We didn't blame the clinic for being cautious. Luckily, we passed the first test. The support we got from our self-insemination group meant so much to us. They understood and shared with us.

I had a hysterosalpingogram, which is an X-ray of my Fallopian tubes, to check for abnormalities and a meeting with a counsellor. She didn't counsel as I understand the word, but told us that whatever the outcome and final decision of the clinic, we were a nice couple and would make great parents! Eventually we were accepted on to the donor insemination programme and got an agreement that they would offer us three normal cycle treatments and three with superovulation by the drug Clomid.

I missed the first three opportunities as no one told my ovaries that the clinic was shut on Easter and bank holidays. I finally had my first treatment, just when a client of mine had been killed in a car crash and another was critically ill in intensive care. I rushed to his bedside, having had treatment that morning, and stayed there for two days until he was conscious enough for me to tell him that his best friend was dead. Despite this stress, I found that I was pregnant two weeks later, just as I set off with another group to canoe and bivvy in the Lake District. My timing has been mad this year. I hadn't told anybody at work so I couldn't opt out easily.

One month later, I went for a scan and found that I had a blighted ovum. There was no foetus developing in my womb, just an empty sac. I felt guilt and pain but got great support from the clinic. They suggested a medical evacuation, which was like a termination. It was so unfair to experience this when I'd wanted a real pregnancy. We duly went ahead and again fitted it in around work without telling anyone at work where I was going. Thankfully, two weeks later, we went on holiday and had time to talk and share our anger, grief, guilt and love. I was also able to windsurf and 'abuse my body' with alcohol which I'd not done for the last three months.

I was next fertile on a Sunday, so I couldn't have another treatment until the month after. Again I conceived. This time we were determined not to be optimistic too early but I did feel more pregnant. Again my timing was off – I was the only one drinking elderflower cordial over Christmas, the Millennium celebrations, and my birthday. Having been someone who enjoyed a drink, I was now aware of how so many of our celebrations in our society focus on alcohol.

When I went for my scan, they said it looked small and asked me to come back the next week. At the second scan, it was less obviously a foetus. The third scan provided definite confirmation that there was an abnormality.

The staff at the clinic were very supportive. When I told them I was dreading going to hospital for the medical evacuation, they suggested I wait and my body would do it naturally. How do you respond to people who know nothing of what's been happening and ask how you are in an offhand way? I didn't want to say, 'Oh, I'm just waiting to miscarry.' I finally miscarried at home at eleven weeks. It did feel it was much more like nature's way and I was less guilt ridden than when I went into hospital.

Yet again my timing was off. At work I was running the project on my own as two colleagues had left. I managed to miscarry on a Saturday and return to work on a Wednesday. I shouldn't have gone back to work so soon. I was drained and anaemic and in physical as well as emotional pain. As if that weren't bad enough, I was acting as a supporter and advocate to young women whose children were being taken into care or who were pregnant themselves.

This miscarriage was especially hard on Lesley. Before the scan with the first miscarriage she had been concerned, while I had not seriously considered that pregnancy loss could be a possibility. This time I was more scared before the scan and she was more optimistic. She also saw me running myself into the ground with work. She tried to care and support me but couldn't make me take time off, pigheaded person that I am. I know she wants to save me pain and feels guilty at her part in wanting us to have children. I feel guilt and failure at not succeeding. Through talking and sharing our feelings, we came to understand and love each other more. I'm sure relationships go through stages. Having children is one stage that takes it on to a new level. Shared adversity seems to be another.

Our friends have been so supportive, but I've found myself shutting off and not contacting those who could have given so much. I couldn't be in touch. It's been so hard living a lie, but it's hard being open about our relationship in a small conservative community. These people know nothing about the trauma we've been through. No one expects a 42-year-old lesbian to have had two miscarriages in one year!

I returned to the clinic for our third treatment. Lesley did the inseminations this time. But yet again, it was not meant to be. As I went to visit a young mum who had given birth and was having her second baby put into care, I felt the familiar premenstrual cramps starting. The boundaries between my life and my clients are blurred. My pain is mirrored in those I'm caring for. I know it's not healthy for me but I certainly have empathy for those mothers who are refused the chance to parent.

We are off to the clinic again tomorrow to discuss treatment. They suggested six cycles and so far I've only had three. I'm not ready to give up yet, but I also need to be realistic and think of how we cope with failure.

Our life together didn't feel like failure before this and we need to get back to focusing on our successful life together.

If only I had accepted my sexuality much earlier. Then I would have been able to consider being a parent earlier. Maybe future generations will have more chances. It took me till I was 35 to see the light, a couple of years later to meet the wonderful woman I wanted to share my life with and another couple of years to feel that our love could be shared to nurture others. If I had seen the light at 25, then it would have been OK.

My advice to lesbians is:

- Don't leave it too late! We all think we can get pregnant anytime, even at forty. Even when the information is there, we don't believe it.
- Be warned! It takes a lot longer than you plan it to take.
- Face the reality – not the doe-eyed fantasy of having a newborn baby. You need to know how hard, stressful and complex it can be.

Even if it turns out to be hell, like it was for us, it can still be a positive experience.

Giving up – Andrea's story

I interviewed Andrea in 1991, when she had decided to stop trying to get pregnant.

Four years ago, my partner and I joined a group of women who were interested in, or already starting to try self-insemination. Someone had a copy of the first edition of *Getting Pregnant Our Own Way*, and we were all so excited to find that there were not only other women to talk to about what we were planning, but someone had actually written about how to do it. We all bought a copy. I read mine from cover to cover, re-read it, kept it by my bed and read it on the bus. All of it, that is, except the bits written by women who didn't get pregnant. Superstitiously, I thought that if I read about them, then my chances of conceiving would be smaller, and anyway, I was excited, optimistic, curious, nervous; I didn't want to read about failure and disappointment. It would be like having the hangover while you were still tipsy.

But here I am all the same, having failed and been disappointed, having grieved and battled and refused to give up, and failed again and again and again. No baby to show for all that effort. No reward, no just deserts, no child of my womb. No new status, no joining in with the others, no belonging.

My hangover lasted for a very long time, although I know that many other women's have been longer. I tried to conceive for over three years, self inseminating, using donors I knew or had at least met. By the time my partner and I met, I had already decided that I wanted a baby and I chose the first donor. My partner disliked and distrusted him; it was a disaster, the first real conflict in our relationship and a fundamental test of our love and loyalty. I felt, by saying that she didn't want to use him and with no other donor on the horizon, that she was trying to take my baby away from me. A timely holiday in Crete provided us with respite and a compromise: to approach an acquaintance, already a donor. He and his wife happily agreed and we embarked on the monthly ritual of counting, measuring, calculating, a two hundred mile round trip, sleeping on their floor and taking days off work, waiting, downfall.

I don't think that anyone else except other lesbians in the same position really can understand what this does to you. It's obsessional, exhausting, it strains every relationship you have, it's odd, you don't fit, it feels mad and weird or hysterically funny and all the time you are working against your own and everyone else's conditioning which says you shouldn't be doing this thing that matters so much. In the midst of all my waiting, of course, heterosexual friends around became pregnant, gave birth and I couldn't express to them the real extent of my jealousy and fury.

My worst time was always the point at which the first period pain told me, so soon, that the hoping was over again this month and then having to wait for the bleeding, knowing it would come. Every month I felt that I had lost another baby, another one had died. Every month my partner, not quite comprehending my needs but seeing my pain, would hold me until I could face it again. I couldn't let it go, not allowing the possibility that it wouldn't work eventually.

In the end we persuaded the donor, already the father of three, to have a sperm count. It turned out to be zilch, so low as to be non-existent. We waited while he got treatment and started again. His wife conceived. I didn't.

There were tests and more donors. There was nothing wrong with my body that anyone could tell, but after the laparoscopy, I'd had enough. After a break of several months, I couldn't face a return to more tears and heartache, and I had a life to live that was now gradually being wasted. I expected sadness and regrets, uncertainty and ambivalence, but that wasn't how it was. After a shaky time and some numbness and distance from it all, I feel as if my hangover is well and truly over. I am well, happy, full of beans, creative and am even – amazing thought! – enjoying the glimmerings of relief and pleasure at making plans which don't involve the patter of anybody's tiny feet!

Losing Connor – Justine's story

When Justine decided to have a baby, she thought carefully about what she wanted, made her plans and went into action. Until the day before her baby was born, everything appeared to be going to plan. She met Simon, a single gay man, through an ad in the Pink Paper. *They spent six months getting to know each other, set up a co-parenting arrangement and began inseminating in 1995. Justine conceived quickly and had a normal pregnancy. Then misfortune struck. This is a lesson about not taking anything for granted. Justine told her story in 2001.*

I got pregnant on the second cycle we tried. I had a trouble-free pregnancy with a couple of minor hiccups. The odd thing was that all the way through the pregnancy, I could never envisage myself with a baby. I could never see further than the birth.

I was planning a home birth, which was OK with my midwife and GP. The consultant was not so happy and I was relieved I had only seen him once early on, an automatic referral for first-time mothers of my age (34). I'm not into the medical model. I had booked a birthing tub and had got to 37 weeks of pregnancy before my midwife put her foot down and insisted that I get checked by the consultant before she would deliver a first baby at home. So I booked an appointment with the consultant for the day after Simon and I were due to return from a short holiday with our families. We left for our break the same day the midwives delivered the home birth pack. After they dropped off the pack, I had an antenatal appointment with my GP. He put the monitor on my belly and said, 'We're all agreed that's the baby's heartbeat, aren't we?' Simon and I agreed. It was an absolutely fine, run-of-the-mill antenatal appointment. That was the last time we heard Connor's heartbeat.

Later that day, we were in the car, listening to Armistead Maupin's *Babycakes* on tape. A phrase from the book stuck in my mind: '… apart from the obvious. How apt this phrase turned out to be! The baby wasn't moving around quite so much, but bearing in mind how normal everything had been, and that babies often don't move as much in late pregnancy, I didn't worry. We had five lovely days with our families. We knew the next time we saw them we would have our baby with us. Our holiday was over. It was a beautiful sunny evening and we were in the car driving home, when suddenly I felt that somebody had walked over my grave. I'm sure that was when Connor died. I mentally checked myself over. Everything seemed OK but I was overcome by a wave of anxiety. I said nothing.

The next day I was restless and tearful whenever I was by myself. I was resentful about having to see the consultant and expecting a row about having a home birth. I put my anxiety down to that. When I saw the consultant I was not very happy with his bedside manner. The only reason I knew he was going to do an internal exam was because I had been told to take my knickers off. I was saving this for the 'frank exchange of views' I was expecting later. He did the internal exam, then tried to find the baby's heartbeat and couldn't. Absolutely deadpan, he said, 'We've been having problems with this equipment today. Let me go and get another piece of equipment.' He came back with another piece of equipment and tried once more. Again he couldn't find Connor's heartbeat. This time he said, 'Oh, this one doesn't seem to be working either. I'll send you up for a scan.'

I was made to wait until the midwife who had booked me in to the clinic was available. I had already told her I was feeling anxious when she booked me in to the clinic. We walked to the sonography room and I remember wanting to pee again. I was lying on the table and we had a trivial discussion about how the gel they use for these scans is warmed up.

I said I couldn't quite see the screen. The sonographer moved it so I really couldn't see the screen. She carried out the scan. The sonographer said 'no' and she and the midwife left the room, leaving me with an assistant. I knew what they were going to tell me when they returned. I think I had known for about 24 hours, but even so, when they came back and the sonographer said that my baby had died, my reaction was to scream no. It felt like it was happening to somebody else, like I was watching it from a long way off. I cried a lot. So did the midwife.

I asked the midwife to call Simon, but not to tell him why he had to come right away. A couple of my friends came to stay with me at the hospital until Simon arrived. They sat me in a small room until the antenatal clinic had finished about an hour later. Then I went back to see the consultant. I asked my friends to come in with me, as Simon had not arrived. The consultant was going over and over my notes and kept saying he could find no reason for this to happen. He was very sympathetic and professional and said the appropriate things, but I don't think he coped brilliantly. I don't think the information I was given was particularly good. He gave me the choice of having labour induced the same day or coming back the next day. I was told I would be given maximum pain relief. I was asked if we wanted a postmortem and I said yes. He said we could arrange the funeral ourselves or the hospital would do it for us. That was it.

Simon arrived shortly after. I think that up to the point he arrived and when my friends left the room without speaking to him, he thought I was about to have an emergency section. I had already told the midwife that it was my responsibility to tell him. I told him his baby had died. Then we had to decide what to do. We decided to come back later that day, but we needed to let our families and friends know what was happening. We drove home and a little later a friend of Simon's arrived from London to offer him support and a change of clothes.

I wish I'd had more information to prepare for Connor's birth. If I had known how important it was, I would have taken some baby clothes and a camera. Except for a cuddle bathrobe, we hadn't bought anything for the baby to wear yet. It didn't occur to me to take any clothes. We were given some in the labour ward. Although a friend turned up with a camera shortly after Connor was born, the faces of babies who are born dead bruise very quickly. You need to take photos within an hour of the birth.

We didn't know this and we weren't told. I also don't remember anyone telling me what my baby would look like when he was born.

I felt desperately ashamed of what had happened. I know how irrational that is, but I felt it was all my fault, as if I'd done it on purpose. I found it so difficult to ring my parents. I knew my dad was out and I didn't want to tell my mum when she was by herself, but in the end I had to. They were in their late sixties and I had visions of them tearing down the motorway, being involved in an accident and dying too. So I told them not to come until the next day. I don't know what I was thinking. I wish I'd asked them to come right away. My mum feels very sad that I didn't.

Simon's friend drove us to the hospital about 6pm and my labour was started at about 9pm. We were booked into a large room with a big bath. As well as Simon and two of my friends, several members of Simon's family – his two sisters, mum, dad, and brother-in-law arrived. They were there throughout the labour. His family wanted to be together – the first grandchild in their family (Simon's sister's son) had died at three days.

The consultant who started my labour is a lovely man and has a lovely bedside manner. He said all of the right things. We knew our baby mattered. He put us at our ease and had a sense of humour. I asked to be referred to him when I became pregnant again. The midwives were great. They made us lots of tea, were very discreet but spent lots of time with us. I don't think many stillbirth labours are like the one we had. Even though it was awful, there were moments of lightness. At one point, I needed the commode and no one could find it. Finally, we realised that Simon's mother was sitting on it.

My body would not let anything out from before the start of my labour. I had wanted to have the same kind of birth I planned at home, with minimum intervention. I laboured in the bath for a while but my full bladder and bowel made the contractions more painful and I was exhausted with grief. I eventually asked for an epidural, a catheter and an enema. They could not fit an epidural to me so I was given morphine. The labour went on for twelve hours. My son was born weighing 5 lb 4 oz, at 8.20pm on 4 June 1996. He was perfect, he had lovely red hair, he was everything we wanted '… apart from the obvious'. We were very proud of him. He was born less than 24 hours after I'd been told he'd died.

I held him while he was still warm and wet. I have a photo taken by the midwives straight after the birth. The midwives washed and dressed him as I was too dopey from the morphine. I would have liked to have bathed him. They also took some photos of him and prints of his hands and feet. I'm not unhappy with the choices we made but I know that if I'd had more information, I would have made different choices. We took photos. We talked a lot. My parents arrived. Everybody held him and cuddled him. It was a beautiful sunny morning. It was very emotional. We cried a lot. It was so unfair.

The staff were lovely, apart from two unfortunate incidents. A doctor came to get our signatures for the postmortem. She wouldn't look me in the eye and hadn't written Connor's name on the form. I objected and told her his full name. She crossed out Baby and wrote Connor, spelling it wrong. Given that Connor's not going to get many bits of paper with his full name, it was important to me to get it right. When my friend raised her voice saying she should use a new form, the midwives realised something was amiss, whisked the doctor away and sorted out the paperwork. Simon signed it. The other incident was when Simon took Connor down to the X-ray department. Without even looking up, the woman behind the desk said, 'Just put it over there.' Simon said, 'He's not an it. His name is Connor.' The woman looked up and realised she was dealing with a parent. She was very apologetic.

The hospital's bereavement officer came to explain the choices we had to make and the legal process. We decided to have him cremated. We arranged the funeral and the hospital paid for it. The hospital chaplain was a wonderful woman – she visited us at home and we planned the service together. Neither Simon nor I believe in God, so she did a funeral service in 'plain clothes' without mentioning God. She helped us to find some lovely readings and poetry. One was read by my dad at the funeral. It was very moving. Afterwards everyone came back to my home. We had put all the flowers and cards into the nursery as well as our photos and his stillbirth certificate. We had a book for people to leave messages in for us. The vicar has said to me since that it is one of the nicest babies' funerals she has ever done.

There is absolutely nobody to blame for the fact that my baby died. The postmortem said that he'd been dead between 24 and 48 hours. I think it may have been closer to three days. His weight was within the normal range. They found no physical or genetic reason for his death at 38 weeks of pregnancy. I don't think there's any point going over what could have been done differently. I was well cared for all the way through my pregnancy. It was nobody's fault.

Losing Connor changed my perceptions. I can never take anything for granted anymore. I know that life does not come with a money-back-unless-you're-satisfied guarantee. Anyone who's ever had a baby fears that something could go wrong and it's true that bad things do happen. But I still believe that pregnancy is a normal process for most women. Things go wrong much more often than we are led to believe. We just don't talk about them. But talking about them seems more honest than pretending they won't happen. I was frightened that something terrible would happen if I had another baby, and that the fear would grow if I waited too long to get pregnant after Connor's death. I got pregnant within three months. Declan was born less than a year after Connor. Although nobody said anything, I feel sure that people made value judgements that it was too soon, that it wasn't the right thing to do. I felt more anxious as the pregnancy progressed, but I don't think that would have been any different if I had waited longer to get pregnant after Connor's death. During my pregnancy with Declan, I had so many scans. Each and every one was traumatic because I had been lying on the scan table when I was told my first baby had died. They did pick up a problem, gestational diabetes, in my second pregnancy. I know any future pregnancy will be closely monitored.

We talk about Connor to Declan. There are pictures of Connor in both of our houses. Recently, Declan pointed to the photo and said 'baby'. I told him it was Connor, his brother. I worry that Declan might feel he was a replacement for Connor. Declan would not be here if Connor were alive. That's the top and bottom of it. My fear is that Declan will think we didn't want him, that we only had him because his brother died. But it could not be further from the truth. We always planned to have more than one child but I would never have done it within a year of the first. Declan is a bonus, something really nice that we weren't expecting. He's so precious. I cannot imagine how I could possibly love anyone else as much as I love Declan.

One of the things Connor taught me is that forever is a very long time.

The death of a child is not the sort of thing you get over. When Connor died, it felt like somebody switched off the colour. Everything I saw was in black and white and grey. I remember screaming that I wanted to die too, in those first few days and weeks. The colour started to come back when I found out I was pregnant with Declan. Every day that you survive with it, you find a way of dealing with it. You start to appreciate the small things that you didn't appreciate before everything went horribly wrong. You change your perspective on what exactly is the worst possible thing that could happen. I'm not so scared of some things that I thought I was. I will never ever regret having Connor. If I were offered a different life with the option of this not happening, I'd have him every time.

Part III

Adoption and Fostering

There is an alternative to having a child of your own, and that is to foster or adopt. Although plenty of lesbians have done this successfully, there is still a fear that we will face discrimination. This part of the book looks at the reality.

Adoption 125   Fostering 143

8

ADOPTION

If you are considering adoption, this chapter should help you prepare for the process. In particular, the suggestion that you find an agency with experience of lesbian adopters could save you a lot of trouble. The second half of the chapter explores the conflicts of adopting a child from overseas.

The good news and the bad news

The good news is that it has become much easier for lesbians to adopt children within Britain and to do so openly. There have been changes in public policy and practice which make it worthwhile for lesbians to consider this route to parenthood. Many adoption agencies have equal opportunities policies that include sexuality. Scattered throughout the country, there are well-informed and supportive social workers who recognise that lesbians are a valuable resource for children in care who need to be adopted. Lesbian and gay social workers in adoption agencies are chipping away at discriminatory practices. There are judges who do not accept that homosexuality is a reason to refuse to grant an adoption order. There are birth parents who have no objections to lesbians adopting their children. So good practice does exist. The many lesbians who have adopted children are proof of this.

The bad news is that a prospective adopter's sexuality is still an obstacle to adopting in many adoption agencies. While there is no overt discrimination in law, public policy favours married heterosexual couples, with lesbian, gay and single people often a last resort. You still hear the Government making divisive and unhelpful proclamations that a family headed by a married couple is the best for children. By law, the right to adopt is restricted to married couples and single people. Only one partner in a lesbian couple may be the legal parent. The other can acquire a limited form of parental responsibility through a joint residence order but this is not the same as that acquired through an adoption order. Leaving aside the policy, good practice is patchy and bad practice is common. A lesbian prospective adopter may have success in one agency or with one social worker but not with another.

Adoption policy

In July 2000, the government published its White Paper on Adoption initiating the "biggest overhaul of adoption law in 25 years." This may turn out to be good news for lesbians.

"The aim," says the White Paper, "is to modernise legislation and to set new targets to speed up the adoption process to help more children find new families. Last year there were 2,400 children waiting to be adopted. These children need the safety, stability and loving care of a permanent new family. And they need that stability as quickly as possible. That is not the case at present. Children stay in the care system far longer than they should. Over 28,000 children have been in care continuously for more than two years."

The government recognises that there is a crisis in the world of adoption. Whether it recognises that lesbians are part of the solution remains to be seen.

In the solutions proposed in the White Paper, there is no specific mention of lesbians, but there are proposals to treat prospective adopters with respect and without discrimination:

"Written eligibility criteria will be provided. People will not be automatically excluded on grounds of age, health, *or other factors* [emphasis added], except in the case of certain criminal convictions. These factors will however be considered, in terms of their ability to look after children in a safe and responsible way, as part of the whole picture."

This still leaves plenty of scope for discrimination in practice, but at least it doesn't automatically exclude lesbians on grounds of sexuality or marital status.

Special people needed

Anyone considering adoption in the UK has to realise that it's unlikely that an agency will place an *infant* with you. Most adopted children are older and have been in care. The average age of children when adopted is four years and three months but since adoption takes a long time, they are usually younger when first placed with their adoptive parents. However, only a quarter are under twelve months when they start living with their adoptive parents (according to a survey by the British Association for Adoption and Fostering). The more general truth is that it is children who are in need of families, not babies.

Children are inevitably affected by separation from their birth families and may have had years of neglect or abuse before they come up for adoption. If you enjoy children and are not a social worker or a child psychologist, you may not realise the full implications of adopting a child rather than a baby.

I have personal experience of this. When my partner and I decided to investigate adoption, we were told to forget about babies altogether. Naïvely, I didn't mind. I even allowed myself a brief fantasy about our new child, remembering how adorable my birth daughter was at three and how much fun we had when she was five. My partner was less sanguine, having worked as a residential social worker for children in care. It wasn't until we went on the adoption preparation course that I realised how different it is to raise your own child from birth than to care for someone else's possibly very hurt child.

Our course facilitator was determined that we go into it with our eyes open or not at all. During the four-day course, I learned that children may have challenging behaviour, learning difficulties, emotional difficulties, mental health problems and/or delayed physical development as a result of separation, loss, abuse or neglect they suffered from their birth family. Even a young toddler may suffer from these problems if the trust-building stage of development which takes place during the first year of life is disturbed or interrupted. I was surprised to learn these problems may not disappear once the child has settled into the new family. The hurt may be lasting, even into adulthood. Or the child may appear fine until hitting adolescence and then go completely off the rails.

When you adopt, you are taking on the job of meeting the needs of children who have been in care. That includes maintaining meaningful contact with the child's birth family as well as dealing with the difficulties resulting from their early experiences. Most people who want to be parents would be excellent birth parents but that does not mean they would be good adoptive parents. For this reason, the process of assessment and placement must be thorough and careful. The worst situation for both the child and the adult is if a placement falls through because the adopters are stuck in their fantasy of family life and are unable to meet the child's needs.

The adoption process

The entire process from initial contact to the placement of a child may take several years. The Adoption White Paper suggests time scales for each stage of the process, with eight months stated as the recommended time from the applicant's first enquiry to the agency's decision. It took us a year and that was without any delays. It was a busy year of continuous and thorough assessment, at the end of which our social worker knew us better than we knew each other.

Details of where to find out more about the assessment process, post-adoption support and agencies to approach are listed in the Resources section. Here, I am focusing on the issues for lesbians at each stage of the process. There will be some differences of approach in different agencies.

i. Initial interview

In the past, lesbians only got through the adoption process by omitting to mention their sexuality. I don't think that would work anymore nor do I think it's a good idea, given the lengthy and intimate contact you're going to have with the adoption agency. The social worker will be interested in how willing you are to co-operate with the agency. During our initial interview, we shared what we considered essential information with the social worker, in particular that we are a lesbian couple who intend to co-parent any child that we adopt. We asked her to find out if this was possible within the agency, since the local branch had no experience of assessing lesbians. She took an anonymous case study of our situation to the panel and discussed it with social workers at other branches. She was able to reassure us that it was worth our while to proceed.

ii. Training/preparation course

The course is a valuable opportunity to think about this most important decision realistically with access to the full facts. The one we went on lasted four full days. There were twelve of us and, as commonly happens, we were the only lesbians. Although we felt awkward coming out in the group, there weren't any overt expressions of hostility towards us. But some lesbians have felt unsafe and exposed on adoption courses and some have had to educate the others about lesbians, or been used by social workers to test the attitudes of the other participants.

We had to write a portfolio at the end of the course demonstrating what we had learned. We were judged on our participation in the discussions and exercises, our ability to think about the past and to understand its effect on us, our willingness to change and develop, our knowledge of children and their development, our ability to work with the agency and significant people in the child's life, our ability to put ourselves in the child's place and our respect for difference.

iii. Assessment

For the most part, we were assessed the same as any heterosexual couple but there were a few differences because we were a lesbian couple. As we were the first openly lesbian couple this branch of the agency had assessed, we took some responsibility for educating them on the issues. Our social worker went away with piles of books and articles we gave her on lesbian motherhood. These she gamely read and discussed with her colleagues.

I had also recommended experts for the social worker to consult, one of whom suggested extra questions for lesbian and gay applicants. These were:

- Write about your experience of homosexuality, your own and your family's response historically.
- How confident do you feel in relation to your sexual orientation? How comfortable are you as a lesbian or gay man?
- How have homophobia and heterosexism impinged on your lives? How do you feel you've dealt with this, and what coping devices do you now use?

I was annoyed that not all applicants, particularly heterosexual men, were asked about their sexuality and their attitudes towards homosexuality. But I agreed that there should be space to talk about how lesbian and gay applicants deal with homophobia. The strategies we use to challenge homophobia as childless adults are bound to be different from the strategies we use when we have children. We do need to reassure the social workers that we could help a child deal with homophobic bullying at school, for example.

The question of male role models is commonly asked of lesbians, so be prepared to come up with an answer that will satisfy them. Our social worker was sure the panel would be concerned about it and she was right. Our answer was, that although we didn't keep a male role model in the house, we did have contact with our brothers, fathers, uncles, nephews, male friends, male neighbours, male colleagues, male teachers, and male doctors. We also joked that we would promise not to turn off the TV whenever men appeared! That seemed to satisfy her.

iv. The panel

The final decision is made by a panel who may or may not accept the social worker's recommendation. The usual practice is for your social worker to present your case on your behalf, but the Adoption White Paper says you should have the chance to attend the panel and be heard.

Having noticed this, we went before the panel. We had to face ten complete strangers, each of whom had read our completed form and knew everything about us. We were asked a few questions, including the inevitable "How will you provide a male role model?" Already a bit unnerved by the occasion, I snapped, "We won't." I wouldn't recommend that way of answering the question because we could easily have been turned down on the strength of it. But luckily for us, the man who asked the question nodded and admitted he knew many boys who had been placed in all-female households and thrived. So that was that. We were approved.

v. Placement

Once approved, the next major obstacle is to have a child placed with you. Given the publicity about the thousands of children waiting to be adopted, you would think this stage would be quick and easy. But it is often the most difficult. Children awaiting adoption have their own social workers who make the decision about what type of family would best meet the child's needs. If the social workers are homophobic, they overlook lesbians and look for married couples, even if this means keeping the children in foster care for years.

vi. Legal process

This is the stage where you get full legal parental responsibility via an adoption order granted by a court.

Setting a precedent – Adopting Rachel

In 1997, a High Court judgement categorically stated that homosexuality is not a reason to refuse an application for adoption. This is the story of the lesbian mother whose case set this precedent. To protect the family from Sun reporters who took an unhealthy interest in the case, there is a seven-year injunction to keep their identity secret. For that reason, all names have been changed and no details have been given of their whereabouts. "Adopting Rachel" first appeared in Diva *magazine in September 1999.*

Until she was in her forties, Chris had not wanted to be a mother. But she changed her mind as her circumstances and lifestyle changed. Her partner, Alison, worked in the field of fostering and adoption. She knew that lesbians were being approved as potential adopters by some London authorities and suggested adoption as an option for Chris to consider. Chris was open to the idea. "I didn't think of it as second best," she says. "For me it was a very positive move. I thought it might well meet my needs."

Chris rang the adoption and fostering team at her local authority in the north of England. Intending to be open about her sexuality from the start, she told them she was a lesbian. They had never knowingly assessed a lesbian before but agreed to start the assessment procedure. Chris made it clear that she and Alison were a couple, with Chris to be the mother and Alison the co-parent. Only married couples can adopt *jointly*; Chris and Alison were assessed in the same way as co-habiting heterosexual couples. Both were interviewed extensively.

They decided on an older girl, age eight to twelve. "I was much more interested in a child who could verbally communicate and because I was working, I wanted a school age child," says Chris. "It does mean, however, that you're getting a child who has been through some bad experiences."

The training they attended emphasised the fact that older children have probably been abused, if not sexually, then emotionally or physically. Chris felt that she and Alison had something very positive to offer and proposed to the agency that female households can be particularly supportive and safe for girl children who have been abused.

Once the assessment was completed, their social worker, who was extremely positive throughout, recommended to the adoption panel that Chris be approved to adopt. The panel agreed, having questioned Chris's age (she was 47), rather than her sexuality.

The next hurdle was to have a child placed with them. This is the stage where a potential adopter has to make a decision based on the haphazard and patchy information written on the child's form by the social workers. The forms say something about the child's history and problems but can't give a real picture of what the child is like.

Eventually the social worker showed Chris the forms and a photograph of an eight-year-old girl named Rachel. Rachel had had eight different homes since she was four. She had been living with assessment foster carers for a year and had two failed adoption placements and many different foster placements. Chris was instantly interested and agreed to meet her.

The couple prepared a family book explaining who they were and where they lived, which the foster carer showed to Rachel before their first meeting, having been prepared by her own social worker to expect a lesbian couple. Fortunately, this was not a problem for her and she gave Rachel a good impression of her adoptive parents. Rachel herself didn't seem fazed by the fact that she wouldn't have a daddy or that she would be living with two women. She seemed more comfortable with women than with men.

At the first meeting, Rachel said hello to Chris and ran off to play. Soon she came back into the room, sat down next to Chris, laid her head on Chris's shoulder, and ran out to play again. "It was such a touching gesture," says Chris. "You could see how very much she needed a mother."

A six-week introduction period was planned. "Looking back, it seems very short to be making a decision about living with somebody you don't know. At the time it seemed like forever. I got deeply interested in Rachel very quickly and she did in us, so it became a kind of waiting period which was hard to handle. I thought about her all the time. It was such a powerful emotion to me. I was surprised and taken aback by it. We bonded very quickly."

The social worker had stressed the importance of continuity in Rachel's life and Chris agreed to maintain contact with Rachel's birth mother, Julie, and her maternal grandmother. When Chris eventually met Julie, they got on well together. Julie had been told that Chris and Alison were lesbians and had no problem with it. She could see that Rachel was happy with Chris and Alison.

When Rachel moved in, she was frightened but not closed off. She responded well to Chris's comfort and presence. "We went through hell when Rachel first moved in, but it was also a honeymoon because there were many nice times. As well as tantrums and some self-harm, she couldn't bear to have me out of her sight. She'd panic if I went round the corner in the park. I'm glad I wasn't doing it on my own. I took the brunt of it but Alison was an essential back-up."

Chris found the constant high level of emotional interaction and intensity very tiring. "It was completely and utterly exhausting. People talk about how tiring it is to have a baby and I'm sure it is, but it's also very exhausting to adopt a child." After about six months, Rachel started to settle in but shortly afterwards, they became involved in an even more stressful stage of adoption – the legal process.

Rachel had not yet been freed for adoption. A freeing order was needed to remove her birth parents' legal rights before the adoption order could be made. A hearing was scheduled before a local magistrates' court. Chris, Alison and the entire adoption team thought it would be straightforward.

"The social workers had done their assessment," recalls Chris. "They'd approved us to adopt. Rachel's birth parents were clearly unfit and were not going to win custody back. There was no question of that."

Nevertheless, the magistrate referred the case to the High Court. Although no reason was given for this, it was obvious that the magistrate felt he couldn't handle a case involving adoption by lesbians.

In the High Court, the QC representing Rachel's birth mother, Julie, argued against the freeing order on the grounds that it was not in the public interest for lesbians to adopt. He claimed that when the laws on adoption were made, the lawmakers had not intended for lesbians and gay men to adopt. Julie contradicted herself in court, saying to the QC that she objected to lesbians, something she'd never said before. But she also admitted that she was happy for Rachel to stay with Chris and Alison. She just didn't want to lose her rights altogether. The QC even questioned the judgement of the social workers who had approved Chris and Alison. But he could not produce any evidence that they were not good carers.

Chris gave evidence, concentrating on what was in Rachel's best interests. She was cross-examined by the QC. "He was vile, a complete and utter bastard. He asked whether Rachel would be sexually abused by us and, at the same time, why we didn't foster her instead of adopting her." It was clear he knew nothing about adoption: Chris and Alison had been assessed as adopters, not foster carers. "I wasn't prepared to make the enormous changes to my life for a temporary placement," says Chris. "In any event, adoption was what Rachel wanted and needed."

Chris found the court case traumatic. "I've never been a person who couldn't cope, but I couldn't cope with this. I started having panic attacks. I knew that there was a lot of anti-lesbianism out there. I was scared that if it became a big political issue, they would take her away. By this time we were very close to each another. I had promised this child that we would be together."

The local authority adoption team were as supportive as they could be, but it was outside their control. Chris saw that they were mystified and shocked. "They were heterosexual and they just hadn't encountered this stuff before. But I knew how nasty it could get."

The months of waiting for the verdict were difficult for all of them. "During this time we had to hold Rachel together and that led to scenes," says Chris. "I was frightened but she was completely devastated. I would not have put her through this if there had been any other way, but we couldn't compromise."

In the end, the wait was worthwhile. In a landmark decision, the judge concluded that the law "permits an adoption application to be made by a single applicant, whether he or she at that time lives alone, or cohabits in a heterosexual, homosexual or even an asexual relationship. Any other conclusion would be both illogical, arbitrary and inappropriately discriminatory in a context where the court's duty is to give first consideration to the need to safeguard and promote the welfare of the child throughout his childhood." [Re W (a Minor) (Adoption: Homosexual Adopter) Before Justice Singer, Judgement 11 April, 1997.]

The judge demonstrated that the lawmakers had deliberately chosen not to exclude lesbians and gay men. The freeing order was granted and the adoption went straight through.

"Rachel was very pleased when the adoption order went through," says Chris. "It's been four years since she's been living with me, but I've still got to reassure her that nobody can take her away." Before Chris adopted her, she had been placed with people who said "this is forever" and "we love you" and then she had been rejected. Her ability to trust was damaged, but fortunately not destroyed completely.

Chris remains committed to helping Rachel remember her history. Rachel hadn't seen her birth mother since before the court case started – sadly, Julie died three weeks after the judgement. Rachel still has her maternal grandmother. "We are lucky that we get on with her nanna. Her nanna thinks that Rachel has done well with us. She's very happy for her. It is wonderful to have that support," says Chris.

"Rachel knows that we're lesbians. Most of our friends are lesbians. We didn't talk about it a lot at first because it wasn't an issue for her. She's able to talk about it quite openly now. I don't think she talks about it with her friends at school; she's not confident enough. At some point it will come up again. We talk about racism and about accepting people for who they are. There's a lot of bullying at school about everything but at least she's got some ammunition. If anyone has a go about her having a lesbian mother, she can say, 'that's your problem, mate.'

"Apart from the court case, adoption has been such a joyful experience for me. It's a lot of effort, very demanding, but Rachel is wonderful and gives so much. Anything you give is returned tenfold. I feel very lucky. There are so many older girls out there who need adopting. I'd like to encourage lesbians to think about doing it."

Inter-country adoption

In Britain, it is rare for lesbians to adopt children from other countries. A major hurdle is that every foreign country (with one exception) has strict eligibility criteria that excludes same-sex couples. It is possible to adopt from abroad if you pretend that you are single, but you won't get a child if you are openly lesbian. The exception is South Africa, which does not discriminate on these grounds.

The procedure for adopting children from abroad is described on the Department of Health website (see Resources). The issue for lesbians is that the assessment has to be approved by a local authority panel, as for domestic adoption. The difference is that for an inter-country adoption, you not only have to pay and wait to be assessed but you also have to keep quiet about your sexuality.

In the States, there are private adoption agencies which facilitate the whole process, including finding a child to adopt in the foreign country. Some of these agencies knowingly accept lesbians and gay men but portray them in the home study in a way that will be acceptable to the authorities in the foreign country. Basically, they don't ask and the couple don't volunteer the information, leaving the agency in a position of plausible deniability should it ever come out.

UK law allows only local authorities and some voluntary adoption agencies to handle inter-country adoptions.

The issues involved in inter-country adoption are different from in domestic adoption and it is best not to go into it naïvely. Although the system in Britain often fails its looked-after children, there is a commitment to try to meet the child's needs. In some of the poorer countries of the world, there is a market in babies in which the best interests of the child are not considered. There are unscrupulous lawyers and agencies procuring babies from women who have seen a way to make money. Even if you adopt through an established agency, you are still uprooting a child from his or her homeland to be raised in a drastically different culture. To help develop their own identity, they need close contact with their country of origin, culture, language and people of the same race and ethnic origin.

Marian's story illustrates the dilemmas in trans-racial, trans-cultural, inter-country adoption.

Never quite there – Marian's story

Marian adopted a baby girl from a Latin American country and a few years later, was asked by the birth mother to adopt the girl's baby brother. Marian wrote this in 2001 when her daughter was eleven and her son, seven. She felt it was important to share their experiences, although she and the children would ideally prefer not to broadcast their lives.

I am a lesbian mother with two overseas-adopted children and, whilst recognising the contradictions (and the privilege of having two children), I am deeply opposed to overseas adoption. I have not written this piece to persuade people not to do it, but to raise some issues which I think are critical, but which are rarely addressed.

My thoughts about the politics of overseas adoption have developed over the past ten years. They come from what I would call the politics of pain, contextualised within an understanding of global inequalities.

The rich (overwhelmingly white) take the babies of the poor (overwhelmingly brown/black or East-European Romany), under the guise of giving them a better life, more opportunities or a home which is thought to be preferable to an institution. All of this is no doubt true, albeit couched in dishonesty, because the real reason why everyone does overseas adoption is that they want a baby. And no, I don't think it's OK for white people to adopt white babies from the former Soviet Union, for whom there is a huge market, particularly in the United States. Adopting a baby deals with your own needs in the moment; it doesn't necessarily deal with your growing child's needs.

I think now that the primary issue for children adopted from other countries is the recognition that they were not wanted by their birth mothers, either for reasons of gender (such as girl babies dumped in Chinese orphanages or in latrines in countrysides all over the world) or for reasons, ostensibly, of poverty. Neither of these is the 'real' reason why babies are abandoned, or given away for adoption. Of all the children I know who have been able to trace their birth families in their countries of origin or whose adoptive families knew something of their circumstances, none come into the category of really dire poverty (in the context of their particular country). The long-term psychological damage of feeling that you were not wanted by your birth mother (as opposed to her not being able to look after you for reasons of alcohol or drug abuse) has yet to be researched. Yes, this also begs the question of rejection by birth fathers, who, in the main, have upped and fled way back when. ... But show me a society where fathers have the kind of central importance to children as mothers do. Odd exceptions don't count.

I have been actively involved in socialist/feminist/lesbian politics for many years. Before I adopted my first child as a baby, ten years ago, I thought that overseas adoption was sort of OK, provided one was absolutely committed to giving the child access to her culture etc. Being a right-on leftie, I did all this: she went to Latin American nursery, I spoke Spanish to her, read her books and watched videos in Spanish, kept up contact with her birth family, made regular visits to her country of origin including visits to the family.

Her birth mother had another baby and asked me to adopt him as well. By this time, I had some understanding of the importance of 'blood' – of how important it was that a child had someone in the family who was a blood relative, someone to relate to on a plane that I could never hope to. My children so adore each other and so hate each other in a wonderful healthy way that, although it drives me mad, it daily reminds me how glad I am that they have each other.

After years of internal battles, external discussions and psychic war in general, I decided that it would be a great idea to go back and live in the children's country of origin (where I had lived and worked prior to adopting my first child). So, although in some ways it was very hard, I think that it was probably one of the really good things I have done for them (and me). For the children, it dispelled all fantasies about how life would be perfect if only we lived there. They actually had a very nice time but the political challenges were much harder for them than they were for me. On a daily basis, they saw babies and children living in families even poorer than their own birth family, where these children were visibly loved and cherished. I saw my poor babies internally acknowledge the reality of all this. Neither of them ever verbalised it, and to my shame I never felt able to open these particular flood-gates until my younger child did towards the end of our stay. They recognise very clearly that they were given up for adoption because, like so many, they were not wanted.

I want to add another slant to the debate on inter-country adoption. I don't think there are any specific issues for lesbians other than that having a lesbian or gay parent is yet another thing for our children to deal with. When I solicited the opinion of my friends, the only ones who made this point were those with overseas-adopted children, and lesbian mothers of much older children. If there are any issues around inter-country adoption for lesbians, it is that we must think of our children's needs, not our own.

If we choose to prioritise the gay issue, whose needs are we addressing when we fight the fight? We feel we need to be recognised, but our children want nothing more than a bit of peace and 'normality' in their lives. None of us has ever made a big deal of it at school, not wanting to 'burden' our children further.

This does of course bring into question the issue of coming out at school, but more critically the question of coming out as adopted at school. A heterosexual friend of mine, who has three overseas-adopted children, told me that when her daughter started secondary school three years ago, she announced that she was going to tell no one she was adopted because she couldn't hack all the flak.

I asked my children this morning what they felt was the most difficult thing about being adopted from another country.

My seven-year-old son (also adopted as a baby) was very clear that it was having to come to terms with the fact that his birth mother obviously hadn't wanted to have children and he didn't understand why she had had two and then hadn't looked after them. My eleven-year-old daughter initially focused her reply on her birth father having disappeared without a trace but, as she spoke, she was overwhelmed with the pain of it all and moved the focus to her birth mother's rejection of her. I asked her if she felt that being brown when I am white was a problem. She was very clear that the only problem is that other children ask why she has a white mother. They aren't always easily fobbed off by being told her father is brown, but go on to ask probing questions that she doesn't necessarily want to answer. She then talked about a white girl in her class who was adopted at the age of six because her mother died. She thinks it would be terrible to have your mother die, but that it is better than 'just being adopted anyway'. My daughter feels that it would be better to not know you were adopted until you were much older (just before you leave home) because it's 'very hard.'

I have come to think that many overseas-adopted children live in a kind of emotional diaspora. They are never quite 'there', never quite connected to the world in which they live. Both my children at different times have told me that the reason they find it hard to concentrate is that they are always thinking of their country of origin. My daughter first expressed this in a voice which said, 'How could you possibly not know what my head is always full of?' I have had so many discussions and arguments over the years about children living in different countries to the one they were born in, but it's not the same because adoption always comes back to a tragic quintessential loss and rejection which no other forms of 'living abroad' contain. I often meet people and think 'they're adopted' and within an hour or so it emerges that they are. Their levels of psychic pain are very high. I can pick out kids in the park, and I'm nearly always right.

I am aware that what I think comes from years of minute observation of my children who have always had a lot of emotional space to express their feelings. They are also (believe it or not!) happy, loud, expressive children, pleased with and proud of themselves. I found a poem my daughter had written to her (mutually adored) dying grandmother, which ended with 'I wish you were brown like me'. These feelings are not those of trans-racial relationships and mixed-race children – I truly believe they come from a deep pain and longing just to be and to belong.

9

FOSTERING

Although many lesbians have fostered successfully, most local authorities are not ready to assess them on an equal footing with straight people, as this chapter shows.

What is fostering?

The fostering process is very similar to that for adoption, but you do not become the permanent legal parent of the child and do not have to go to court. You have a continuing relationship with social services and get an allowance for your services.

There are various types of fostering, including:

- *Respite care* to give the child's main carers a short break.
- *Short-term or long-term care* of a few months upwards, until the child can be returned to her or his birth family or moved on to adoptive parents.
- *Long-term permanent care* until the child is ready to live independently.

Do they want us?

'Good with kids? Ready for a challenge?
Fostering could be right up your street.'

In the year 2000, the desperate shortage of foster carers drove the government to fund a £2 million recruitment campaign. Co-ordinated by the National Foster Care Association, the campaign included an appeal to lesbians and gay men. It seemed as if the government had finally recognised that the ability to care for children has nothing to do with the carer's sexuality.

Some lesbians have the time, skills and desire to foster children, and respond to these recruitment campaigns in good faith. And it's true that social workers with experience in this area believe that lesbian and gay foster carers whose motivation is "child-focused" have a higher capacity to hold on to very difficult children and meet their needs.

Often it works out brilliantly. There are lesbians throughout the country who have been approved to foster and who are working well with the local authority. But few local authorities are ready to assess lesbians and gay men on an equal basis with heterosexuals, and most have not even started putting good policy into practice.

Some agencies have good policies and good practice but prefer to keep it secret. My partner and I were approved by a local branch of a national childcare agency to offer respite foster care. Five months after we were approved, we were still twiddling our thumbs, waiting for a child to foster. At this time, we received a letter from the agency asking all their approved foster carers to help with a massive publicity drive to raise the profile of the agency and to encourage people to become foster carers. They wanted us to approach the national and local media with our stories. No problem. I was glad to help out. I wrote an enthusiastic article for *Diva* magazine to encourage lesbians to think about fostering and to emphasise how positive our experience had been with this agency.

At that point, it became obvious that the letter had been sent to us by mistake. Head office would rather the agency not be named in a lesbian magazine. They were prepared to assess us as an openly lesbian couple and to approve us on the basis of our competence to look after children, as long as we didn't shout it from the rooftops.

We felt unsupported and wrote to the agency, expressing our distress at this hypocrisy. It was clear from the reply that the agency is deeply divided. Some people are urging the agency to stand by their decision to apply skills-based assessment, even in the face of negative publicity. But others within the agency are acting from fear and prejudice.

Check out the agency

The following story shows how poorly agencies sometimes respond to lesbian applicants. But many lesbians have been approved as foster carers – they have been assessed relatively quickly, have been open about their sexuality and have fostered boys as well as girls. If you are interested in fostering, check out the agency first and make sure it has experience of placing children with lesbian and gay carers.

So unfair – Janet and Teri's story

Janet and Teri had an unfortunate experience with a local authority that had not even begun to think through the implications of accepting lesbians as foster carers. They had been together for five years when Teri got a sudden urge to have a baby. Janet was taken by surprise and objected strenuously, feeling that it wasn't fair to subject a child to prejudice because of their sexuality. Interview in 2001.

We agonised about having a baby for ages. It was a really emotional time: we were so confused and mixed up, and it felt too scary to talk about rationally. We went for counselling.

After ruling out having our own baby, we thought about adoption, but decided against it because it was too permanent, too big and too much like having our own child. Eventually we reached a compromise which was fostering. It's not as huge as adoption – we wouldn't be getting a child for the rest of its life. We would be helping children out as and when they needed it. The way we rationalised it was that kids in care have got a really shitty life and it can't be more shitty coming to us – we might be the best of a bad lot. Somebody else has taken the responsibility for bringing them about and we would merely be ameliorating what had gone wrong. The funny thing is that during the assessment, we came round full circle and became open to the idea of permanency. At the end, we decided that after fostering the child for a couple of years, one of us would adopt and the other take out a residence order. It came down to the fact that we would both have been happy to adopt had we got the right kind of child.

In January 1998, we phoned one of the London local authorities that we'd heard good things about. However, the department had never assessed a lesbian couple before and right from the beginning there were delays. They sent round a social worker to check that we weren't aliens. It turned out that she was PC and very enthusiastic about us, so this initial pre-visit visit went really well. We tidied the whole house up but she didn't look at the house.

At the official first visit, she explained the different types of foster care. She started by suggesting that we take pregnant teenagers, thinking we might like having a baby around. We both said no to that. She then proposed emergency short-term foster care: you could be rung in the night and be sent a child for anything from a few weeks to a few years, it might be one child or five. We said no to that. She finally decided that the kind of home we would be good at providing would be a stable home where we could look after one or two children, help them with their homework, be very supportive.

Soon after this, we had another visit from her and her manager. They wanted to talk through the implications of assessing a lesbian couple. Same-sex carers weren't written into their equal opportunities policy. They gave us the option to wait until they'd written one or to proceed in tandem with them re-writing it. We went for the tandem option.

They took our case to panel. Here was another delay as the panel only meets every couple of months. The panel had a little think and said to go ahead.

Finally, they started the assessment process. We went on a week-long course and started the interviews at the same time. On the course we felt more out on a limb for being too middle class than for being gay. We felt more similar to the people running the course than to the other participants.

The social worker who did the interviews was as keen as the first one but not as experienced. From day one, she asked us questions relating to our sexuality. She admitted she wouldn't ask straight couples about their sexuality, but she had to know what we would do if the child were embarrassed by us holding hands. She wanted to know whether we would impose our sexuality on the child. She asked about male friends and whether our support system was mixed in terms of race, sexuality and gender. She admitted she wouldn't ask a straight couple whether they have straight friends. All the way through, there were questions that were meant specifically for us. The questions sounded crass to us, but she was ignorant – she hasn't got any gay friends. We didn't mind on the whole because she was on our side and wasn't coming from a nasty place. She was responsible for filling in Form F1 so the better she knew us, the better job she could do filling it.

What we really resent now is that at no point did anyone say to us that it would count against us that we hadn't had children. We'd seen adverts to recruit foster carers which clearly say you don't need to have children of your own to foster. We understand that they are placing kids from hell and if they think you're going to crumble at the first obstacle, they're not going to want to trust you with those kids. But they shouldn't have approved us if they thought we couldn't handle it. We were quite shocked at how much of a handicap it turned out to be. We do wonder how much of it is an excuse for homophobia.

Race, religion and culture came up, but not class. We would not be allowed to foster a child from a different race. We were asked what we would do if they were to place a Catholic child with us whose parents really wanted the child to go to church. (Teri said that would be fine. Janet said, 'over my dead body', as she has a lot of problems with the Church.)

Then our social worker's boss wanted to know the sexuality of the single man and the single woman we had named as babysitters. We thought this was outrageous. You have to nominate babysitters as they have to be police checked. Nobody ever nominates a man to be a babysitter; most people nominate female relations or friends. Our social worker said we didn't have to answer it, so of course we didn't. The fact that this was brought into question at all left a very sour taste in our mouths.

The department was clearly nervous about assessing lesbians. They were worried about the media getting hold of it. We were told not to tell too many people that we were fostering and they insisted we meet with their lawyer to discuss what we would do if we were held hostage in our house with the media outside.

We finished Form F1 in April 1999, sixteen months after we first contacted the department. It went to panel in May. We didn't have to go in person; our social worker went on our behalf. She phoned us, exhausted, just after. It had been the biggest grilling she'd ever had. We were approved for one or two siblings of school age, for long-term foster care with a view to permanency. We didn't get officially approved until October of that year.

Over the summer, we got a new social worker. Although she was perfectly pleasant, she didn't convince us that she was on our side. Her job was to find us a child or at least that's what we thought her job should be. We don't know what usually happens but she left us to do all the phoning around to ask about children. She gave us the impression that if we wanted kids, we should pull our fingers out.

It's very difficult to do the phoning yourself. You have to come out as lesbian in that initial conversation. We had to say, here's the bad news – we're lesbians – and then sell ourselves. We felt it was our social worker's job to promote us and it felt inappropriate that we had to do it.

We looked through magazines that had pictures and short descriptions of the children. With every picture, you imagine that child living in your house so, rightly or wrongly, that makes you really picky. We didn't lower our standards. Our social worker thought we should go for any child that looked at all suitable, but we didn't. We were drawn to boys but by picking boys, we seemed to be handicapping ourselves from the start. Whenever we phoned, we were told by the children's social workers that we would not be suitable due to a lack of a male role model or due to our lack of experience, having no children of our own. They were damned if they were going to give us any boys. We made between fifteen and twenty phone calls. All said no, until the last one.

The one enquiry that got as far as a visit was about a brother and a sister of primary-school age who had moderate learning difficulties. They lived in the north of England. We thought they looked nice, so we phoned and spoke to the placement social worker. As usual, we came right out and asked if being a gay couple was a problem – she couldn't see that it would be. She did tell us there was another couple interested in those children. Nevertheless, she agreed to come to London with the children's social worker to meet with us and our social worker.

At the meeting, in the interests of openness, we laid all our cards on the table. First we brought out the gay thing. They said the birth family would probably not take too kindly to it but that didn't matter because the kids could do with getting away from their birth family. They thought it would be good for the kids to come down to London. We then asked if it would be a problem if we moved out of London in a few years' time. They both said, 'God no, as long as you don't move while the kids are just new and settling down. If they're part of the family and the family moves, no problem.' We also said we were exploring the possibility of maybe one day having our own child. Again they said they didn't see why that would be a problem as long as the kids were settled.

We all thought the meeting went really well. Our social worker was brimming with pleasure. They had already seen the other couple and said they would decide on the long train ride back home and give us their decision right away. They left all smiles. We didn't hear anything for at least two weeks.

Eventually we phoned them and were told they had decided to place the children with the other couple but would put us on the back burner in case that went wrong. Our social worker was as pissed off as we were and requested feedback. We were shocked by the reply. They had decided not to place the children with us in view of the fact that we had no experience with children, that we might move out of London, that we might have our own child and that the children's birth family wouldn't be happy about us being a gay couple. All those positive, reassuring messages we'd got in the meeting had completely misled us. We were stunned to realise that we shouldn't have been so open with them.

In August 2000, we finally decided to withdraw from fostering. We'd been approved for a year and a quarter and still hadn't had a child placed with us. Our social worker was sympathetic to our decision. She said that if approved carers haven't had placements after a few months, then it becomes harder to place children with them. People start asking questions about what's wrong with them. We were a bit disappointed with her response. We wanted her to say, 'Oh come on, now. Let's give it another go.'

It's so unfair for us and the agency. They had us as a resource and they lost us. They spent all that time and energy getting us approved and then couldn't use us. We were so up for it and we would have done a brilliant job. Most local authorities are desperate for foster carers. What made us cynical is knowing that there are so many children in need of foster care. It's madness to turn away approved foster carers because of ridiculous fears about a lack of a male role model. We believe that homophobia is at the root of our experience.

Part IV
Family Relationships

This part of the book is a glimpse inside some lesbian families. They talk about step-parenting, ex-husbands, coming out to children, being disabled, raising boys, having lots of children, single parenting, shared parenting, domestic arrangements and lots more.

Leaving a Straight Life 155   Coming Out to Children 167
We Are Family 173

10

LEAVING A STRAIGHT LIFE

If you are married with children but would rather be in a relationship with a woman, this chapter should help you to plan what happens next at this difficult time. Then the following chapter looks at how and when to explain your sexuality to your children.

Breaking up is hard to do

Many women become lesbian mothers when they leave the heterosexual relationship in which they had their children, as we see in the stories in this chapter. Their new-found sexuality may be a surprise, as Jess and Caroline discovered or, like Myra and Susan, they may have given their partners plenty of advance warning.

Leaving any relationship is painful, but when homosexuality and children are involved, the leaving can be particularly difficult. Homophobia is sometimes an issue – indeed, sexuality has been used against women in custody disputes. Read the stories of Amanda, Emily and Rachel for the experiences of children whose lesbian mothers were caught up in traumatic court battles.

Custody

Gill Butler is a family law solicitor who has many years of practice working with lesbian mothers' custody cases. She says, "I still get calls from women who think that because they're lesbians, the courts will give the children to the father. But the situation has changed. I am confident in saying that the courts take a consistent attitude towards lesbian mothers in custody disputes with their heterosexual partners. Although the mother's sexual orientation is a factor, it is not a very significant factor. Since Susan Golombok's latest research was published [see, for instance, F Tasker & S Golombok, *Growing Up in a Lesbian Family – Effects On Child Development*, Guilford Press, NY/London, 1997], most judges are satisfied that there is enough independent evidence to know there is no risk to children from a mother's lesbian sexuality. Although there is still the slight risk of finding a homophobic judge, the attitude the official bodies now take towards lesbianism is that it is not a reason to take the children away."

Gill recognises that some men may still threaten to use a mother's sexuality in divorce proceedings. "Part of my job as a family law solicitor is to give women confidence. I say to them, 'Don't give in. Hold on. You're not going to lose. He won't get the children.' If you let your ex-husband control your life, he's getting what he wants. You've got to give him the impression that you are strong. Otherwise you'll be dominated by the spectre of court proceedings. I don't see how you can live your life looking over your shoulder, anticipating that someone is going to take you back to court."

One piece of advice if you are thinking of leaving your husband – take your children with you. If you leave them with their father, he may not want to give them back to you when you are ready to have them, and he may well be granted a residence order by the court on the grounds that it's in their best interests not to be uprooted. Regardless of your sexuality, judges definitely take a dim view of moving children from pillar to post.

Staying on good terms

Leaving your children's father may be the end of your intimate relationship with him but it is not the end of your co-parenting relationship. The main goal at this stage is to separate in a friendly and harmonious way so that you and your ex-husband can continue to be there for your children.

When parents divorce, children will often but not always suffer. On average, they have more problems with behaviour, self-esteem, relationships with other people and achievement at school than children who have not experienced divorce. None of us wants our children to suffer because of decisions we've made – and it's not inevitable. Studies into the effects of divorce show that suffering is not caused specifically by having a mother turn into a lesbian, by the loss of a father, by economic hardship or by the number of stressful life events the children experience, but rather by the amount of conflict between the parents both before and after divorce. It is the way the divorce is handled that affects our children. An acrimonious divorce followed by continuing conflict causes more problems for children than amicable separation followed by co-operative co-parenting.

Mediation can help separating couples to work out what's best for all involved. Most mediators offer an unprejudiced service (see Resources). Of course, both of you have to want to co-operate if the separation is to be amicable. To find out how some lesbian mothers have managed ongoing relationships with their former husbands, read the stories of Caroline and Lynn, Cathy, Jess, Susan, and Myra.

Trying to be honest – Susan's story

Susan had two children, Tom and Louise, when she was married. She became a lesbian mother when she found herself attracted to women and left her husband. She became a lesbian step-mother when she got involved with Tracey, who had a one-year-old son, Samuel. She became a lesbian co-mother when Tracey gave birth to Ruth. At the time of the interview in 2001, the children were thirteen, eleven, five and fifteen months.

I was twenty-two when I got together with my husband and thirty when I left him. I did warn him that if I split up with him it was because I was going to have relationships with women, so he did have a bit of warning – which I considered to be fair play. In my late twenties, I started to feel more and more attracted to women. It got to the point where I couldn't keep to the monogamy part of marriage anymore. I knew that if the opportunity arose, I would probably sleep with a woman. I guess it was quite hard for him to take, but I felt that at least I was being honest. He was prepared for what was to come.

I went on a couple of women's camps, met a lot of lesbians and started exploring that part of my identity. He wrote me a letter when I was on one camp saying he thought we had a great relationship and how he really missed me, which was sweet. But when I came back from the camp, I started talking with him about ending our relationship. We went off camping together for three weeks with our children, who were then six and four. We were working out how to end it amicably.

But all my attempts at honesty and assertiveness went wrong when I was contacted by a woman who was attracted to me and wanted us to be lovers. It was unfair to my husband because I went off with her and effectively ended the relationship that way. It was an inappropriate way to end a relationship, but that's how it happened. It was messy for me and for my children and for the woman who became my lover at that point, and put a lot of stress on my family.

From my experience, the ideal thing is to leave heterosexuality, deal with being a single parent and being a lesbian mother, and then find a partner. I can understand why women don't do that. For me it was about falling in love with the first woman who came along. It would definitely have been better if I'd finished being heterosexual and then moved on. The kids could have come to terms with that. Looking back, I see that I used my first woman lover as a way of getting away from heterosexuality. It was clearer and easier for me. But I don't think it was the best thing for the children.

In terms of coming out to the children, I was very tactless about that. It was not what I would recommend to others. It was all confused to them. Basically, I split with their dad, went off with a woman and became a lesbian all in the same week. I didn't take my time about telling them. They were only six and four and weren't particularly interested in all the gory details. I spent at least the next year trying to smooth it over, especially with my son. I think the circumstances of my leaving his dad and becoming a lesbian made it difficult for him to come to terms with it all. I remember him saying that he hated lesbians. When I asked him why, he said, 'because they're all women'. It all got confused in his mind. I had to spend a lot of time supporting my son and showing him that there was some positive side to the lesbian community. There was a lesbians and children network then but he didn't want to go to events and didn't want to meet other lesbians, whereas my daughter was quite relaxed about it all.

It was also complicated by the fact that I had a long-distance relationship with my first woman lover. We didn't do any of that dating business. She would come and stay with me at my house and be there for a week and then go off. In general, it's probably better to introduce the woman lover to your family in a slower way, so you're dating that woman and then introducing her to your children, rather than involving them right at the very early stages of a relationship, which is what I did. With my present woman lover, I dated her and got to know her a bit and then introduced her to my children as a woman who I was dating rather than someone who was going to come and stay in our family home for a week at a time. I used a bit more tact.

Becoming a step-family is a different thing altogether. My current lover already had a son, who was one, and my children were six and eight by the time we met. I wasn't particularly aware that we were about to become a step-family. It's only with hindsight that I realise that that's what we were doing.

We planned our fourth child together. We found a man who was willing to be a known donor. I consider myself to be Ruth's co-mother rather than a step-mother to her.

Keep talking – Jess's story

Jess had two sons, Richard and Stewart, when she was married to John. Although she recognised there was something different about her sexuality by the time she was fifteen, she didn't come out as a lesbian until she was forty. At that time, her sons were ten and thirteen. She has been living as a single parent in a small English country village for the last seven years. This interview took place in 2001.

I came out as a lesbian while I was still living with my husband. By that time John and I already had separate rooms. We'd had trial separations within the house several times before and several reconciliations. For a long time we thought the children needed us to live together in the same house and that we would have our separate lives, but that didn't work at all. John absolutely hated it. He became depressed.

We went to counselling to see if there was anything we could do to stay together. But the counselling just made me realise that I needed to be true to myself. Then my aim was to part amicably. I was very clear that although we were no longer a couple, we were still parents. John was shocked and hurt that I was having a relationship with a woman, but he wasn't homophobic. He was just jealous that I loved someone else. He recognised and still does that the boys needed an ongoing relationship with both their parents. They had it before and they needed to continue it.

The boys were used to me being a lesbian by then. They had somehow believed that we could go on living in the same house and were upset that we had to live separately. They felt bereaved. I had done my crying and grieving some time in the past. By the time we got to the point of separation, I just felt relieved. They had to accept that we were allowed to have different feelings. Eventually the boys got to the point where they also felt relieved. Initially, Stewart had an extreme stress reaction – he took to his bed for six weeks and didn't leave his room. Richard took it differently. He wanted us to sort things out so he could get on with his life.

I took advice from friends whose parents had separated. I wanted to find out what had worked. My friends said that what they hated was having to plan access. What you want as a teenager is to be able to just drop in on the other parent. You don't actually want to have to make appointments. The ideal thing is to have the other parent near enough so you can choose. I found a small flat in the village about ten minutes' walk away and encouraged John to go and live there.

That did work for us. We tried very hard to make sure the boys had unlimited access to their father. He worked away a lot so they were used to not seeing him all the time. He dropped in and was around – the boys drifted in and out. He's there at the end of the phone. He will drop everything and come if I need him to be with the boys. When they were younger, he would come and live here so I could go away on holiday.

It works quite well because we're both good communicators and we're committed to our children. It has been painful at times. If we hadn't had children, I probably would have made a financial settlement and made a clean break. We both recognise that once upon a time, we loved each other and we were happy together. That helps. We've both been there for each other through difficult family times. We had a good history. We didn't ever get into the blame culture. We were able to reframe it, to admit that we're not a couple anymore but that we are parents. My tip to any married lesbian is to keep the parents bit at the front of your mind and to keep talking.

No regrets – Myra's story

Myra considered herself to be bisexual when she got into a relationship with James. She decided to start living with him when she was five months pregnant with her first daughter. She also had a relationship with Anna for five years during the seven years she was with James. She left James when her daughters were four and six years old. Nicole is now nine and Chantelle is twelve. Myra sees herself as a single parent and a lesbian mother. Interview in 2001.

I came out as a lesbian when I was twenty, when I started going out with a woman. When it broke up I started going out with James. I wasn't bothered about having a baby but when I became pregnant I thought I would move in with him, although my mum had offered to let me go and live back home and have it. He had said he was bisexual, so I knew he would be open-minded about my sexuality and if I wanted to keep my options open in the future he would understand.

I lived with him for seven years and had two children in that relationship. After about two years, although I still loved him I was spending more time with my best friend Anna, who I went on to have a relationship with for five years. When I told him, it became very difficult. He didn't try and stop me though because he only wanted me to be with him if it was what I wanted, but he was upset and unhappy and I felt guilty that I was hurting him. For the last three years, I felt very confused. I wasn't sure if it was the right thing to leave him. I didn't want to break up the family and deprive them of their dad. I felt a lot of affection towards him, but I was getting my emotional support from Anna. He went off briefly with another man, but I felt stuck. I felt I was the bad person in the relationship.

Anna was married with three children. She left her husband, I think because she wanted to be with me. I wasn't ready to leave James yet. Instead what I did was invite her into a sexual relationship with me and my husband. I wanted to be honest and open. I felt guilty about hurting people and not being able to commit to either of them. It was magical at times but I'm sure we were all jealous of each other. He fell in love with Anna. I remember comforting him and stroking his hair as he was crying, when she didn't want to sleep with him anymore, only me. He hated me then.

I had to leave him in the end. I couldn't make it all right for any of us. I was trying to wait until he was all right, but in the end I had to let go and realise I was powerless over his feelings and how he lived his life. My life had become unmanageable and I had to go.

When I was married, I made a lot of the decisions. He was working full-time while I was at home with the children. I was the one getting up in the night, doing the washing, sorting out their clothes, putting them in the nursery school that I chose. It was quite a traditional relationship. He was only around in the evenings and weekends. He made money, I spent it: took the children out and saw my women friends. That's how I made my decisions, by talking to other mothers, finding out what they thought and how they ran their lives. He was around, but like another child. I went to counselling at one stage and we talked about my relationship with my husband. It came out that I felt alone and unsupported. That's when I questioned what I was doing in the marriage and that I wouldn't be any more lonely as a single parent.

Anna and I had a deep and strong love but unfortunately it got too complicated. It never went the way it could have done. It's quite a sad thing. My life with Anna became more meaningful to me than the life I had with James. Anna will always have a special place in my heart

I must have spent the last two years of my marriage going round and round in circles. I spent ages with my lesbian friends, trying to justify to myself breaking apart a family. My friends gave me a lot of space to talk and cups of tea. They listened but didn't tell me what to do. You can't force someone to come to an understanding. It had to come from me when I was ready. I am so grateful for that space and for not being judged because I was coming from a heterosexual place. Some of my lesbian friends had also come from broken marriages. When I did leave, I left knowing I'd done as much as I possibly could to make everything all right. I said that I would go as soon as I finished my teacher training course. All he said was 'Fuck off, then.' Fair enough, really. I wanted to talk about it – he didn't. We never talked about it. A week after I finished I was in private rented accommodation with the kids. I didn't leave with much, mainly money from the joint bank account.

Three months before I left, Anna decided she didn't want to be with me because it had got too heavy, and went off with another woman. It was the best thing she could have done. When I did leave, I left on my own. If she had come with me, I would have gone from one dysfunctional relationship to another. I still see her now and again. I said to her, 'Thank you so much for not being there because it made me do it on my own. It made me be strong.'

I never ever regretted leaving my husband. I was so relieved to get out of there. There was nothing I could do to make it better for him. It wasn't fair to live with him and have women lovers. It was hurting him each time I did that. I felt too cruel. He was very angry for a long time. I wish I hadn't waited so long. I would say to anyone, get out, if that's what you really feel like. Don't try to make it all right. You can't.

Dutiful wives – Caroline and Lynn's story

Caroline and Lynn were married with six children between them when they met at their children's school and fell in love. They divorced their husbands and moved in together, along with three of Lynn's four daughters and Caroline's two sons. They have been living together as a family for the last six years. Interview in 2001.

Caroline: We first met through the children. They went to the same nursery school. My oldest boy was very keen on Lynn's youngest girl and invited her to a party. I used to save a seat for Lynn every week when we went to the pre-school.

Lynn: We were both living with our husbands and we had all become friends. They played golf together and we had dinner parties with all four of us. I eventually realised that I liked Caroline. There was something about her. On her birthday, I cooked the best meal I'd ever cooked. The next day we went with our husbands for a walk. Caroline linked arms with me and said, 'Thank you very much for last night.' Something inside went ding. It was like fireworks set off. From then on, I knew I was falling in love with her. I was really confused about my feelings then. My God, I was married with kids. I'd fallen in love with a woman. What was I going to do? I had fallen in love with a girl before when I was thirteen but my parents caught me and since then, I had steered completely away from it.

Caroline: I was so confused about my feelings. I'd never had an attraction to a woman before. My husband was the only partner I'd ever had. It was getting to the stage where it was painful seeing Lynn. I cried when she went on holiday. She must have thought I was mad. You don't cry when your friend goes on holiday. I had to say something, so I went up to Lynn in the playground and said to her, 'I have to tell you something. I think I love you. It sounds terribly corny but I'm getting too old to play games. This is just how I feel.' For me, that was quite brave. She could have completely flipped. I just knew that we were so comfortable with each other. We were happy when we were together. I had no idea she cared for me in any way.

I was honest with my husband. Our relationship was going nowhere. It was platonic by this stage. Two years previously, I'd made my decision that we would separate. I was very old fashioned. Being married with children, I would have stayed with him because that's what I thought I should do. We had decided we were going to separate but we were waiting for the right time. I told him about Lynn and it didn't seem to bother him. He was fine at first and said good luck to you. He was very matter of fact, very adult, very mature. Things didn't stay that way.

Lynn: My husband was completely hostile. I had the kind of relationship where I was the dutiful wife – his tea would be on the table, his washing would be done, his shirt would be ironed, his shoes would be polished and my body would be available to him 24 hours a day at any time when he wanted it. As my feelings for Caroline grew, I started to withdraw from him and would cringe when he tried to have any sexual relationship with me. My feelings for Caroline were so intense I couldn't bear for this man to touch me. I went away for a week with the Brownie camp. I led the camp holiday with two other guiders and Caroline. Caroline was my assistant. All four of us talked about our relationships with our husbands. During the week, we got the chance to talk to each other about how we felt. Caroline said she was going to separate from her husband and that things were bad between them. I had no intention of leaving my husband.

When I got home after seeing off thirty Brownies and their luggage, the first thing I got from my husband when I walked in the door was, 'You're late. Where have you been?' I looked at him and thought, 'I can't cope with this.' He tried to kiss me and I turned away. I just stood there and said to him, 'I want to separate from you.' He hit the roof; he hit me. We had the most terrible row. I slept in another room that night. The next day we had another stinking row and he hit me again. I walked out, packed my suitcase and called Caroline to collect me and the children. A few weeks later, I moved back to my house. He used to hit me in the past when I didn't do what he wanted me to do so I just did what he wanted. When I moved back, he kept being violent towards me. One morning, he hit me one time too many. I went straight to a solicitor and got an injunction served on him that same day. I knew then that it was over.

Caroline: By this time, my husband had moved out. He realised that Lynn and I were serious about each other.

Lynn: We had a granny flat attached to our house and my husband moved into that. He wasn't allowed to come in through the connecting door. It was a very strained situation. I agreed to go out so that he would come in then and see the children. Every day he came in, he would forage through my things, steal my jewellery.

My divorce came through in three months. I got 52%, which wasn't a huge amount considering I had three of the children and he only had one.

I moved in with Caroline. He threatened to raise it in court that I was a lesbian but he didn't do anything about it. He said that it was a phase, that nobody would be my friend anymore, everyone would hate me, I wouldn't be able to hold my head up in the street. He kept saying that I would come back to him.

As soon as he realised that I was serious and wasn't coming back to him, he got another lady friend. As I moved out, he took possession of the house. She moved in and they had a baby the following October. I was easily replaceable. He got another cook and bottlewasher and bedwarmer. It hasn't mattered because I have Caroline. That's what I wanted and we've gone on and made a new life. The people who were friends when I was married who are not friends now – well, they're not worth bothering about. I don't feel that I've lost anything. I've gained heaps more than ever I had before.

Caroline: My husband and I went through mediation. After the press incident [described in Chapter 17, p293], it became very nasty. I saw a side of him I'd never seen before. He used to reduce me to tears nearly every mediation session. We had an excellent mediator. She wasn't homophobic. She was very supportive of me and Lynn. My husband said and still maintains that if my relationship with Lynn affects the children, then he will remove them from us. Should that happen, I wouldn't object to that. My interests are for their welfare also. If they were being badly bullied at school, we would ask that they live with him. Of course, if any problems did arise, I don't think we would let them get that far. Both of us agree that they would live wherever it's best for them to live and wherever they want to. Neither of us regret having left our husbands. With mine, I lived a lie continuously. All the way through it was a platonic relationship.

11

COMING OUT TO CHILDREN

If you have been in a heterosexual relationship, then moving to a lesbian life raises questions about what to tell your children, which this chapter aims to help you answer. There is more on this topic in the stories in the next chapter too.

Guidelines

In general, it's better to come out to your children than to keep your sexuality a secret. However, some lesbian mothers are in situations where they feel it's not safe or where they couldn't handle the consequences. The following suggestions are for you to adapt to your circumstances only where appropriate.

Accept yourself

Before you come out to your children, you need to come out to yourself and accept who you are. Most lesbians find that as they come to accept their sexuality, their sense of well-being increases, despite any prejudice they may encounter once they come out. But for some of us, self-acceptance is a long way off. Don't wait until it's complete before you come out to your children – they may well have grown up and left home by then!

Be honest about who you are

Your children deserve to know the real you. Not disclosing something as fundamental as sexuality causes anxiety about being discovered and guilt over misleading people, and it results in distant and false relationships which would otherwise be more intimate. Although the research is limited, most writing on coming out to children asserts that it tends to improve the relationship even if the child does not accept the parent's homosexuality.

Be positive about your sexuality

Children will learn not just what we tell them, but what we convey to them indirectly and unconsciously. It is not only a matter of choosing the right words and the right timing. Children's reactions are also influenced by the approach you take. If you feel positive about your sexuality, your child is much more likely to feel all right about it. You will be giving them a model of positive self-esteem. If you don't feel positive about what you have done and who you are, you will have a much harder time putting across a positive, affirming message to your child. It will also be much more painful for you to handle any negative reactions from your child. You may find that you thought you were clear about your choices until you are faced with your child's grief and rage, at which point, you may suffer from guilt and uncertainty.

A distressingly large percentage of British people suffer from homophobia. If you are proud to be gay, your children need not suffer the same fate. Most people raised by lesbian mothers are accepting of homosexuality, open-minded about sexual diversity and often questioning of their own sexual identity.

Children are growing up in a changing society where there is a wealth of sexual identities, cultures, lifestyles, types of families and values. By being out, you will teach them by example and by explanation to value diversity, to be empathic with people who are oppressed and not to be afraid of difference.

The younger the better

Some lesbian mothers wonder whether they should wait until their children are in their teens before they break the news. In fact, the younger the children are when they learn of their parent's sexuality, the easier they find it to accept. They are never too young to be told.

Children conceived by donor insemination to lesbian mothers have lived with no other reality and most do grow up accepting their family as the norm. But there are many other influences on children, even very young ones. They will inevitably be exposed very early on to propaganda about heterosexuality and what is considered a "normal" family.

You have to tell them what is appropriate for their age and level of understanding. It is best to make your explanations simple, straightforward and matter of fact. The younger they are when you start telling them, the less likely they are to pick up society's homophobia. If you have a choice, tell them before they start secondary school. If your children are already teenagers, all is not lost. You can still get your message across.

Lesbian mothers from the USA claim that, "deliberate verbal acknowledgement and legitimation of an array of sexual orientations, conveyed in conversations that occur prior to puberty, can 'inoculate' children against a potentially lethal bout of internalized homophobia when adolescent questioning of sexuality occurs. Acknowledging – not just to gay people and their families – that people of the same sex can (and do) love each other, can (and do) have and raise children, can (and do) 'live happily ever after', can (and does) assure children that they can be who they are regardless of sexual orientation, that they can have a sense of personal worth and a life of value." (V Mitchell, "The Birds, the Bees and the Sperm Banks: How Lesbian Mothers Talk with Their Children about Sex and Reproduction", *American Journal of Orthopsychiatry*, 68 (3): 400-409, 1998.)

Tell them yourself before they find out from someone else
It is better to hear it from you than from someone who thinks that homosexuality is perverted and wrong. If your children are told by a hostile informant or if they work it out for themselves, they may well be upset that you did not trust them enough to come out to them directly. They may also get the message that your silence on the subject means that you are ashamed of your sexuality.

Keep on coming out

Explaining what it means to be lesbian, about insemination, and about donors is a long-term process. Like any other information you give your children, you will have to tell them again and again. One conversation may be followed by months of silence, then by a question out of the blue. Don't force the issue on them when they're not open to talking about it, but be prepared to seize the opportunity when they bring it up.

Accept your children's reactions

No matter how positive you are, you cannot control how your child reacts. Not only is your child a separate person with their own feelings and thoughts but their position in the family is completely different from yours. They haven't chosen to have a lesbian mother. They may feel a sense of loss or anger at you. They may blame you for breaking up the family if you left their father. If you got pregnant by anonymous donor insemination, they may feel hurt that the donor is not interested in them. They may complain that they didn't choose to be different. Eventually they will learn that nobody chooses their families and that a good many families are different in one way or another.

Every mother will have her own ways of helping her child understand her reasons and of giving the child space and permission to react. It can be very painful for a mother to see that she has caused her child's suffering. We so much want our children to be happy that we are often prepared to do nearly anything to take away their disappointment, frustration or grief. But if you can listen to your child express whatever they feel without being thrown by it and without denying it, then you are giving them something very valuable – the message that painful emotions can be endured, that they do not destroy you.

When you first come out to your children, your task is to acknowledge their feelings, not to argue and point out where they're wrong. Here is an example of how not to do it:

Mother: The reason I left your father is because I've realised I'm a lesbian and can no longer live with him. But he's still

Child: Lesbians are disgusting and perverted. I don't want a lesbian for a mother.

Mother: Well, you've got a lesbian for a mother, so you better get used to it.

Child: I hate you. I don't want you to be my mother.

Mother: Don't you dare talk to me that way. There are lots of lesbian mothers. There is nothing wrong with it.

Child: Well, I think there is. I don't care how many mothers are lesbians. I don't want my mother to be one. Why can't we be a normal family?

Mother: You think normal families are so great. That shows how little you know. In normal families, there can be child abuse, wife beating, neglect, pressure to be heterosexual.

Child: You've ruined my life.

Mother: Compared to lots of children, you've got a great life. I don't know what you're complaining about.

Child: I hate you. I want to go live with Dad.

Here is an example of a better way to do it:

Mother: The reason I left your father is because I've realised I'm a lesbian and can no longer live with him. But he's still your father and you will continue to see him often.

Child: Lesbians are disgusting and perverted. I don't want a lesbian for a mother.

Mother: I realise it's hard for you hearing this. You've heard lots of bad things about lesbians but I'm still your mother. I love you and always will love you.

Child: Well, I hate you. I don't want you to be my mother.

Mother: You sound really unhappy about this. I understand that you might feel worried about what it means that your mother is a lesbian.

Child: Why can't we be a normal family?

Mother: We are a different kind of family but we're like normal families in a very important way and that is that your dad and I both love you very much. I am still your mother and we'll still have lots of time together. We will work this out.

Child: You've ruined my life.

Mother: I accept that this will be difficult for you. You are quite angry, aren't you?

Child: Yes, I don't want you to be a lesbian.

Mother: I understand that. I am happy as a lesbian and I hope that you'll start to feel happier about how things are. Do you want a hug?

Child: Yes.

Tip 1 – Offer lots of hugs and reassurance.

Tip 2 – Don't get defensive.

Tip 3 – Don't be guilty.

Talk about strategies for self-protection

Coming out is not just about telling them it's OK to be lesbian. You also have to explain that there is a lot of prejudice about and that they will come across people who can't accept lesbians. Armed with this information, they can choose whether or not they come out to their friends, classmates, teachers, grandparents and neighbours. (See Part V for a fuller discussion of strategies used by children with lesbian mothers.)

Introduce them to other children with lesbian mothers. Join or start a lesbian mothers' support group which organises activities for children. Help them find a penpal who also has a lesbian mother. One useful aid is to provide books which portray lesbians and gay men positively, which show children with lesbian mothers and which raise the issue of donor insemination. Seeing their kind of families validated in print can have a positive impact on young children, not to mention on mothers. Although they have their faults, it is wonderful that these books are available and that there is beginning to be a choice. (A booklist is available from PinkParents – see Resources)

There is always the risk of rejection, but the benefits of coming out usually (or eventually) outweigh the risks.

12

WE ARE FAMILY

We have all kinds of families and we don't always have words for them. A woman who starts a relationship with a lesbian mother, for instance, may become a step-parent, even if she doesn't describe herself as such. This kind of relationship is explored below. The stories later on in this chapter also describe going it alone and sharing the parenting with ex-husbands.

Stepping up to step-parenting

"Step-family" is not a label many people choose to use about themselves, whether gay or straight. But the fact remains that there is a lot we can learn from heterosexual step-families about family change and step-relationships.

Much is known about the processes needed for building successful families and the strengths as well as the stresses of step-families. Most step-family literature advises that the changes take at least *five years* and that what's needed is good communication, respect for each other, relationships skills, tolerance, flexibility and space to deal with losses and change. If you can get past the insult of lesbian and gay invisibility in virtually all the mainstream step-family literature, you can pick up some useful tips that may well rescue your new family from the most common mistakes that merging families make.

There are obvious differences – lesbian step-families face different issues about gender, sexuality, definitions of family and social acceptance than do heterosexual step-families. Adding another female parent places the lesbian step-mother in a unique position, unlike that of a heterosexual step-mother who may expect or be expected to replace the mother role.

The issues are different enough to make it worthwhile reading Janet Wright's book, *Lesbian Step Families – An Ethnography of Love* (The Haworth Press, New York/London, 1998). Janet is herself a birth mother and a step-mother of five children in a lesbian step-family, but the book is not about her own family. She studied five American lesbian step-families, getting to know them through family and individual interviews, by observing them at get-togethers, and by reading their diaries.

What emerged from this intensive investigation is a fascinating discussion of the issues. She explores several themes about family life, including "normal" family problems such as discipline disagreements and jealousy; how a lesbian couple acts as head of the household; how the families created the step-mother role and redefined the mother role; and the strategies they developed to cope with anti-lesbian prejudice in a straight world.

This is an academic book, aimed at professionals and sociologists. However, it is readable enough for non-academic members of lesbian step-families to recognise themselves, and to set them thinking about the positive steps they can take to build a successful family.

Here are the key points to bear in mind when you become a parent by joining an existing family:

Don't take on a parenting role at first

Don't try to set limits or discipline the children. Try to avoid telling them off. Leave that to the birth mother. You can support her and back her up but don't take over her role. When you are looking after the children, consider yourself the babysitter.

Prioritise building a warm, friendly relationship with the children

Do fun things with them. Enjoy each other's company. Concentrate on getting them to like you. Spend time just with them, doing things they like to do.

Build a strong couple relationship with your partner

Make sure you have child-free time together. Communicate well with each other. Own your own feelings and don't blame each other. It's natural to feel jealous towards her children, and they may well try to set you against each other.

Don't criticise the birth mother

It's not good for your relationship with your partner to tell her how you would have done it better. Even if you know you're right, try to be supportive rather than undermining. Your partner will be much more open to your suggestions for improvement if she knows that you respect her as a parent. It's a rare mother who doesn't already feel guilty for getting it all wrong, so be careful not to make her defensive. You don't know that you would have done it any differently if you'd been in her shoes.

Spend time together as a family

Establish a history together as a family. Build up a store of joint activities that you can look back on. Set up your new family rituals and ways of doing things.

Have realistic expectations

Be prepared for rejection. Don't take it personally if the children are hostile towards you. They are bound to be jealous that you are taking their mother away from them. You are never going to have the same close bond with them as their birth mother has. It may be an advantage to their mother to have a partner, but not necessarily to the children.

Expect it to take a long time

Be patient. Most step-families have not fully merged until they have been together for at least five years.

Beware!

Don't jump into parenting without reading more about how to make it work. Look at the Resources section and at the following stories, which describe different kinds of lesbian families, including step-parenting, co-parenting, the involvement of fathers and going it alone.

Forming a new family – Susan's story

Susan and Tracey are parents to four children in a lesbian step-family: each is step-mother to her partner's birth children. Susan's birth children are Tom, age thirteen, and Louise, eleven. Tracey's birth children are Samuel, five, and Ruth, fifteen months. They live in separate households in a small village in the north of England and have been together for four years. Interview with Susan in 2001.

A step-family starts happening when somebody starts dating a parent. From what I've since found out about step-families, it takes at least four years for a new family to form. It has taken three years for Tracey to become a step-mother to my children. That's possibly because they were six and eight at the time we got together and their dad was involved in their lives. He had them certain nights of the week. Tracey and I don't live together, so I guess that complicates things.

I wish I'd known about step-family formation before, so we could have talked about it. We would have had an awareness that we were forming a step-family. We would have known in the very early days of dating, that if a conflict arose, it's not appropriate to step in and have your say with each other's children. You must have a positive relationship with someone's children before you can criticise and discipline. As step-parents, we should be working on creating a positive relationship where those children trust you and know that you like them. Otherwise, when conflict arises, you step into the wicked step-mother role. If you plunge in and discipline children who feel you don't like them, it's disastrous. The birth mother should do all the telling off, until you've formed a positive relationship with your step-children, at which point you may start to take on an active role in discipline issues.

I've been more active in step-parenting Tracey's children than she has been with mine. I've looked after them while she's worked, whereas mine are of school age, so she's never done that. She's had very little one-to-one time with my children. There's always been an inequality and imbalance about it, which has made it hard to gel as a family. Her relationship with my children was quite distant for the first two years, but for the last two, she has been closer to them. She has supported the children in little ways, doing things that I don't do with them. She's helped Louise with cooking and baked cakes with her. I don't like cooking. She's mended their bikes. I don't mend bikes. In those ways they've come to trust her and see her as a positive force in their family. And that's how she's built up a close relationship with them.

It didn't worry me at first that their relationship was so distant. At first I didn't even want her to be a step-mother to them, because I was quite possessive about them and they already had their father. But then as the years went by it seemed that she gradually became more like that anyway, and I did want her to be closer to them. In recent months, it's got a lot easier, and the kids themselves say positive things about Tracey.

I see myself as Samuel's step-parent, but Ruth's co-mother. The difference is that we embarked on having Ruth together. Ruth brought the whole family together, in the sort of idealistic way that people hope it will when they have a baby. Everyone's so fond of Ruth. She's our child, she's no one's step-child. I breast-fed Ruth, and I was there when she was born, and you can't get much closer than that. I have her for twenty hours a week when Tracey's at work. I never had Samuel for quite that amount of time.

In our family, we've got a lot of different relationships and different dynamics going on. I think what we've got going for us is we do all genuinely enjoy each other's company and we have a lot of fun together. Tracey and I have different parenting styles, but it's not a huge source of conflict. I tend to see us as a gay family who've got a lot of jobs and a lot of children and a lot of animals and a lot of pressure on us. We don't row about the little things much, because there's a lot of big issues that we focus on dealing with in our day-to-day lives. I see a lot of positive qualities in how she is as a parent; I guess she would probably say the same about me. We don't live together so we don't have conflict about how she's left the washing up or I haven't cleaned up or whatever. She's got a lot to give my children, different from what I give them.

I would very much like to live with Tracey at the moment. We don't because we haven't got enough money to get a big enough house with our four kids, and partly because of the homophobia that my children perceive. We live in a rural area, and my children are not out with their friends at the school, so if we live together they think that that would make it all a bit obvious. We've just had a baby together without it being obvious, but that is because we don't live together. If we did, I guess more questions would be asked.

I very much hope that Tracey and I will live together before my kids leave home. It's very difficult not living together. Practically we don't all squeeze together into either of our houses. We spend about five nights a week together, but the kids are squashed when we are all together.

Tom's got his GCSEs coming up and he'll need more room and space, so I am currently thinking of renting a bigger house. But the financial pressures on us are quite big, and I think it would be a lot better if we shared a house. We would save a lot of money. I have pointed out to the kids that they would be a lot better off if we could pool our resources in that way, but they are frightened of homophobia. It is quite a barrier to us being able to live together. They are old enough so I don't feel I can just ignore what they're saying, but I do feel quite confused about it. I've thought about coming out to the local housing association and trying to get a house on Tracey's estate next door to Tracey. We'd still be maintaining separate households. But whether the housing association will take us on as a whole family or agree that we have those needs, I don't know.

I have concerns about bringing up a son without a dad. Those are my personal views from my professional work in parenting education as well as observation of our children. I feel unhappy about Samuel not having anything to do with his dad. When he was four, he expressed the wish to have a man about and asked for a dad more. He has got a biological dad who hasn't seen him and hasn't contacted him. Tom and Louise have an active dad, and Samuel has said to us, 'I wish I had a dad who I could go camping with.' That is a bit silly because he does go camping with both his mums, but he misses having a dad, and there's no way around it. My guess is that a girl won't miss that in quite the same way, that it's a boy thing. I've yet to see with Ruth. But from what I've noticed with other people's children, I think all children to some extent miss a dad, because 'normal' people have dads. We would both like it if Samuel had a man in his life who was there for him. We haven't got that at the moment and it's something that we talk about trying to get. It's not that he needs role models.

Maybe it would just help if he had another person in his life, a godmother or godfather. Samuel would quite like to have someone else who was close to him and wanted to spend time with him and was committed to him apart from me and Tracey – an uncle or even an aunt. I think that all children could do with having other adults who are interested in them, aunties or uncles, who are actually there for them rather than living hundreds of miles away and not really caring that much. Tom and Louise go off to another parent who cares about them and does things for them. Samuel would like to have that as well, and we'd like to have it, because then we could possibly get a babysitter for Ruth and go out! We completely ruled out advertising for someone on that score. We meet people but it never seems right to ask – it seems like too big a thing, in a way. My sister recently moved to our village, so we've got more of an extended family. Samuel is quite close to my sister's little boy, so it is building up in that way.

When we came to have Ruth, we thought long and hard about it and decided that it wasn't right for us to have an anonymous donor. All children will have questions about their dads. I want to be able to give the children answers to those questions. But I do think that dads are as likely to create problems for their children as they are to be supportive to them. I've worked with over two hundred families in the past few years in my work in parent education and that's what I've observed.

Tom and Louise have a close relationship with their dad. They go to his house two or three nights a week. That generally works quite well. Because the kids are going to and fro, he and I usually talk about what's going on and every now and then we get together and have a chat when they're not around. That's been straightforward and positive. We did have to go through mediation when I moved out of the city where we had been living, because he didn't want me to move. I'm lucky with him in that he's into equality and doesn't see me being a lesbian as a problem, and he's able to deal positively with the children about that.

For the son of a lesbian, I think self-esteem is more at stake than for the son of a mother who isn't lesbian. A son growing up with lesbian mothers might have questions about how acceptable he's going to be. You need to reassure him and come from a strong position, that men are part of your life, and when he's grown up, he'll be a man and he'll be part of your life. I don't think we can afford to involve women in our lives who basically don't like men and don't want to have anything to do with men. I don't live in a lesbian ghetto. I like men as friends, and I've got men in my family. I've come across women in the year 2000 who think that the separatist scene is cool. They sit around slagging off all men. I go out of my way to avoid lesbians like that and I don't let them around my son.

I think it's positive for children to grow up in a lesbian family. It's positive for children to have two mothers, because we both bring all the intelligence and wisdom that women bring to parenting. Of course, we both think we know best because we're both birth mothers. Tracey feels that she knows best all the time and she should have the ultimate say. But as the birth mother of two children, one of whom is already a teenager, I tend to think I know best. That is the thing about a lesbian family with two mothers. You are both mothers and mother knows best. It's not like a mother and a father, where a father could stay in the background anyway, because that's what fathers do.

Step back – Angela's story

Angela is a single lesbian mother living in rural Wales with her seven-year-old son, Liam. She had her son with a known donor when she was in a relationship with a woman. She ended the relationship when she couldn't cope with her partner's unreliability. This interview took place in 2001.

I was in a non-monogamous relationship with a woman when I decided to have a baby. We never lived together. She was a traveller, so she was coming and going quite a lot. We didn't make any concrete agreement about co-parenting. We didn't sit there in advance and come up with anything that you could refer back to. She was really into the idea and said she wanted to support and help me. She did find a donor by asking a friend of hers. But her yearning to have a baby and the promises didn't match up with the reality. The relationship started breaking down during the pregnancy. After Liam was born, the relationship broke down within three months, but we struggled on for probably two years trying to maintain contact and allowing her to see Liam. I will admit it's hard to take a breastfed baby away from its mother for any length of time and he never got the hang of feeding from a bottle.

She didn't support me through the whole of the pregnancy and rarely visited me. She never came to antenatal classes. When I was pregnant, I was not well, was very tired and spent some time in hospital. I was also desperately trying to get work to get a mortgage to get somewhere for us to live, so I turned inwards while she just carried on as normal. I did not have the energy to travel to where she was.

Miraculously, she turned up for the birth and was supportive for at least 24 hours, left within the week, flitted backwards and forwards and made loads of promises, none of which she kept. She came and went, never stayed for long. She was not committed and wasn't supportive, but swore blind to everybody that she was Liam's co-mother and that I was the difficult one. She used to turn up late to take him away. I would ask for help with childcare and she'd never contact me, or she'd say, 'Oh, I can't possibly do it then.' If she was to bring him back at four, she'd bring him back at eight. She paraded him around a couple of times at camp saying, 'Look, I've changed his nappy!' She'd take Liam off for a couple of hours to give me a break, and then I'd track her down and find that somebody else had Liam. I got ill and depressed, so I got paranoid about people stealing him. It wasn't a healthy situation. There were no boundaries. It was just like what many heterosexual women go through with their men. I couldn't get a clear answer from her, apart from how much she wanted to be Liam's mother and how much she wanted to care for him. It was a mess.

In hindsight, I should have been more sensible. This wasn't a change in her character. Being pregnant makes you change but not being pregnant means one doesn't have to change. It's very much like how men act when they become fathers – they have a role, but they don't know what it is. I can see a lot of similarities. She didn't quite know what to do. Things just got worse and worse, and I got more and more upset. Eventually I wrote to her and told her to fuck off, that I never wanted to see her again. Then I moved house for three months and disappeared. For me that worked really well.

She kept sending messages to anybody that remotely knew me, trying to convince me that she'd got something to offer. I thought, no way! I was heavily criticised for cutting her out of Liam's life. I have had her friends come and say to me, 'Look, can't you give it another go? She's offering this, and she's offering that.' And I'd say, 'Yes, but will I get him back on time? I've got a child-minder who is there when I take my son and is there when I come to pick him up.' I knew she was too unreliable to trust my son with.

I went through a lot of guilt. Politically, it's not something I should have to do – I'm denying a woman a child that we'd said we'd parent together. It felt wrong that we had an agreement and I couldn't cope with it. But now whenever I hear her talking about it, it just makes me cross. Her line was that I had all the rights and she didn't have any, that it wasn't fair. If she'd have gone to court, I would have fought her tooth and nail. But there are rights and there are responsibilities. We were basically incompatible people, in terms of our values and our way of life.

The donor and I have become quite reasonable friends since. He didn't know whether he wanted involvement or not. He said he wanted to see as it evolved. I felt fine, because I knew enough about him to know that he was never going to try for custody. The court would have to be completely mad to hand over custody to him. It turned out that once Liam was born, he got more and more into the idea. It was quite a surprise to him. And as Liam's got older, he has found it much easier.

Since I told my girlfriend to leave, Liam's father has toed the line. Anything I say, he does. He lives in Ireland and has Liam every summer and every other Christmas. He helps out financially occasionally. He's more like a doting uncle. There's nothing in writing, cast in stone. His family treat Liam as their own grandchild. They don't know what the set-up is. Liam benefits a lot out of it and it's working out for me very well. I probably will send Liam over for a term or two at an Irish school. It's a nice lifestyle out there. He gets a much better summer holiday hanging out in Ireland than he would here hanging out with a child-minder.

My main issue as a single lesbian parent living in rural Wales is my total invisibility. To my son and to everybody else, my lesbianism is invisible. People might know, but it's not the same as walking arm-in-arm with someone, being at a party and kissing them. It's hard to keep asserting my lesbianism, particularly around here. There's not a lot of lesbians and they're mainly closeted. If I go to parties run by alternative-type heterosexual people, you take your children. But it's not done to take children to lesbian events. I don't mean taking them to clubs; I mean camps, or weekends away, even walks in the countryside. I rang up one of the walking groups and was told, 'Nobody's ever asked to bring a child before... people bring their dogs!' I find getting babysitters really hard. I have asked daughters of friends of mine who I know are unfazed by my being a lesbian but I'd not ask any of the local girls, as I'd not want to have to de-dyke my house before they come round.

I don't think there are very many lesbian mothers around here. I've got one lesbian friend who is just about to become a grandmother; but a lot of the younger women leave and the blow-ins are older and long in the tooth. We've heard by word of mouth of lesbian couples living up in the hills, but they're perfectly happy together, and they're not really looking for a scene. It's hard to find them. There are the Welsh lesbians who are around who may or may not have children. I've found it very difficult to break into their network.

It's very much insiders and outsiders here. I'm English and used to live in London, so I'm one of the blow-ins. It's very hard to get to know who people are. It's not automatic in the street, you can't recognise people.

I'm not encouraging Liam to be aggressive. I'm not encouraging him into being a boy or a girl. I'm letting him be. His personality is such that he'll sit and play with paints rather than rampage round the room jumping on the furniture. He likes art. He likes playing with girls. He does play football and ride his bike, but he's not a great rough and tumble, loud person. He has come back from school many times complaining about the 'bad boys' who are rough. He's a very small seven-year-old, so rough and tumbles just means that he gets shat on. I'm not particularly worried about him. His teachers tell me that he's popular at school.

Looking at the male role models round here, I'm very glad he hasn't got any! He can't avoid them, but I've had a few men that have offered, saying, 'Well, of course, if you need a male role model.' I think they were saying that he needed to be tougher, and I think that's a pile of shit. There's a guy we know who takes Liam out occasionally. He rides a motorbike, and he's a big, six-foot, hairy guy. Liam thinks he's wonderful and has fun with him. They trot off picking flowers. I'm not quite sure what male role model's acceptable. Liam's father comes from a well-off family and has no practical skills whatsoever. He's not particularly macho.

I'm trying to avoid the worst kinds of male role models. I used to spend a lot more time with various heterosexual couples because we had kids the same age, and I started backing off when I realised I didn't like their children or their men. The women were OK, but their men were horrors. It's not a very alternative area around here – people are still twenty to thirty years in the past. When some women set up a women's group, it caused a riot amongst the men. It was unbelievable. This was just a women's group, not a lesbian group. And it wasn't even a consciousness-raising group. It was really an excuse to get somebody to mind the kids. I sometimes challenge people about sexist attitudes, but I'm learning not to. I find it much better to keep quiet, because I've had a few comments back about my strange politics.

Riding the storms – Jean's story

In 1992 when Jean gave this interview, she and Cathy were living together in London with their two daughters, Alice, age seven, and Elaine, two. They had both girls by anonymous self-insemination.

When my lover, Cathy, decided to get pregnant, we didn't sort it out in any depth. We didn't think about the pros and cons. She never talked to me that plainly about her feelings at the time, until after it had happened. It was something that Cathy decided she wanted to do. She hadn't even decided on self-insemination. I thought she might go and have an affair with a man. She just wanted to get pregnant, any way would do.

I knew I would love Cathy's baby, but at that point I wasn't even sure what would happen if Cathy slept with a man. Would that man be involved with the baby? It was a real fear because I didn't really want him to have anything to do with us.

How Cathy got pregnant is very indicative of how our relationship functions. In fact, the same thing happened when I wanted to get pregnant. I remember saying, 'Right, you've got yours. My turn.' I very selfishly went ahead without a lot of discussion.

I had Elaine when Cathy's daughter, Alice, was two and a half. It was absolute hell, with little moments of sublime joy that made it all worthwhile. Alice felt displaced. I breastfed Elaine for a long time so that Cathy felt excluded from a relationship with Elaine. I know that I did really want this intense relationship with my baby, but I wasn't very honest about what I was doing. I didn't feel that I should or could have it. It was quite destructive.

I don't think we thought about roles. The roles are quite clear when there's only one child. Cathy was Alice's biological mother and was very generous with her in a way that I wasn't with Elaine. I fed Alice, I was very involved with her as a baby, but when Elaine came along and Alice was still very demanding, the family split down the middle and stayed like that for quite a long time. We were all exhausted. To minimise the exhaustion and just out of ease, I breastfed Elaine in bed because it meant that she went to sleep faster. There was this whole thing about Elaine being in bed with me and Alice getting into bed with Cathy. Alice didn't sleep through the night at two and a half; she was never a good sleeper.

I feel very different about my own child, Elaine, than I do about Cathy's daughter, Alice. My relationship with Alice is much clearer. Having your own child opens up a whole can of worms. The relationship between the mother and the daughter is immensely intense. I made it intense and I loved that intensity to start with, but of course it doesn't go away. It's not like a relationship that you can end. It also made me confront issues about my own childhood that I would have managed to forget. The issues around parenting that came up with Elaine because she was my child were quite different to those with Alice. They were to do with boundaries. I didn't have clearly defined boundaries in my relationship with my father and I found it enormously difficult as a mother to Elaine to define boundaries between us. That led to a messy relationship where I was responding to Elaine's rages as if I were another child, which was completely inappropriate. That didn't happen with Alice. I had an emotional distance from Alice that didn't interfere with my love for her and made it clearer how to respond to her.

It was relatively easy being a family of two adults and one child but as soon as Elaine came along, we felt like two exhausted single parents who happened to be living together. During the baby stage when they are very demanding, it didn't seem to make a lot of difference having two adults. As they get older, it does get easier. But having two kids is twice as hard as having one. When one of us wants to go off and give the other partner space, there are two children to take. It's very easy to go off with a seven-year-old on your own. It's not the same taking a seven-year-old and a four-year-old on your own.

Until Elaine was about three, we had a very difficult time, but it is becoming much easier now. My relationship with Elaine is less intense. After the first few years when Alice behaved like a typical jealous sibling, hating the baby and not being able to bear her, now there is an immensely strong bond between them and they get on really well. It has made life so much easier. They both get up in the morning and play together. We can lie in bed for hours on weekends. When they were babies, that's something we never thought we would have in our lives again. We thought it would just go on and on and on. We have emerged from that time as a strong unit and as four separate individuals with strong relationships with each other.

At the moment, the relationship between me and Cathy is strong and the relationship we have with the girls is better than it ever has been. But we've had bad patches. We've rowed in front of the girls and seen how destructive that is for them. All of our problems can be traced to a breakdown in communication, compounded by exhaustion. We just stop talking about the important things. Cathy tries to initiate discussions but it's fear that stops me talking. The fear is that if we talk, we will wreck it and I want it to continue. We know that we can keep going. We've been together for fifteen years and we know that we're actually very good about being a household and that we're all very fond of each other. I'm frightened of delving any deeper than that. If we talk and reveal things, then I fear that we'll no longer be in control, and things could explode. Whereas I'm quite good at the superficial maintenance – keeping things ticking over, like cooking, shopping, thinking ahead – I'm not so good at major overhauls.

As I get older I become less frightened of experiencing the pain as well as the pleasure of intimacy and also realise that we just have to go through it together. The base line is that we love each other and our children, but we also have to work hard to keep it all going.

I'm pleased that Alice and Elaine have had to grow up in a larger unit than a lot of single parents have. They've had to adjust to the dynamics of four people in a household instead of two or three. Also neither of them are the sole focus of two adults, which I think is actually difficult for a child. It's not as big a family as Cathy would like. I think she would like more children. I wouldn't want any more because physically we're too old. We started too late. There are other things I want to do with my life now that I've got through the baby bit and have more energy.

Over the years I have realised how particularly stressful it is to be lesbians bringing up kids. We live as a family unit in a small friendly street full of family houses. We have close heterosexual friends who are bringing up their children in nuclear families, with whom we have much in common in terms of the day-to-day parenting. But we are not what we appear to be. Our incomes are much lower, we are not homeowners, and our lesbian relationship has little in common with the relationships of our heterosexual friends. So when Clause 28 identified 'pretend families', it hit a raw nerve. We know we are different but, in order to be supportive to us, 'real' nuclear families tend to overlook the differences and they 'pretend' we are just like them.

The other thing I find stressful about lesbian parenting is an enormous pressure not to talk about how awful things can be. There are issues that I feel we mustn't talk about, like violence towards the children. I feel we can't be completely open because we should be doing it better than heterosexuals. We've set this up. We've done it ourselves. We're going to do it perfectly. We're not going to fail. I think I've internalised that pressure. That puts us under as much if not more pressure than heterosexual families, which makes me wonder why we berate ourselves about our parenting!

Sometimes I'm envious of lesbians who have children on their own, because they appear to have more time to themselves. Single parents have to be far more organised about childcare and seem to make more effort to involve other adults with their children. It's easy to be careless when there's two of you and to rely on each other too much, but this puts a great strain on the relationship. It's easy to go out separately but harder to go out together.

Recently a young lesbian said to me, 'I realise I'm in a privileged position. I don't have children and I can offer help to lesbians who have children.' I nearly wept. I had not heard that in ten years. When I got involved in women's liberation, I was always helping out heterosexual feminists with their kids. The consciousness around being a mother and how mothers were oppressed in heterosexuality was really high on the agenda. We thought, 'poor women, what awful lives. I'm a lesbian and I've got more time. I must babysit for free.' Now you're a lesbian mother and other lesbians say, 'It's your choice.' I didn't turn around to heterosexual feminists and say, 'You didn't have to fuck a man. You didn't have to get married.' Lesbians are not seen as being oppressed as mothers. At the moment, I feel so grateful that if another lesbian or gay adult shows any interest in my children, I could hug them. I think it's awful that I feel that desperate.

Even though we've had rough patches, in fact we do function as a unit very well and I adore both girls enormously. They're good fun. We have a lot of laughs, the four of us. There are family in-jokes. There are roles that we take – Elaine is the clown, which is common with youngest siblings. Most of all, those girls give an enormous amount to us. Our relationships with them are getting better and stronger as they get older and we're able to discuss issues and our views of the world. You don't expect this when you have babies. It's wonderful. You can talk about issues like homelessness with a seven-year-old. I find it very exciting. I'm really looking forward to them getting older.

Growing family – Audre's story

Audre is a lesbian mother of mixed Nigerian–English parentage who is co-parenting her eight-year-old son Tyler with his father. Her girlfriend recently moved in with Audre and Tyler and they are gradually evolving new family relationships. She was interviewed in 2001.

In the first year after I left Tyler's father, I found it difficult to adjust to my status as a single parent. I got into a relationship with someone who had not been involved with a woman with a child before. We were not really sure how to work out the logistics of childcare. She was more used to a lifestyle where she was able to just accept invitations to things. She would ask if I had childcare and I often didn't. We didn't get to the place in our relationship where we negotiated childcare and socialising and so it caused tension. I was quite anxious at the time, having just left Tyler's father, and was afraid that my changes would cause the situation to become more volatile. But in time, the situation changed. Our relationship was by now ending, and on reflection we both felt we could have done with discussing the impact of my having a child within the relationship earlier on. She now has a very close relationship with Tyler and they spend time together regularly.

My current partner spends time with Tyler and has formed a relationship with him. We haven't got to the point where we're talking about whether it's parenting or co-parenting. It feels quite new still, and she and Tyler are creating their relationship as it goes along. There isn't that much difference between what she does or what I do or what his dad does. Although his dad and I still make the major decisions, my partner is involved in the process. I think that will change about some things over time. I talk to her about important things. Our family relationships, including that with Tyler's father, are evolving. It's taken a long time to reach this decision about living together, and it might seem soon, but the stress of being in two separate places in a relationship is just unbelievable. She hardly ever got to sleep at her place unless we all three went there together. It got so complicated. Amongst the reasons, logistically, living together seemed the next step.

When I think of my childhood I had with my heterosexual parents, I get really frustrated about the grief people have about whether lesbians can be good parents. The emphasis shouldn't be on whether the mother is a lesbian or not. I remember from my childhood that what I wanted was to be in a loving home with people around from whom I felt love and felt safe.

I was adopted by a dysfunctional white family that was struggling with issues of abuse, both emotional and sexual. I had a difficult relationship with my parents. We lived in a white area where my black identity was not nurtured. It was also at a time where black and mixed-identity children were encouraged to assimilate into white society. This was alongside the idea that if adopted into a [white] family, all would be well. I did struggle within the family and issues of my racial identity were not discussed except when we were in crisis. It was there that I realised that I wasn't like them i.e. white and so had to gradually define my identity in other ways as I grew up.

I grew up with a very, very negative self-image. It's taken me a long time to turn that around. I couldn't begin to think about who I was and what I wanted because I had such a lot of confusion going on just trying to get through day-to-day life. I didn't feel good about myself at all. I spent my childhood trying to fit into something that didn't work for me and it led to me being quite depressed and anxious for long spells. That began to change when I identified what I needed in terms of people around me and the lifestyle I wanted to adopt. I feel much happier and have made choices for myself which fit who I am, not who I am 'supposed' to be based on my earlier years' experience.

When raising a child, we've tried to be stable and loving and consistent. There have been changes that have meant some disruption, but that is how things are. There are many different versions of family – one is not superior to another, but it is important to be aware of the differences around us. Lesbian and gay people are here and parenting and are able to provide good family environments. Tyler will grow up with a range of families around him and he must work out for himself how it fits into his world. He does have different ideas developing in his world and he is different from me. I think that the role of parent develops as it moves along and as things progress. I have become aware that my world has less men in than I would like and I am working that out with Tyler's dad. He [Tyler] is growing and developing and becoming very much more aware that he is growing into a man. We would like to have some more children in the family and for Tyler to have brothers and/or sisters. I was recently pregnant and lost the baby during the pregnancy. Tyler was very excited and was beginning to think about how the family would grow.

Frightened of parenting – Cathy's story

Cathy unwittingly became a mother when she got involved with Penny, a married woman with two daughters. They moved in together when Deborah was twelve and Jo was fifteen. The couple have been together for twenty years. Cathy was interviewed in 2001.

I met Penny in 1975 at Sappho, a lesbian social group. Penny was 35, heterosexual and married with two children but had written to Marjorie Proops, the agony aunt, saying, 'I don't know what's up with me. I'm unhappy and I don't really know why, but I just keep thinking I feel drawn to women.' Marjorie Proops told her about Sappho. When she came to the group, I was there that night. That's how we met.

Penny and I knew each other for about six years before we actually got together. We'd been in an on-off relationship during that time. She still thought she was heterosexual. The main problem for me was that I couldn't see myself taking over two children. I was frightened by it. I've never wanted to have children. I never thought that I was the maternal type. It wasn't that I disliked children, I just never wanted any of my own.

When we eventually got together, she left her husband and we moved in together. He was devastated, although he'd known about our relationship before they broke up. They remained good friends for the children's sake and he was very much in their lives as a parent. So when I came on the scene, I didn't come as a parent because they had a mother and a father already in their lives. When there were problems I stayed completely neutral. I didn't get involved. I didn't have any confidence in myself as a parent. In any case, the worst or the best of the parenting had been done by Penny and their father.

A few months after I moved in with her, Penny had to go into hospital for a hysterectomy and there was me left with these two teenagers, completely on my own. I had been friends with the children for six years, before I moved in with Penny. They knew me as a favourite auntie and I was very fond of them – took them to the theatre, played games with them. So when I moved in, to them it was like favourite auntie moving in. Penny was in hospital for about three weeks. Her husband came at weekends and took the kids back with him sometimes. I'd always been spoiled at home, and I was quite ill equipped to be running a house. I never knew how to work the washing machine or do anything domestic. So the kids and I had to figure it out together. We were like three teenagers. I was quite pleased with myself – I got them up, got them to school on time. That was the first taste that I had of parenting and of having full responsibility for children. Fortunately, Deborah hadn't yet entered adolescence in earnest. A couple of years later, and I'd have hung myself if I'd been left alone with her.

Because I didn't take on a parental role when I first moved in, I was able to step in later when Deborah was fifteen and the problems really began. She went through a punk stage where she came in late, smoked cannabis at school, and stayed out all night. The rows were terrible. If we said black, she said it was white – everything was an argument. There was nothing smooth about anything. It was a nightmare for three years. Her father had his own problems by that time and he was removing himself from the parental role. He couldn't cope with any of it. When he stepped back, that's when I stepped in more.

Penny was absolutely desperate, especially the time Deborah stayed out and didn't come back all night. We discovered that she was in a squat with roadies who were a lot older than her. We found out where this squat was and at five o'clock on a Sunday morning, we went banging on the door. This bloke with rings in his nose came to the door and said, 'Deborah's not here.' We just burst our way in, like the SAS, and of course, she was there. We dragged her out and took her home.

She went straight to her room, which was like a pigsty. I'm sure there was penicillin growing in some of those mugs! I went up after her, gave her a cigarette, and sat down with her. I said, 'Look, let's just talk about what's going on.' And we sat upstairs, smoking these cigarettes, me and this fifteen-year-old girl – God, the social services would have my guts for garters now! But I was trying to bridge the gap somehow, and I thought maybe if I came to her level it might help. She kept saying there wasn't a problem with her mother. She didn't really know what it was, she was just being a normal teenager. But she cried a bit, and that was good, because she was getting things out. And then we reached a sort of compromise. I said that we were happy to give her some freedom, but there had to be trust on both sides. I told her that we worried about her and that we loved her, all the usual things. And it started to work. Now she's 32 and laughs about that time. Recently she said, 'I can remember you coming up and sitting in my room smoking cigarettes. It did work. Because it was lovely just to sit there and talk for three hours.'

If I could put the clock back and do things differently, I would say maybe we didn't talk to her enough at the beginning, when I first moved in. Perhaps we should have sat her down and talked to her. The beginning was difficult for a number of reasons. Deborah says now that she probably had about a year of feeling insecure after I moved in. She was insecure about her father leaving, insecure about the move out of London, insecure about me moving in. But she was also relieved to have the arguments removed from the house and to see her parents getting on better. The girls were eventually able to see their parents as two human beings who did have a lot in common and liked each other, but found marriage impossible. Their father was a really nice, decent man but he was quite weak. He didn't take a lot of responsibility.

During that time, Penny and I had our own set of problems. We both worked in London, and had pressurised jobs. I was finding it difficult to adjust to the lack of privacy and the lack of money. I had a good job and I was used to spending all my money on myself, going to the theatre, eating out. Suddenly I couldn't do that any longer, because there were two kids to think about. I bought half of the house, so I had a mortgage.

All these things were going on, and maybe Deborah got overlooked in it all. I do think that we could have taken more time to spend with her. She was probably lost, a little bit too much on her own. She didn't get enough attention. That day I sat down with her for three hours was a turning point. We made up for it then and she has come out the other end absolutely fine. As a human being, as a person, she's lovely. I have an excellent relationship with her now.

Penny told Jo, the oldest one, that she and I were a couple before I moved in. She didn't mention the word gay. She put it to her like, 'I still love your dad, but he and I don't get on. I love Cathy and she's going to come and live with us.' Jo cried a little bit for her father, because she didn't want to see him hurt. But because they'd known me for six years before I moved in, I wasn't as big a threat as a complete stranger just walking in. I had a warm relationship with them. The important thing I would say is to be friends with the children before. I think it worked because I didn't take a parental role at the beginning. That wasn't a conscious decision, that was just me not knowing how to.

We didn't come out and tell Deborah. Penny's policy was to answer every question when a child asks. Deborah was about thirteen when she happened to come out with, 'Mum, are you gay?' Penny was so taken aback that she said, 'Well, I don't know if I am or not, but I know that I love Cathy.' She accepted it. They never had any problems about that, neither of them.

I feel guilty about it now, but sometimes I did find myself resenting the fact that I felt tied, that I wasn't as free as I had been. If we went away for a weekend, I would just want to go for a holiday but we'd always have to think about the kids and have to take them with us or make arrangements for them. Or if we went to stay overnight at a friend's, we had to come back the very next day for the children. You've got to be so aware of that, as well as the lack of privacy. I had come from not being used to children, and suddenly they'd burst into the bedroom! I don't think we had a sex life for a while. They would tap on the door and walk in. They'd want to sit in the bed and chat. Penny was used to that but I wasn't, not on a Sunday morning. Now, when Deborah's over for the weekend, we're practically all in the bed, looking at photographs and chatting. It doesn't bother me now.

They had no troubles at school, probably because if anything had to be done at school, Penny always went and their father was around for a great deal of the time. During the cannabis smoking incident, Penny and her husband went to the school. Penny's friends knew about us, but they were the sort of friends that wouldn't have given her a problem anyway.

My little chat with Deborah was the start of my role as a parent. At first I got as angry as Penny and then tried to find answers to it all. Most of the parenting came from Penny. If there was any telling off to do about the room or whatever, I would step in later, after Penny had nagged and nagged and nagged. I would say, 'Are you going to do something to the room?' In a funny sort of way, sometimes she took more notice of me than she did of her mother.

Penny has been a good mother. She wishes she hadn't spent so much time making sure her children were quiet and well mannered. She says, 'I wonder now, looking at today's style of parenting, whether I've eroded their confidence a bit.' They both did have a problem with confidence when they were teenagers. I think we all did. I was brought up in a very strict household with my parents saying, 'Sit down, shut up and don't talk unless you're spoken to'. Today's parenting is to encourage the children to come out of themselves. I couldn't really find fault with Penny's parenting.

The girls are both lovely and she's done a good job with them. They are extremely polite, well-mannered, kind individuals. I don't think you can do any more than that. If you bring your child up to be a decent, nice human being, that's got to be successful. We're still together and we're still happy. Now I get Mother's Day cards as well, so that's nice! My experience of family life has been positive.

Mummy no. 2 – Bernadette's story

Bernadette, her fourteen-year-old daughter, Jade, and her partner, Ronnie, are a mixed-race lesbian step-family dealing with issues of racism, homophobia and step-parenting. Bernadette wrote this piece in 2001.

I met Ronnie nine years ago, on a blind date arranged by mutual friends. Jade was five and had never experienced me having a partner. She was always a possessive child and easily got jealous if I even cuddled another child, so all hell broke loose when she realised that Ronnie wasn't just for Christmas!

Even though Ronnie joined our family gradually, Jade was very resentful. She reckoned Ronnie had a cheek inviting herself round and making herself at home! It was really hard work trying to establish a new relationship and dealing with Jade's fury at having to share her mummy with someone else. She needed a lot of reassurance that I loved her the same as always, that she was my 'number one girl'. Sometimes they had terrible rows and Jade would scream, 'You're not my mum. Get out of our house!' At times I felt very low and wondered if it was worth all the stress of being constantly caught in the middle and trying to balance everyone's needs. Somehow we ploughed on through lots of fights, lots of talking, lots of patience, lots of shouting, lots of forgiving and loads of cuddles and love. Now Jade accepts Ronnie, and has come to depend on and love her as another parent figure. On Mother's Day, she sends a card to 'Mummy no. 2'. They still have flare-ups, but now that seems more normal, to do with teenage stuff and their individual personalities, rather than Jade feeling threatened and resentful that someone is taking her mother away.

Ours is a racially diverse family. I am white from an Irish background, Ronnie is black from a Caribbean background and Jade has Nigerian/Irish heritage. We are very aware that racism is a reality in our society. Rather than focus on our difference, we get our strength from the common bonds we share as the children of immigrants who came to Britain to escape poverty and have a 'better' life. This experience in our original families gives us a similar outlook on life and a fantastic sense of humour!

When Jade was younger, I tended to over-protect her from the harsh realities of racism: partly because I didn't want her to feel hurt in any way and partly to avoid my own discomfort. For example, if there was a story on the news of a violent attack on a black person, I would turn it off. Ronnie felt that I wasn't helping Jade to understand what she was up against and so be able to develop skills and defences that are necessary for black people to cope with and survive racism. We talk about issues in a positive way and try to teach Jade not to internalise things if she experiences racism, that the problem is to do with the fears and prejudice of small-minded people, and nothing to do with who she is as a person.

In many ways, our family life is very conventional. Ronnie goes out to work and pays the bills and I'm the housewife. I do all the cooking, cleaning, shopping, ironing, and decorating. This works very well for us as a family. It means there is someone there for Jade and no arguments about whose turn it is to clean the bog! When I worked, we argued more about chores and it was stressful working out childcare. Even though there isn't much money, we have a fairly happy and relaxed home life. We have a strong moral outlook on life in that we teach Jade the importance of good manners and respect towards other people. We always have our dinner together because it's a time when we can reconnect and talk. As Jade gets older she can see that compared to some of her friends, she gets a pretty good deal, in that her feelings are listened to, she's involved in family decisions, and we are not as strict as her friends' parents. Compared to my youth, my life now as a mother is very quiet and ordinary. I do get a twisted little thrill at school parents' evenings when we introduce ourselves as Jade's parents. It's hilarious watching all the various expressions until they finally settle on the 'right' one!!

Now that Jade is a teenager, we face some new challenges as lesbian parents – 'the teenage girls' sleepovers'! When she was younger, it didn't matter that we were lesbians, because her friends' parents were our friends and it just wasn't an issue. Now she goes to a fairly tough girls' school, where it is a term of abuse to call someone a lesbian, despite pop stars and *Brookside*! While we don't want to hide what we are, we don't want Jade to be worrying about how to explain things to her friends. It's a bit of a dilemma at the moment but like everything else, I guess we will manage to steer our way through. We see ourselves as a normal family with normal ups and downs. Sometimes I take a step back and feel really, really proud of the loving, supportive family that we have created for ourselves.

You can't win – Jess's story

Jess had two sons, Richard and Stewart, when she was married to John. Although she recognised there was something different about her sexuality when she was fifteen, she didn't come out as a lesbian until she was forty. At that time, her sons were ten and thirteen. She has been living as a single parent in a small English country village for the last seven years. Jess was interviewed in 2001.

When I told Richard I was lesbian, he was ten. He said, 'I know.' I said, 'How do you know? It's taken me 25 years to find out.' He said, 'It's the way you look at people and touch people.' Often our children have a sense of us being slightly different even before we know. Neither of the boys had a problem with me being a lesbian, although Stewart said he had a problem with other people knowing about me being a lesbian.

I've learned that you've got to choose your moment and allow for the fact that your children will have different feelings from you. I felt relieved when I separated from my husband and when I came out. My life was opening up. But my kids were upset that their father was leaving. I felt isolated in that I wanted to be joyful but a lot of other people around me were not quite ready.

I found that you have to be careful about introducing your new girlfriend to your children. Even though people had told me this, I still made the mistake of introducing someone too early. That created a lot of anger and jealousy. It's much better to allow your kids time to grieve and change, at least a year. They won't want your girlfriend there having breakfast with you. It's better to come out slowly, incrementally.

The question of how my partners relate to my children is very difficult. I think 'you can't win' is the answer. Even if you're low-key, you don't live together, she just visits once a fortnight and your kids actually like her, you can't make it work out for everyone. My experience is that the kids are happy only so long as she's a guest.

I've been with Gillian for the last six months. As our relationship deepens, Gillian inevitably becomes part of this family and starts to feel free to comment on the boys' behaviour. They can be quite rude and dismissive. I occasionally pick them up on this, but mostly it goes over my head. Gillian finds it jarring and tells them off for the way they speak to me. They do not like that at all. They say it's not her place to interfere. She doesn't want to be a step-mother. On the other hand, I know how it feels to hear someone you love and care for spoken to in a dismissive, rude way. When she highlights to me that my boys behave badly, then I feel a failure as a mother. I know in my heart that I'm not the world's greatest mother but you don't want someone to point this out to you.

I don't know any easy answers. We have tried quite hard. We can't live near each other at the moment because of our work commitments, and our weekends become very important and intense. We spend a lot of time talking to each other on the phone but you can't give someone a hug on the phone. Words matter, so saying things like, 'You let your sons walk over you' comes across as a criticism of me, not of the boys. She's not a mother. She must be thinking, 'I would have done this differently.' Maybe she would. I'm quite a laissez-faire parent. I remember reading that the greatest difference is not between men and women but between people who have children and people who don't.

We have to be careful of each other's feelings; we can inadvertently cause each other a lot of hurt. We have to keep the lines of communication open and sometimes not talk about it. I think that if you want to live together in harmony, the partner should not discipline the children or tell them off. Privately, you've got to be free to speak. She's the one with the problem about their behaviour. Every mother does the best she can but you don't realise when they're small and you're sowing the seeds how it's going to be when they're teenagers. Even if people tell you, you still don't know.

My boys are seventeen and twenty. There are going to be issues between me and Gillian around the boys for years. Having got this far with them, they are a major part of my life. Even though I can imagine them living independently and I look forward to that, I will have an ongoing relationship with them.

I don't know how Gillian fits in. I want her to be friends with them, because you want the people you love to love your children. Recently Richard was fantasising about the future and having a baby. He said he would come to show his baby to Granny and Granny. He started making Granny and Granny jokes. He used to imagine me as a lonely old lady living alone with cats. Now he sees me living with Gillian so that frees him up.

In control – Myra's story

Myra left James, her husband of seven years (with whom she now co-parents), when her two daughters were four and six years old. Nicole is now nine and Chantelle is twelve. This is her story, told in 2001.

Because my children had been around women all their lives, I don't think they had any particular problems with me being with women. When I left my husband, I told them I loved women and that I didn't want to be with men. They were fine, but they were only four and six. They were happy as long as I was happy. Nicole, the youngest, was fine because she wanted to be with me anyway but Chantelle had nightmares for about six months about me leaving her, too. She was missing her dad. She was his little princess and got a lot of attention from him. She still has pictures of the family together on her bedroom wall. Quite recently she said that she wished we were together still, even though she remembers arguments where things got thrown around the room and times when we didn't speak to each other, when you could have cut the atmosphere with a knife.

One time she said to me that all she wanted was to be 'normal' and why had I done this to her. That was difficult. I said about women beaten and killed by their husbands every week. She's got this unreal view in her head about what normal is, and thinks I could do better for myself in the women I choose. Chantelle thinks their dad is better than my girlfriends so far.

I used to wonder if Nicole would grow up to be a lesbian, but I don't really care. She'll grow up to be whatever she is. I'll find out eventually. When she first went to school, Nicole changed her name to Nick, wore boy's swimming trunks and boy's underpants. I worried that her teachers would think she was doing it because I was a lesbian. I was so worried about it, I even took it to parents' evening. I said to Nicole's teacher, 'I know I'm a lesbian and my daughter wears boy's underpants. I didn't encourage her to do this.' I was really paranoid when I first came out as a lesbian that I would be accused of bringing up my children to be lesbian man-haters or something. That's what I thought they'd all be thinking of me. But the teacher was great – she gave Nicole a pair of Superman underpants. I was so relieved that she was so accepting and that we'd got it out of the way.

I co-parent with the children's father. James lives around the corner and they see him twice a week. I've had the same arrangement for the last five years. When we used to have arguments about access, I was worried that he would take me to court. But if he did try that, I could report him to the Child Support Agency. That's my little lever. When we separated, I wrote to the CSA and said that I refused to co-operate as a political decision, not because he was violent. We wanted to come to a private arrangement which the CSA doesn't let people do. I knew that we'd have a better quality of life if he paid because he wanted to pay, instead of having to pay me a certain amount of income determined by the CSA. He would probably have to pay a lot more than I ask him for and then he would feel that he had a right to more access.

I want to be in control. I am the main carer and I want to make sure that I stay that way. It's very important for me to be a good mother and to give them a better upbringing than I had. James works full-time and it takes a lot of arranging for him to work at home. He can't suddenly look after the children. In theory he could, but he hasn't done because I've always found other ways of doing it. When I was in hospital last year for six months, they were living with my mum in my house and James had them at weekends until he made arrangements to work at home. Even though I was near death, in hospital one hundred miles away, I was on the pay phone trying to organise childcare, asking my mother to have them, arranging when they'd swap the children over. My mum and James don't talk to each other much, so I had to be the mediator. It was a nightmare and it was ridiculous. I must have been spending about £5 a day on the phone. I finally had to let go of all that and trust them to sort it out in the best interests of my children.

James is a lot happier since he got a girlfriend. He accepts my lesbian friends now. At first he didn't like the children seeing my friends and he wouldn't talk to them. My friends were worried when I was ill that my children were going to get dragged into his heterosexual world and cut off from them. They made a big effort to ring my husband and see my children who, after all, were part of their lives as well. James was shocked at me being so ill and actually pleased to get so much support and help bringing my children to see me.

I haven't lived with anyone since I left James. I don't particularly want to. When I see lesbian couples, I think how nice that is but I'm getting a lot of my needs met, anyway. I get support from my friends and I have great sex with a woman friend of mine, when we get together sometimes, but I haven't got into any traditional one-on-one relationships for ages. Partly I don't because as the children get older, they want to know more about what's going on in my private life. If I have lovers, they want to know where it's going and where they are in it all. If they don't like the lovers, they don't want them round the house, whereas before they'd just accept it. I need to respect their views, too – after all they live with me. So we talk about things. Also I've had enough emotional stress, nearly dying. I'm still trying to find myself after being ill. I don't want anyone to feel they've got to be responsible for me. I've been through so much in my life, dying and then not dying. Having an intense sexual relationship is too much for me emotionally. Sometimes I think I should be more traditional, but then being a lesbian I don't have to.

Sometimes I feel invisible as a lesbian because I don't have a partner with me. In the lesbian mothers' support group I go to, everyone is in a couple except me and one other woman. There, a lot of the dynamics going on is between partners. For me, all the dynamics is between me and my children and how I get support around dealing with them and how they get support dealing with me. What is really helpful is knowing other lesbian mothers and the kids knowing other children of lesbian mothers so they can talk about their situation if they want to without having to explain what it is like having a lesbian mum.

All my women partners have been involved with my children as far as they and I want. I wouldn't go out with somebody who didn't like children or be friends with them, but I don't expect them to form attachments with them. I said to one girlfriend that if we split up she could only see the children if they wanted to see her. They didn't so she didn't. I think she found it hard, but in the end it's me and my children who are always together and I have to look after them.

I always talk about my parenting with my partners. It's a major part of my life. I find it hard bringing up children on my own without anyone to refer to. If anyone is around that I can talk to, then I will. But I make the decisions. I always did. Anna used to look after my children and me sometimes – I was with her for five years when I was with my husband. She was very kind. We used to cook together – as I find cooking boring day after day – and then take the food back to our separate homes to eat. Chantelle still talks about her. I think it is important for the children to have close adults to talk to other than me. When James split up with his woman, she wrote to me to ask to see them, which was fine as they liked and missed her. She's back with him now, so they see her regularly.

Except for Anna who was another mother and feminine, I tend to be attracted to quite butch women. I find them sexy. One butch woman I was involved with was sometimes mistaken for a man – she let the children drive her car, she was very strong, had big muscles in her arms and thighs and a masculine build. None of the butch women I was involved with were mothers, but they were still into children. When they were growing up, they did boy things and played with boys. They identify with Nicole, who also likes boy things. She loves collecting wood, making things, painting and decorating. She looks to them as role models.

I haven't come across any anti-mother stuff among lesbians but I don't get out on the scene much. I once saw an ad in the personals section saying 'no bisexuals or lesbian mothers'. I just thought, 'OK, I'm not interested in you, either.' With one of my girlfriends, it took six months for us to get together. She was worried about getting together with a mother. She thought you had to be so much more committed and take it so seriously. She was scared because she'd have to get involved with the children as well. Taking on a family must be quite daunting.

I think you change your circle of friends when you have children. I go around with other mothers mostly or with women who like kids. The lesbian mother friends I go out with are great. Since I've been on my own, I don't have anybody to share the good things with. When Nicole scored a goal in league football, I was so happy that I went and phoned another lesbian mother friend. I really want to share the good things as well as the bad things.

When I was in hospital, I tried to keep everything stable for Chantelle and Nicole. I got a lot of support from my friends. I knew that mentally I had to hand my children over, to let go and trust in the universe that they would be looked after, that my spirit or the goddess or whatever would look after them. I had to take them out of my head and put them aside. I let go as part of my preparation for dying. I did it on my own. I prayed a lot as well. I'm more of a pagan. I'm into any healing spirits.

When I eventually came back home, I found it difficult to connect to my life. It was like I had been living on another planet, then dropped back on earth again and told to get on with it. I was scared to see the children after mentally saying goodbye to them. I didn't know how I was going to physically look after them and emotionally reassure them. I had to reconnect; I think it was a two-way process.

My illness and being away in hospital was very disruptive and scary to my children. Nicole had things from my bedroom stashed in her room – my jumper, my clothes, my coat. She didn't even remember taking them. Chantelle was off school for months with stress and some virus when I got home. Every time I went to hospital for a check-up, she didn't know if I was coming back. I had gone into hospital when they were on holiday with their dad, and when they got back, I had disappeared. She said that if she hadn't gone on holiday it wouldn't have happened. Obviously I didn't want her to feel responsible, but after that she didn't want to go on holiday without me. A good friend of mine helped her a lot – she took her on holiday and let her ring me every night. Chantelle took a photo of me, and was reassured that I would still be there. She felt angry with me for being ill and not being with her when she started secondary school. She's quite protective of me now.

Going it alone – Sheila's story

Sheila got pregnant by self-insemination with an anonymous donor in 1979. She raised her son, Tim, on her own. (His story opens Chapter 14 on page 227.) Sheila gave this interview in 1993.

I chose to do it alone. I know lots of women who want a baby but who first of all want a partner. It was never like that for me. This was my own life decision, something that I was choosing for myself. Being part of a couple with somebody has never been a major goal in my life. If it happens, OK, and at times I do feel more drawn to it than at others; but it's not a part of my basic life plan. Therefore the decision to have a child wasn't made in that context. It was more that I was choosing whether or not I wanted to do it for myself. It didn't feel like a second-best solution.

When I first decided to get pregnant, I was lovers with a woman named Liz but we didn't see ourselves as a couple. We had no intention of being together for years and years. That wasn't our philosophy. We were lovers for about four years but we didn't live together until she decided to move to the town where I was living and spent ages looking for somewhere to live. She ended up living in my flat, but we still tried to maintain separate lives. When I made the decision to get pregnant, Liz was against the idea. She moved out and we stopped being lovers shortly after Tim was born.

I feel happy that the decision to do it alone was right for me. It was the best thing I ever did, the best life choice I ever made. In terms of my relationship with Tim, I think it's brilliant. That side of it is easy. But I do think it is hard doing it on your own, especially the practical details. It's hard having no money when you're the only one there to pay all the bills. And living with other women has its own hassles. I've tried both and I'm happier living on my own with Tim.

I suppose a lot of single women think that eventually they will meet someone, but I've never had that expectation. It is difficult not having support for me that's automatically built into our living situation. I have had to learn to be my own strength, to cope alone with things. There's good and bad in that, because it makes me more isolated, yet at the same time I have learned to get emotional support from a number of people rather than from one.

I strongly value those support networks and close friendships with other people. It makes me sad when women in couples let those friendships drop. It's not just important for the mothers, but for the children too. I can't quite imagine how the children would cope if they thought they were the only ones with a lesbian mother. I go to some lengths to make sure that they have those relationships. When I was young, I had lots of cousins and we went on outings, birthdays, and parties together. I suppose that the way I grew up influences what I want now. I always had the idea that I would make that for myself and choose my own family.

I used to say to my friends that I wanted our children to be like cousins to each other. I feel really happy that we've managed to do that. Most of my closest friends are other lesbian families. Some of them were in the original self-insemination group with me and those children are twelve or thirteen. We are also close to other younger children and their lesbian mothers and we spend lots of holidays and weekends together. This loose network – my 'chosen family' – is an important part of my life and Tim's. It makes me feel really pleased and proud of what we have done and how we have managed to struggle with those relationships. They haven't always been easy. It is really like my mum and her sisters. You have rows, but you come through them and stick with it. That's a commitment I've made for the children and for me and my friends.

Since Tim was born, I have had long periods of not having a lover. In the past I worried about whether it would be difficult when I do have a lover. What happens in reality is that Tim has always been very welcoming to the lover. It amazes me how really easy and nice Tim always is about it. He's so warm and encouraging to them. I think it's because he thinks I'm happier with a lover and that he sees it as a bit more fun than our boring old life with just the two of us. I've never lived with a lover, so it doesn't ever get to be ordinary.

We did go through some quite difficult times with the first lover I had in his life. He was six when I got involved with her. He sometimes felt left out, and sometimes I felt quite torn between my needs and his needs. One thing I learned from that first relationship is that I expected her to love him as much as I loved him or as much as she loved me. I felt critical of her for not loving him enough and it took me a long time to realise that that was an unreasonable expectation. It took somebody else who was lovers with a mother to say to me, 'Of course the thing is that the mother always thinks you are going to love their child as much as them.' I had a flash of realisation of how it felt to be in the other position. Years later I had a relationship with a mother and I think there's quite a difference between having lovers with children and those without. The dynamic is different. Having any kind of lover requires quite an adjustment. It is a shift in the balance of relationships. Luckily Tim is into talking about it.

A lot of people have the idea that children can only cope with long-term relationships. I don't agree with that. I think children can and do cope. Anyway, what can you do about it? It's life, isn't it? There are all sorts of situations where you have close friends for short periods. Children do that too. My attitude with lovers is to let it develop into a close friendship if it is going to. I've never kept a lover away from Tim. I make sure I do have time with lovers when he's not there, but not only. I couldn't imagine just having a lover who wasn't involved with him as well. I think it's very nice for them to develop a close relationship but if it ends, then it ends.

An important person in our family is my close friend Anna. She was my first lesbian lover and we went on being friends after we were no longer lovers. Although she wasn't welcoming of my pregnancy, she quickly became involved with Tim when he was very tiny. All three of us – Tim, Anna and myself – have seen her as a kind of second mother, though not perhaps as an equal parent. If I die, Tim would live with her. She's been very involved in his life. I think it's really important for him to have other adults whom he is close to apart from me. So from that angle, I am committed to making sure that their relationship goes on. If he goes to her for a weekend, I will do what needs to be done to organise it and get him there.

We've had some conflicts. When I moved out of London, she felt really angry and powerless about it, saying that I was taking him away from her. In fact, we've made it so that he spends whole weekends with her and holidays. Like any other relationship, there have been times when I've felt like saying we should forget it and let go of it. But I'm strongly motivated to keep on with it. That's because I believe that it's right, even though I feel angry with her about some choices she's made in her life. I just have to respect their relationship and let them get on with it.

Because a single parent needs other people to be with their children, sometimes those relationships can develop much more than if the mother had a partner. I needed holidays alone or with my lover and Tim would go off with someone else or spend time with other people. It's a normal part of his life to do that. There wouldn't have been as much space for Anna if I had had a partner or if Tim had had another involved parent. I've seen it happen with children I know, where there's so much adult input at home that there's no need for any other grown-ups outside the immediate family. So the children don't learn to be flexible. That's something Tim has learned – to be really flexible, to make the best of any situation, to really enjoy different experiences. I've seen some children who find that very difficult, partly because they're not used to it. I'm happy that he has had that.

Full house – Caroline and Lynn's story

Caroline and Lynn were married with six children between them when they met at their children's school and fell in love. They divorced their husbands and moved in together, along with three of Lynn's four daughters and Caroline's two sons. They have been living together as a family for the last six years. They gave this interview in 2001, and prefaced it by saying:

Children are a big part of our lives. However, had we met prior to being married, we probably would not have had children. We only have a small part of our lives for each other. We wouldn't lose any of the ones we've already got, but our relationship suffers because we have so many children and so much responsibility.

Caroline: There were no tensions between my husband and me about me being lesbian. I still to this day don't really know what sparked off his animosity. He is still so hostile. He maintains contact with the boys. He considered giving up work and challenging me for their care but that wasn't because he objected to the way we care for them. It's because he cares for them so much himself. He has them every other weekend.

Lynn: I haven't spoken to my husband for six months. I try to speak to his new wife. I don't like speaking to him. He makes me very agitated and upset. He's so horrible. He has never shared responsibility for the children. He has never come to a parents' evening at school. He's not interested in anything the children have done. He originally had the children from 6pm on a Saturday until 7pm on a Sunday. That's changed – now he has the youngest from school on a Friday until Monday morning every other weekend. My other daughters sometimes go to their father on Saturday night. Their father will pay half towards two major trips each year, but refuses to pay anything else. As far as he's concerned, he'll pay their maintenance until they're sixteen and then they're out.

There are totally different sets of rules at our home and his. Here, we sit at the table to eat; we don't eat in the front room. The children have treat night on a Wednesday. At their father's, they can eat in the front room; they don't eat as a family. They can eat sweets any time during the day. It's totally different morals. They're not expected to bathe every day and keep themselves clean. Here they are. They're expected to change their clothes, keep their bedroom tidy. At their father's if they don't make their beds, that's up to them. They're allowed to watch TV until all hours. Here, the younger ones can't watch after nine o'clock. They're expected to read. There, they're not even expected to do their homework.

Lynn: My twelve-year-old daughter wouldn't come with us. She stayed with her father. I lost my eldest child. She had nothing to do with me. She will be eighteen in January and she still hasn't come round fully. She's more accepting, but she only visits two or three times a year, and she'll phone occasionally.

Caroline: I don't think she's homophobic. She has lesbian and gay friends at school and she's very supportive of them, which I think is a positive response to me and Lynn. Unfortunately she sees me as the enemy because I brought about the split. When she visits, she's lovely towards me – but I don't think she'll ever allow me in. She's determined to make Lynn suffer for breaking up the family.

Lynn: In the beginning, she tried to insist on seeing me on my own or not at all. She gave me the ultimatum – either Caroline or her. I weighed up the pros and cons and said to her that she's welcome to come and live with us and that I still love her but I love Caroline. In a few years she's going to be grown up and go away. I don't want to wait. I couldn't allow a twelve-year-old to run my life. Her father had run it for long enough and I wasn't about to let somebody else run it. I needed to take charge of my own life, which I did.

Caroline: At that time, we were trying desperately for people to see us as a family, that it was all or nothing. It was important to us for people to take us as a package and not as individuals.

Lynn: I think that was the right thing. Otherwise, she would have had me over a barrel.

Caroline: Unfortunately, she was a very immature twelve-year-old. The most important thing in her mind was that we would be poor. She was from a wealthy background.

Lynn: The very first thing she said to me was, 'I can't possibly come with you. We'll be poor.' She didn't say, 'I can't possibly come with you because you're a lesbian.' Her father then did a fantastic job of poisoning her mind. He tried to describe the sexual antics we might get into. The damage he did was unbelievable. She wouldn't come round, so we weren't in a position to tell her it wasn't correct. ...

My youngest daughter and Caroline's oldest son have become like twins. They're the same age and they're inseparable. When they come back after being away at their respective fathers', they're like a little married couple. They shut themselves away. They hardly ever argue. They have an unusual relationship. They've been brought up together and their likes are very similar.

My sixteen-year-old daughter is a happy, healthy, well-adjusted, rounded person, very sensible. We've had our ups and downs, same as every parent would. For a while, she thought the grass was greener on the other side of the fence. She went to live with her father because we didn't get on over silly things, like wanting her to have a bath every night, eat her vegetables.

Caroline: She wouldn't eat anything I cooked. She became difficult every time I spoke to her. Her father lured her back to live with them with false promises. Her step-mother wanted to go back to work and had a young child. They wanted a babysitter. We said, 'you must do whatever you want'. She went back for a year and it was an awful period. We hardly heard from her for the first three months, then she came back in tears – but she didn't move back here for a long time because she felt too sheepish.

Lynn: She said she would never go back to live there again. She hates it there. The insight her father has given her of heterosexual marriage and all that comes with it is a far worse role model than what she's learned about lesbian relationships. She can see how different our values are from his. I hope he doesn't make her afraid of heterosexual family life. She talks to us about her feelings. She talks to us very openly about her relationship with her boyfriend. I know she wouldn't do that with her father. She felt comfortable enough to talk with both of us. Now she's at an age where she chooses to go to her father or she doesn't.

My third daughter has always stuck by me. She's never got on with her father. Now she's fourteen; there's heaps of trouble between her and her father. She doesn't want to go there.

Caroline: My relationship with Lynn's fourteen-year-old is under immense strain. I've never felt this way before. She's causing a huge disruption to the family.

Lynn: My relationship with her is also at an all-time low. She has disowned me. She says I'm not her mother anymore. She will purposely cause an argument. She will stand barefaced and be really unpleasant or she will come to the table and purposely do things with her food that she knows she's not allowed to do. She will sit and swear at the table. She will do it to get a reaction. She's very, very destructive at the moment. She's very angry.

Caroline: It is definitely beyond normal adolescence. She is actually seeing a counsellor weekly and has a social worker.

Lynn: We attribute her behaviour to negligence by her father. When she was twelve and on holiday in another country with him, she was raped. Her father allowed her to go out every night until whatever time she wanted and drink whatever she wanted. We would never have allowed that. With all the professionals helping her, there's never been an issue about us being lesbian. We had an assessment at the hospital together and we're signed up for family therapy.

Caroline: It's tearing us apart. I don't know if it's harder because she isn't my child. For the first time ever, I told her that was it. I'd had it. I think I would have said the same if she'd been my own kid, but I know it caused her immense distress.

Lynn: I've actually told her I hate her, which is terrible. You can hate them, but you can still love them. Her father won't have her. He has so little to do with her and he has such disregard for her anyway. The amount of problems that the other children cause are a fleck on the wallpaper compared to her.

Caroline: She has caused so much damage to my relationship with Lynn. … I treat Lynn's children as if they were my own. I don't have a problem with that at all and I find it easy not to favour. That's the way I am. Out of my two boys, I don't have a favourite. To extend the family was not difficult. Having said that, I would never ever have had six children. I do find it quite depressing to be responsible for so many children. I didn't have my first child until I was thirty. However, they all have the same amount of time. If one of them wants to speak to me, I don't say no. They all relate to me and talk to me quite easily.

We share parenting. Very often it's me that takes the girls to the GP. Sometimes they ask me about boy-related problems. Maybe they choose me because I had five brothers. We tend to do most things together anyway. I never say those are your kids, they're your responsibility.

Lynn: I say I've got six children, unless I don't want to discuss my relationship with Caroline for a specific reason. I always say I've got four girls and two boys.

Caroline: We say that we all live together and are bringing up the children as a family. You can't expect them to live together in a house and not regard each other as siblings.

Lynn: At bathtime, I wash the boys' hair. All five kiss us before they go off to school in the morning and before they go to bed at night. Even the fourteen-year-old who's causing so much disruption does it. She does love us.

We've already lived six years as a family. But as the years go on, we realise that we don't have the rights that other families have. It's quite a terrifying thought.

Caroline: I would like legal recognition of our relationship. Lynn would like to marry me. It would make it better for people to recognise us, silly things like anniversaries. That might sound very twee. But we recognise our own anniversary and the children do – that's nice. I would like to apply for a joint residence order, but I know that there would be obstruction from my husband. He makes it quite clear that if anything ever happened to me, he would take the boys.

Lynn: I would object to that now, especially for the youngest boy. He has lived longer with me than he has with his father. If you split the 'inseparable twins' up, that would be terrible. If something happened to me, I would pray to God that Caroline would keep the girls. I don't believe my husband would want the girls. That's a terrible thing to say, but he has got his own life with a new family. He pays lip service to them. He does what he thinks is expected of him.

I have stated to Caroline what I want to happen if I were to become terminally ill – about the children, donating my organs, etc. My mother has already stated that she will not allow Caroline to deal with it, even though it is my wishes.

Caroline: If I were to die, I don't think my husband would object to the boys having contact with Lynn and the girls. He is a reasonable person.

Lynn: As they get older, about the age of eleven, they have the right to say where they want to live. Certainly if there was some legal way to do it, we would. I know that the two older girls would not want to go and live with their father. They would leave home and where would that leave the youngest one? It's a situation that doesn't bear thinking about. We have discussed it at great length. I know that they wouldn't get the same sort of upbringing with my husband as the boys would get with their father. My feelings for the boys are such that if Caroline suddenly decided that the boys were going to live with their father, I wouldn't stand and take it. If, God forbid, something happened to Caroline, I wouldn't allow their father to take them. It gets harder as time goes on.

Caroline: Like anything, it's a challenge but it's worthwhile. I would never not have the kids now that I've got them. We have lovely times.

Lynn: We do really have lovely children. I do love all of our children.

Part V
Our Children's Point of View

*How do our children feel about having a lesbian mother? What are the
issues for them? Unlike their mothers, most of them did not choose to
create new kinds of families or to assert their sexual identity. So their
perspective is bound to be different – and to interest lesbian mothers and
those who are planning a family. This part of the book presents some of
the issues and then lets our children tell their own stories.*

What About the Children? 217   In Their Own Words 227

13

WHAT ABOUT THE CHILDREN?

This chapter serves as an introduction to the issues raised by the sons and daughters of lesbians, some of whom tell their stories in the next chapter. They all have different experiences of growing up with a lesbian mum and coping with homophobia.

Ordinary lives?

During 1995, I interviewed twenty people who had lesbian mothers or gay fathers or both for a book called *What About the Children? Sons and daughters of lesbians and gay men speak about their lives* (published by Cassell in 1996 and no longer in print). Seven of those interviews are included in the next chapter. Some of the people, especially those who were lesbian and gay themselves, were eager to share their stories and make their case for lesbian and gay rights. Others needed to be convinced that their stories were worth hearing. Many believed that their experiences were unexceptional and couldn't understand how such ordinary lives might provoke such interest.

The sexuality of their parents is the only thing they have in common and it is not a strong basis for solidarity. While lesbians and gay men have a sexual identity which loosely unites them, at least in spirit, the people I interviewed did not claim an identity as a daughter or son of a lesbian. They labelled themselves, if at all, by their own sexuality or their race, nationality, class background, occupation or by any number of characteristics intrinsic to themselves. This is not to say that their parents' sexuality was unimportant or had no effect on them, but it did not define them. It is one characteristic among many about their parents.

I asked the people I interviewed how they defined their own sexuality and in what ways they felt that their lesbian parent's sexuality had influenced them. I wanted to reflect a range of experiences, so I selected people to interview who were at various points on the continuum of sexuality, from exclusively gay to bisexual to exclusively heterosexual, plus a few who were too young or still unsure. You can't draw any conclusions from this sample about the proportion of daughters and sons of lesbian mothers who are gay or lesbian themselves.

Awareness of prejudice

What came out of the interviews is a common awareness of homophobia. Prejudice against homosexuality is pervasive in our society and affects our children as much as it affects us. People with lesbian mothers have developed various strategies for dealing with prejudice and have learned to assess what strategy to use in different situations.

"I'd say the down side of having lesbian parents is other people's attitudes towards lesbians. I feel a sense of solidarity with gay rights issues. It makes me furious when anybody says anything against gays." **Alice, 15**

Strategies for dealing with homophobia

Children are acutely aware of anti-gay prejudice and develop their own strategies for dealing with it. Some persevere with one strategy, consistently taking measures either to avoid or to confront prejudice. But most have an eclectic and pragmatic approach, using whatever tactics they feel safe with at the time.

Children of lesbians have the option to disclose or not disclose their parent's sexual identity. Motivations for keeping quiet may include shame and embarrassment about homosexuality, but are more likely to be self-protection and avoiding the unpleasantness caused by others' prejudice.

"I don't go around shouting about my parents' sexuality wherever I am. Not everyone can take on board the fact that I have two gay parents. Initially I thought it was going to put people off me, so I used to not say anything until I had to." **Kate, 24**

Some children take the view that a parent's sexuality is not for public disclosure; that it is a personal and private matter. After all, most people with heterosexual parents do not routinely talk about their parents' sexual identity with friends.

"In some ways I think it's really important that people know, because telling helps make it more accepted. But then on the other hand, why should people know? My mum's made it quite clear that it's her private business who she's having a relationship with. I completely respect that. There is no reason for me or her to tell people if she doesn't want to." **Zoe, 24**

"Mum's sexuality doesn't come up with close friends very often. It's only when a friend confides in me something that's relevant that I would share something about Mum back. I've talked to my husband and other close family, but generally I don't drop it into the conversation. I got the feeling from Mum that it wasn't something that she wanted known about." **Claire, 33**

As children reach adolescence, they become more concerned about being different and are under intense pressure to conform. They are developing their own personal and sexual identity, differentiating themselves from their parents. In addition to fear of harassment, they may well fear that others will think they are homosexual if they reveal their parent's sexuality.

"Lesbianism is so taboo. As I was growing up, I would hotly deny it if my mum was accused of being a lesbian. None of my friends ever knew apart from [a friend who also had a lesbian mother] and a girl who was like a second daughter to Mum. Mum was aware that I didn't want everyone to know, because it wouldn't have been acceptable in the circles I moved in. She never jeopardised anything for me." **Katrina, 17**

"When you're a child, all you want is to be the same as everyone else. It's only when you're an adult that you revel in being different. Many aspects of Mum's lifestyle that weren't anything to do with her sexuality made our family different from the norm. If I'd known she was a lesbian when I was a child, it would have been one more thing that made us different. I probably would have found it a burden. I was already uncomfortable that my packed lunches were radically different from all my friends." **Claire, 33**

Keeping a parent's sexual identity secret means that children have to control their parents' behaviour as well as their own. This usually involves asking the parent to be discreet in public and some children may refuse to be seen in public with an obviously gay father or lesbian mother.

"For about three years after the custody case, we had a rule that my mum and her lover didn't hold hands, or make any display of their relationship when we went out or were near my friends... I needed boundaries and rules to protect me when I started secondary school. I was not ashamed of Mum's lesbianism. It was purely about my fear of being rejected." **Amanda, 24**

There may be times when the child decides that non-disclosure is the best strategy, but the parent has decided that openness is necessary for their psychic survival. Many lesbian and gay adults have been through a long process of coming out and have no desire to go back in the closet. It can be difficult to find a balance between the different needs of the children and parents.

"My mum wears a lesbian necklace and I remember saying to her, 'You've got to hide your necklace when you come in to school.' My mum always respected the fact that I might not want my friends at school to know, that it was my choice, not hers. I always felt awkward about asking Mum to hide signs of her lesbianism. I think she knew that it was fair enough, but we weren't always completely clear about what were the issues of her life and what were mine. I eventually decided that I love my mother, but she has her own life and I have mine. What she does is separate from what I do, even though she has influenced me in so many ways." **Zoe, 24**

In families where the parents are not open about their sexuality, children are expected to maintain the secrecy. The family may perceive the dangers of disclosure as a greater burden than keeping a secret. Children become adept at assessing the intensity of anti-gay prejudice and of knowing when to tell and who to trust – even young children are able to discern the social acceptability of homosexuality and to determine whether it is safe to come out. Gretel, eleven, tells children at school that her mother's partner is "just sharing a house with us". She says this woman's daughter is her sister, "except at school where I just call her a sort of sister because people there don't understand".

"I only mentioned it to one person at the schools I went to in Gloucestershire. They're all very small minded there and had no understanding at all. No one at my school even knew anyone who was gay. They used to joke about gays. They saw gays as people out there somewhere, as other. So to tell anyone would have been impossible. It wasn't until I'd moved into cities where people are more liberal that it became easier." **Kate, 24**

"When I was just starting at secondary school, I felt nervous about revealing my secret. I was worried that people would hold it against me. I chose a few apparently trustworthy people to tell. Although I was so careful about who I told, when I left school five years later, I discovered that the entire school already knew. My 'best friend' had made it her business to gossip about me to everyone." **Mary, 20**

"I don't tell most people. You have to work out who you can trust. Boys get hit more often. I have to be more cautious than girls." **Lawrence, 14**

Keeping a secret of something as important as a parent's homosexuality is difficult and can have a bad effect on friendships, which are more relaxed without such a burden. Liam, fifteen, felt encouraged by the positive responses he had from the friends he decided to tell and found that "I feel better with the friends that I've told."

Kate, 24, also discovered that "The burden has got lighter as I've grown up and talked about it more. I told my last two boyfriends on the first night, just got it over and done with. They were shocked for about five minutes and then that was it. My boyfriends are interested in me, not in my parents."

One purpose of public disclosure is to change people's attitudes. Presenting themselves as an example, children of lesbians and gay men take on the responsibility of educating others. As Lawrence, 14, said, "We always have to be training people."

"I've never had any stick at school about my mum being lesbian. When people say to me, 'Is your mum gay?', I say, 'Yeah.' That's it. I'm not ashamed about it and if they want to make a big thing out of it, they can. I'm not interested in their opinions about it. It helps other people change their attitudes about gay people when they look at me and think, 'It's not such a weird thing, is it? Her mum is a lesbian and had children. She's a human being.'" **Rachel, 19**

"In my Religious Education class, they didn't know anything about lesbian mothers until about three months ago, when I said, 'You're speaking complete garbage, because you've never met any lesbian mothers. And actually why shouldn't lesbians be mothers? I have three who are my mothers.'" **Alice, 15**

Many children choose friends who share their values, meaning they can be open about having lesbian or gay parents. In certain situations, such a revelation will enhance their standing.

"At school, I chose friends like myself, people who are very open. Some of my closest friends identify as lesbian now. They find it incredibly refreshing to come to my home and see my parents as role models. I wouldn't have a friend who was homophobic, not just because I'm bisexual myself, but because anybody that's prejudiced isn't really worth knowing." **Rosie, 20**

"I went to university, where I met a gay man who became my best friend. He and I went to gay pubs with him and his gay friends. They thought having two gay parents was cool and trendy. Whenever he introduced me, he'd say admiringly, 'Kate's parents are gay. She's great.'" **Kate, 24**

Children are best able to adopt a strategy of openness and of challenging homophobia when they perceive it as a problem belonging to other people and can put it into a broader perspective. Families are different for many reasons, the sexuality of parents not necessarily being the only one or the one most significant to other people.

"There are only disadvantages [to having a lesbian mother] if you care what other people think. Children are affected by what people say, it can't be denied, but it's impossible to go through your childhood and not have anybody say anything bad about you or your parents. Kids will always find something. My family was completely different from the others families we knew in many ways. There was only one black family where we lived, which made us very different. As I grew older, I came to realise that I had an unconventional family, but we didn't worry about what other people said about us." **Rick, 34**

"I have never encountered serious homophobia, so it's strange for me to think that anybody really does mind about people being homosexual. I can't see what the problem is. But I've been taught that society is a bit twisted and that the opinions of ignorant people don't count for much." **Rosie, 20**

How can parents help?

Parents are not responsible for the distress caused to their children by bigotry, but they do have some responsibility for their emotional and moral development. A parent's job is not to give children a good time, to keep them entertained or to see that they are always happy. It is to help them live their lives with strength and humanity, and to be individuals who can stand up for themselves and think for themselves.

Sometimes, the best a parent can do is help the child learn something positive from a bad experience. The issue is not whether lesbians and gay men have a right to have children in the face of universal condemnation of homosexuality, but how they can best make use of these opportunities for the development of strength of character and positive moral values.

In her book *Reinventing the Family* (see Resources), Laura Benkov asks: "How do children flourish and grow amid bigotry? How do parents face the pain of this question and help their children with this task? How and when do parents try to shield their children from pain, to actively advocate for them, to hold back and let them find their own way of dealing, to be present and bear witness to their suffering?" (p190).

The answer is that parents teach these values by the way they live their lives. If they are comfortable with their sexuality, they model pride and self-acceptance. If they know a variety of people and types of families, they teach children to value diversity and to understand that there are many routes to happiness and fulfilment. If they act according to their own standards of right and wrong and challenge injustice and prejudice, they teach that "people of integrity do not shrink from bigots" (quotation from judge in custody case, taken from Benkov). Most of all, they teach reality, a better preparation for life than myths about how the world should be.

"The greatest single problem for daughters and sons of lesbian and gay parents is our isolation. When kids from similar families just get together, regardless of what we do or say, it is a positive experience we can't underestimate." **COLAGE Guide**

Children are more susceptible to the prevailing prejudice against homosexuality when they are isolated and do not know any other children with lesbian or gay parents. Many lesbian mothers place great importance on building a sense of community, forming support networks and groups. They maintain friendships with other lesbian mothers and choose schools and neighbourhoods where they are not the only ones. The need for such contact is appreciated by the children.

"Every month we go to a lesbian parents' group. It's a bit boring. The adults just go and talk and I sit downstairs playing darts. There are lots of other children, but I'm the oldest. I would like a group for kids my age who have lesbian mothers. I don't know what kind of things we'd talk about, the same things we talk about anyway, but at least I would feel safe. In case of a slip of the tongue, saying something about lesbians, it wouldn't matter." **Josh, 12**

"What was missing for my mother and for us was a sense that there was a community of people like us. It would have helped us to feel normal. One of my mother's girlfriends had children and they lived with us for about two years. So we knew that there were other lesbians with children." **Rick, 34**

There are support groups for lesbian mothers in Britain. But there are not yet any run by and for their children. As a teenager, Zoe tried to set up one for children of lesbians:

"At the end of the day I came out of it feeling positive about my mum's sexuality and wanted to pass on my positivity to other people. Unfortunately, the support group didn't ever get off the ground. It's hard to find those children of lesbians who are having difficulties with their mothers' lesbianism, though they're the ones who most need a support group." **Zoe, 24**

As parents, we can't make the world safe for our children but we can help them to deal with the prejudice they will inevitably face. A great source of strength to us and our children is knowing they are not the only ones and that their parents are not ashamed of their sexuality or intimidated by the prejudice.

In the next chapter, the sons and daughters of lesbians describe their lives, including strategies for coping with homophobia.

14

IN THEIR OWN WORDS

These are the stories of seven different people whose mothers are lesbians. As described in the previous chapter, they were interviewed by the author, mostly in 1995.

Prejudice is uncool – Tim's story

I interviewed Tim when he was twelve and again when he was eighteen, in 1997. His mother got pregnant by self-insemination using an anonymous donor and has been single all of Tim's life.

Sitting in the cosy living room of the terraced house he shares with his mother, Sheila, eighteen-year-old Tim struggles to remember when he first learned about self-insemination and how he was created.

"I never didn't know," he says, perplexed by the question. "Sheila always told me everything from a very young age. It was never a secret. Anyway she was proud of it. I eventually met other children who had dads as well as mums, but Sheila had already taught me that there are many kinds of families."

Living in Hackney for the first six years of his life, Tim and Sheila were surrounded by alternative families. They were part of a tight-knit group of lesbian mothers and their children, all born about the same time. For Tim, it was normal for children to have one or two lesbian mothers – and you couldn't easily find families in Hackney with married parents living together with the children they had made. To Tim, diversity in family life was the norm.

Even when they moved to a small seaside town without many other lesbian mothers, Tim didn't find anything extraordinary about his family. They bought a house in the old part of town, by chance right next door to John and José, an older gay couple. Tim remembers them fondly: "They were really cool. I talked to them about loads of things. I needed to find things out about growing up, becoming a man. They'd been through all that."

In the country

A career move for Sheila brought them to a rural village where Tim encountered his first negative reaction. "People in that area were narrow-minded. It was more about Sheila being a single parent than being lesbian. They were all typical families with 2.4 children and a dog. They were shocked when I came to parents' evening with just my mum. I was teased a bit. At that age, I felt insecure, not so much about my family but just about myself. It was difficult but, at the end of the day, it made me who I am. It helped me to build up a thick skin. You know," he adds with amazement, "literally within a month, they'd lost interest. I don't think there's anyone who can say they've never been teased about something, the way you dress, your hair, where you live, whatever. If they didn't tease you about having a lesbian mother, they'd find something else. Young people are very cruel to each other."

Tim wasn't very impressed with the attitude towards lesbians and gay men at his new primary school. "Kids were constantly making terrible jokes about gays and lesbians. This is one: 'there were two men in a bed feeling happy, so happy got out.' It is disgusting. I just don't find them funny. Kids think that gays and lesbians are people to make fun of, that they aren't as normal as their parents. When I was in the fourth year junior, I went to the head teacher about those horrible jokes. I wanted him to come down hard on people who do this. But he is the kind of person who is very understanding and you really feel that you are being listened to and then he does sod all about it.

One day one of my best mates worked out that I wasn't finding the jokes funny. He asked me, 'What's the matter? Don't you find them funny?' That's when I told him that my mum is lesbian. He went all embarrassed and said, 'Sorry about those jokes, Tim.' I could see that he didn't really want to hurt me. I had thought I was probably going to have a bad time of it, but actually it was a good reaction and I felt glad I had told him."

Television appearance

In 1991, the tabloid media generated a big scandal about donor insemination by single women which they called the "virgin birth technique". Tim and Sheila heard various people on the radio saying how selfish a woman must be to get pregnant by donor insemination when she's single. Tim was outraged: "It just makes me think how stupid those people must be. They were telling everyone to ring in if you had any comments on it and I rang in. I wasn't actually on the air – you have to leave a message on their answering machine. I said, 'I'm the son of a lesbian mum. She's single and she used the so-called virgin birth technique and I feel fine about it. I don't see anything wrong with it at all. It's certainly not selfish. In fact, I think I've got a better life than many kids.'"

A friend of Sheila's suggested that Tim ring up the local BBC TV station. Still outraged, Tim phoned up and said he would like to appear on TV. "I told the station that my experience is relevant and that I'm upset and disgusted by what people are saying. The woman I spoke to said, 'Can I speak to your mum? When would you be ready?' At this time, it was about 7pm. They arranged to come over to our house at 9pm.

"First of all they filmed us looking at my photo album of when I was a baby. There were all these pictures of Sheila holding me. They asked me questions like, 'Do you think your mum's being selfish? Do you think you would rather have a dad? Would you like to meet your dad?' There were lots of questions like that. It was really exciting.

"There was a horrible priest on the show who kept saying, 'He's only an eleven-year-old boy. When he's twenty-two, I'm sure he'll have different views.' That made me angry. I felt like ringing him up and telling him that he doesn't know what he's talking about. Just because I was eleven, it didn't mean I couldn't have my own views." At eighteen, Tim's views on this issue have not changed and he can't see why they will.

Appearing on TV had a positive outcome. "I told everyone that I was going on TV, but I didn't tell them what it was about. Not many people watched it because I don't think anyone believed me. Some of the teachers did watch it and they acted quite differently towards me afterwards. I no longer heard them say, 'Give this to your mum and dad.' They started saying, 'Give this to your parents.' I don't think I've heard any of the anti-gay jokes since. I've definitely raised the consciousness of my classmates.

"To be honest, I feel sorry for people who are prejudiced against lesbians. People are definitely afraid of things they don't understand. I can see how at first they might find it weird for lesbians to have children. But I can't see how they can go from that to saying that lesbians *shouldn't* have children. I don't think anyone should be judging people like that."

Just the two of us

Another move brought Sheila and Tim into the city, this time to share a home with Sheila's girlfriend and her children. The long-distance relationship that had worked so well fell apart when the two families merged into one household. "It was wonderful for about five years before we moved in together, but the stress of joining up with another family was too much." A year later, Sheila and Tim were back to their familiar twosome. Tim sighs. "I've never lived in such a nice house. I miss that house."

He has a flair for design. His room is a mess, typical of many teenage boys' rooms, but there's a parachute hanging from the ceiling and psychedelic patterns painted on the walls. "I'm into the way things look. Without all the clothes on the floor, it's quite nice. I like nice surroundings." Music is his real passion and he's recovering from a party he organised the night before. About three hundred people came and danced to speed garage music until 5am. Rubbing his eyes sleepily, Tim says, "I like the idea of being part of a small community of people who are interested in underground, garage and all these new non-commercial kinds of music. I like making music for the love of music, not just for the money."

It's hard to imagine what Tim has missed, growing up with a lesbian mother and no father. "I've never felt a need to have anything more. The only trouble there's been has been other people's problems with it and that's rare. Nobody really cares about it, that's my experience. I'm happy with my life. I wouldn't change any of it." He nods his head toward the kitchen where Sheila is tidying up and cooking dinner. Laughing, he admits, "I've had it cushy really. I know lots of people who are unhappy about the way they've been brought up, who hate their parents. I haven't felt that at all."

Single mothers don't get a very good press these days but that doesn't mean he wishes he'd had two parents. "It's always been just me and Sheila. We have a really good relationship, probably because there isn't another parent around. When we have a mad raging row, neither of us can go up to anyone else and complain about the other one. As soon as we've shouted and screamed at each other, we hug and say we're sorry. Sheila's never had an authoritarian approach. About some things, she says, 'I'm your mother, I make the decisions'. But her approach is to talk it over. I've been taught how to argue by her. She respects my opinion. We get into arguments about me tidying my room, staying out too late and doing my homework. But we've got the bonus that we communicate well. I don't feel restricted in what I talk to her about."

When he was asked at the age of twelve what he liked about his mother, Tim said, "She is really good in emergencies. She makes me have very healthy food. She doesn't let me have any of that Mr Whippy ice cream. I don't mind having healthy food occasionally, but not all the time. She will make me do jobs like washing up and doing the bins. I do appreciate that, though sometimes I'd rather she didn't. She's into fairness. A lot of boys don't cuddle their mums a lot. They wouldn't go in for a morning cuddle in their bed or wouldn't want their mum to come in to their room and give them a cuddle before they go to bed. I do. We're very close and I love my mum a lot."

What's missing?

Many people, including some lesbians, feel that a boy needs a father in order to learn how to be a man. This isn't Tim's point of view. "I can't recall any times when I wished I had a dad. I never thought, if only I had a dad, I could play football with him in the park. Whenever I wanted to play football in the park, I did it with my friends. Playing football is just boring to me but I do like watching it. I've never been to a football match and I'm quite disappointed about that. I'd quite like to see Arsenal play, but I can see it on telly. I suppose it would have been easier if there'd been a man for when I started shaving. I was cutting myself here there and everywhere, but I learned how to do it within a week."

When he was twelve, Tim noticed that a lot of his friends were rougher than him. At the time, he observed, "Their fathers teach them to fight, which makes me very glad I haven't got a dad because I don't get into fights. If a kid is brought up to be tough, he'll go and smash someone's head in if he gets called a name. I'm definitely glad I don't have a dad to teach me that attitude. My mum does not agree with hitting anyone. If she sees anyone else hitting someone, she'll tell them off, which I think is good. However, I'm not the kind of person who can be picked on easily. I do defend myself and I am quite protective of my friends. I don't feel I'm a right softy. I'm just like any other kid. I don't let people bully me."

At age twelve, Tim was not concerned about the identity of his birth father. He didn't feel any different at age eighteen. "I might like to track down my dad and meet him, but I don't really have a strong desire to find him. I'm slightly curious. It would be kind of interesting to find out who this person is. I would like to know his name. Sheila doesn't know much about him at all."

No pressure

Tim dismisses any suggestion that lesbian mothers pressure their children to be gay. "Absolutely not. I'm definitely straight. Sheila accepts that totally." He's shocked that anyone could be so naïve. Then he remembers an incident at school where someone half jokingly, half seriously asked if he was gay, since his mum was lesbian. "From my reactions and those of my best mate, the person felt kind of stupid after they said it."

How does Tim's girlfriend feel about Sheila? "I'd been going out with my girlfriend only a couple of weeks when she first saw the lesbian mother badges my mum had put all over our kitchen wall. I saw her do a double take. So I gave her a hug and said, 'Well, what's your reaction then? Does that bother you?' She was offended that I thought she would even be concerned about it."

Tim acknowledges the benefits he's had growing up knowing other children in similar circumstances. "I think it is quite important to know other children of lesbians. I needed to chat with somebody else about it and to know that I wasn't the only person in the world like this. Sheila started up a lesbian mothers and children network when we moved to the city and I felt more relaxed with those people because they understand. At school there was always a little bit of a burden to carry in case anyone should mention something about my dad.

"I've chosen friends who are open-minded. That's because of who I am. I like to think of myself as not having many prejudices." Does he think his open-mindedness is down to having a lesbian mother? This is a new idea and he thinks about it carefully. "Yeah," he says slowly, "It's bound to, actually. I've never thought about lesbians and gays as being outside of society, as though they're totally different. I've always looked on it as some people are straight, some gay, some aren't anything. Sexuality is just one aspect of life. So, yes, I look on other aspects of life differently too. But I don't know what I would have been like if I'd been brought up by a straight mother. Most of my friends have had so-called normal upbringings. But they're also open-minded. I think it's more the 90s than anything else. The young community is increasingly more accepting of homosexuality and of any kind of differences. It's no longer cool to be prejudiced. That's not just my personal friends, but everyone at my school is like that. Maybe it's the school or maybe it's living in the city. I don't know what it's like in the countryside."

What would he say to people who are worried about children born to lesbians today? "Having a lesbian mother in the 90s is not going to make a blind bit of difference to those children," he says strongly. "My own experience should be reassuring. You hear all the time about straight women getting pregnant by accident. But lesbians doing self-insemination have to spend months and months, thinking whether they really want the baby, and how they're going to cope. It's that much more effort. You can't just fall into it without thinking about it. I would say they're twice as responsible as straight parents. I don't see how anyone can say that's selfish. Being a good parent has nothing to do with the mother's sexuality."

Living with Dad – Rachel's story

In 1995, when I interviewed her, Rachel was nineteen and living in Brighton with her two-week-old daughter. Rachel has an older brother Max, now twenty. Her mother, Linda Bellos, came out as lesbian and left their father when the children were three and five. After a long court case, their father was awarded custody in 1983. Linda has been active in community politics in London; she was leader of Lambeth council in the 1980s, and publicly visible as a black lesbian mother.

My mum's always been lesbian. She came out when I was two or three and I've accepted it as totally normal. Her sexuality was just one other fact about her. It wouldn't have occurred to me to explain why my mum had a girlfriend any more than it would to explain why my dad had one. I wouldn't have thought that needed explaining. I can't imagine what it would be like for either my dad or my mum to have anything but women partners. It's always been that way in my life.

My parents got married when they were nineteen. They were living in London, but decided to move to Brighton so their kids would have fresh air, the sea, culture and a sense of community. My parents were staying with my uncle when my brother, Max, was born. But once I came along, they bought a house and we moved into it. I've lived in that house all my life until just a few months ago.

Problems

When I was three, my parents split up. Mum moved out and lived down the road with her first girlfriend. Six months later, Dad's new girlfriend, Liz, and her daughter moved into our house. Mum stayed on in Brighton while she completed a politics degree at university. When I was four, Mum moved up to London. Until I was six, I didn't see her much at all because of Liz.

My dad's partner, Liz, was an evil twisted woman and used to hurt us. She didn't lose her temper. She contrived reasons for doing it. She treated her own child like a princess. I don't understand how anybody can inflict pain on another person, let alone on a child. She must have been mentally disturbed. Liz had a great amount of power. She was a clever woman who knew how to manipulate to get what she wanted. Liz sent Max away to a boarding school for mentally handicapped children, claiming he had learning difficulties, which wasn't true. He was only hyperactive. My dad took him out of it.

Liz used to make it impossible for my mum to see both me and Max at the same time. If Mum had arranged to see us, Liz would take one of us away from school so that Mum couldn't take both of us. Liz also stopped us from seeing our grandparents. Before Liz moved in, it had been a regular occurrence to go to my grandmother's house, but Liz claimed they were interfering with the way she was bringing us up. My mum and grandmother knew what was happening, but couldn't do anything. Their hands were tied.

Dad was pretty messed up by the divorce and didn't know that Liz was abusing us. He felt inadequate as a male because my mum was gay. He has nothing against gay people, but it made him question whether he was such an awful sexual partner that she had to turn to women. All the things that he could think, he thought. So when he found a new woman partner, he felt like a man again. He was blinkered and didn't look at what was happening to his children. He believed at the time that women know what they're doing with children and left her to it.

I didn't talk to my dad about it. I didn't see much of him during those three years. He was working full-time and as we were so young, it was bedtime at five. Anyway, it's very difficult to tell your parents about bad things that have happened to you, especially if you love them a lot and you know they love you. I would rather be hurt than see him hurt as well.

My dad found out what was happening three years later. He was devastated at what he saw and finished with Liz. Then our life became a lot nicer. Now when I think about what happened to me and Max, I'm appalled. But when you're a child, you take everything as it comes, and you don't realise how horrific it is.

My brother has never talked about what happened. He's very shut up. He's got deep sad eyes, which show a lot of pain. Max was worse affected than me by the whole thing, because he doesn't talk about it. I've always talked with friends, since talking about it makes it easier to live with. Keeping it to yourself never helps.

My parents had a custody battle from the time I was three until I was about seven. They went to court and my dad got care, custody and control. Max and I weren't aware of what was going on at the time. Our parents sheltered us and were careful not to involve us. We just went to school and saw our mum whenever she came by.

Custody

I've always wondered why my mum didn't get custody. It would have been sensible for us to be with her. She applied for custody immediately after she moved out, but the fact that she left and didn't take us with her counted against her. More significantly, she was out as a lesbian and never hid the fact that she was gay. I guess the judge didn't think lesbians should be mothers. What I find horrific is that the judge must have known about the abuse that was going on. Throughout the custody battle, my dad was living with Liz. The Social Services knew about our situation and we were on the at-risk register at that time and until we were thirteen and fourteen. The court would have seen reports from Social Services about us. The judge must have thought that we were better off with someone who was abusing us than with someone who was gay.

I don't know how the judge could ever question my parents' love for us. Both of them created us and both of them love us. You don't have to be of a certain sexuality in order to love your children and to bring them up properly. It's very frustrating how much the system failed us.

My mum was blocked from being a full-time mother to us and I feel for her. Because she came out and said, 'I'm gay', she lost her children and had to stand by and watch the abuse that was going on, powerless to do anything about it. Now that I'm a mum myself, I know that would have devastated me.

I don't regret that my dad got custody. He's always loved us so much. I don't resent my father for anything that happened. I understand. When I was younger I used to resent my mum more, because she wasn't there and I didn't understand why she wasn't there.

Dad has had other partners since Liz, but no more live-in relationships. I was much happier when Dad's partners didn't live with us. I think he realised that partners could take over and that he was ultimately responsible for us. He was working full-time, and ended up working nights as a taxi driver, so whatever partner he'd have would have been responsible for us when he wasn't there. Very soon after Liz left, he had a relationship with a woman until I was about ten. I couldn't stand her, but she wasn't evil, just fanatical. I don't think I've liked many of my dad's partners. Eventually he had a relationship with someone I did like. He's single now. He decided to give up on relationships, saying they're too much hassle.

From the age of six, I saw a lot of Mum. We saw her every other week or every weekend. She often came down for Sunday visits with her girlfriends. It was something to look forward to. Mum has always been fun and exciting. At first, when Liz was there, we only saw her for the day. Later it was the weekends. After Liz left, we'd spend the weekends and the holidays with her.

Even though I used to enjoy going to see my mother, we were closed off from each other. Because of everything that had happened in my past, especially what Liz had done, we found it difficult to talk to each other. We were holding something back. When I got to the age of fifteen, it came to a head. At that point, I felt I didn't have a mum in the way that I needed. I needed her to understand me and to talk to. I wrote to Mum, explaining how I felt. It turned out that she felt the same way. It helped us to make our relationship a lot better and now it's very good. I'm so pleased that we could do that. I kept thinking, 'Oh my God, I've got my mum back.' It was a real identity crisis for me trying to communicate with her. Thank God we sorted things out.

Close bond

Now I have a close bond with my mother. We just naturally know things about each other, we know if something's wrong, we know what the other is thinking. When I fell pregnant, I phoned my mum on a Friday and said that I needed to come and see her on Sunday. She asked whether it was urgent. I said it was quite important and she said, 'You're pregnant.' She knew immediately. It's a mother–daughter connection that happens because we're both females and because she carried me for nine months in her body.

My sexuality isn't influenced by my mum's at all. My mum encouraged us to have relationships but she didn't mind whether it was with boys or girls. I had my first boyfriend when I was about thirteen. I went to France at Christmas time, where my mum had a house with her partner, Lily. My boyfriend had bought me a gold necklace with a locket. We were playing bridge and my aunt asked who bought me the necklace. I replied, 'Oh, just a friend.' Lily started teasing me, saying 'Oh, what's her name, then?' It was good fun.

My parents are liberals. They've been easy about me having sexual relationships with my boyfriends. As a result, here I am with a baby at the age of nineteen! I belatedly realised that there is nothing bad about being a virgin. Sex is very nice, but you don't have to jump into it so young. I felt pressure from my boyfriends and from my friends to be sexually active. I wish that my parents had been stricter. My parents and a lot of my friends' parents were around in the 1960s and 1970s when the message changed from 'sex before marriage is wrong' to 'sex with everyone is cool'. But in fact they all have stable monogamous relationships now.

There have always been gay people in my life. My mum used to bring me and my brother to gay events. In the early 1980s, there were gay liberation marches because gay people were just starting to come out. I used to go on gay marches with Mum as often as I went on anti-racist marches with her. I went on a lot of demonstrations and I loved it. She also took me to all-women parties in Brixton at clubs and at women's centres. It was great fun.

Telling other people

I've never had any stick at school about my mum being lesbian. When people say to me, 'Is your mum gay?', I say, 'Yeah.' That's it. I'm not ashamed about it and if they want to make a big thing out of it, they can. I'm not interested in their opinions about it. It helps other people change their attitudes about gay people when they look at me and think, 'It's not such a weird thing, is it? Her mum is a lesbian and had children. She's a human being.'

Having a famous mum has meant that I've also had some media attention. I appeared on the TV show, *Richard Littlejohn – Live and Uncut*, with my mum and Max last summer [8 July 1994]. Max and I sat in the audience while Mum was on the stage speaking about lesbian mothers. Littlejohn asked me if I'd been taunted at school because of having a lesbian mother. I said that all my friends have been very open and that I didn't come across any taunting or stigma. I explained that having a heterosexual father and a homosexual mother has helped me grow up with no barriers against either sexuality. To me, all of it is natural. He was criticising lesbians who have children by artificial insemination and claiming that those children need a mother and a father. I said that as long as you've got love from your parents and security, I don't see what the problem can be. Children don't need a dad and a mum. Children need love. And that's what I've had.

Avoiding labels – Rikki's story

Rikki Beadle Blair is a black gay man who grew up in south London with his lesbian mother and his younger brother and sister. He was 34 at the time of this interview in 1995. Rikki later went on to produce and perform in a comedy drama about gay parenting called Metrosexuality *that appeared on Channel 4 in 2001.*

I don't have a clear memory of my mother's sexuality throughout my childhood. At no point did my mother march in and say, 'OK, I'm gay now. You've got a lesbian mother.' We don't explain things openly like this in my family. It eventually dawned on us that she was lesbian. I imagine I was the first to know, as I'm the oldest. Also being gay, I was probably more aware than my brother and sister.

My mother got pregnant with me when she was sixteen. I presume that she was leading a heterosexual life, at least until she had my brother at the age of 24. We weren't brought up by a mother and father and then the father went away. We each have different fathers: you could say my mother got sperm donors in her own way. None of us has met our fathers. We didn't stand out by being a one-parent family, as that was common in my area.

My mother always had lots of women friends. She was very sociable, and many women would stay over after parties. But there were some who were clearly more than friends. I could hear them making love when I got up early or woke at night. Gradually I realised that so-and-so was staying often, and then it became apparent that there was a relationship. My mother started to have long-term, live-in relationships with women when I was in my early teens. I was quite grown up. I knew what lesbianism was and I knew that's what she was. It wasn't traumatic for me at all.

My mother never announced that she was lesbian when we were growing up. I don't think she saw it as being in the closet. She's one of those people who says, 'I don't hide anything. But I don't scream it from the rooftops.' She never felt she had to explain herself to other people and as she was the boss of my family, she never explained herself to us. And we never challenged her.

I kept wondering how we could go on not mentioning it. But it remained unspoken for years. Now we can talk about it and she does say she's a lesbian. She's very active within the lesbian community. But it's still surprising to me to hear her use the word lesbian about herself after all those years. It doesn't feel wrong, just unusual.

My mother had to have all her defences up, since she didn't get much support. There must have been gossip about her. She was a young black woman bringing up three children on her own in the 1960s and 70s on a white estate. She came and went when she pleased. When she was younger, she used to love to dress up and go out and dance. They'd tut as they went off to the pub greasy haired and dowdy, while she was whooping it up with her big wigs on. They didn't like it because she didn't behave like a Greek widow and she wasn't answerable to any man.

Nobody would think my mother was a lesbian, especially a woman with three children. Lesbians were invisible in the 1960s and 70s. It was OK for women to be friends, and she and her women friends were seen as tarty women who should have been at home looking after their men.

A mother with passion

I have great respect for anybody who can bring up three children on their own and not completely cave in under the stress of it. My mother is smart and that's worth its weight in gold. She knows how to get on in the world, how to assess a situation quickly and what action to take. She's always been right about people, about judging what their intentions are and about telling you what traps to avoid in life. She taught us to be smart. Of course, when you're a teenager, you think your mother doesn't know anything and we ignored her, but she was always right.

My mother is very demonstrative of her feelings. If she's angry, she throws things, and if she's loving, she hugs and kisses you all over. In fact, she can't really control her feelings. That's either great or not so great depending on what feelings she's having. In many ways, she was very open. She wasn't afraid for us to see her naked, for instance. But we never sat round and discussed things. As children we didn't question her about anything. It wasn't fear of what she might say. It's that we grew up in an atmosphere where we didn't talk about feelings. As a result, I don't know anything about her life before she had me or outside of her life with me. I don't know why she had children, or whether she was lesbian at the time.

She's very different now. She works as a counsellor for young people and I'm sure she's very good with other people, but she wasn't a counsellor for us when we were growing up.

When we were children, my mother wasn't involved in feminist things, though she certainly was liberated. Now she is gung-ho into it. I used to be the politically correct one in my family, but she's way beyond me now. Luckily she's not a separatist, though she skirts with radical feminist politics. When my brother teases her about being right-on, it's an acknowledgement of who she is. As she gets older, she becomes more willing to reveal who she is to us. I suppose the reason she didn't talk about things when she was younger is because she didn't know who she was then.

My mother wasn't perfect. She's a much better mother to her girlfriend's son than she was to us, because she wasn't happy when we were young. Her saving grace, and it's a considerable grace, was that she wasn't pretending to be somebody she wasn't and that she passed on passion to us. We never felt that she was cold toward us. As long as there's passion, the family bonds are strong. There's no chance that somebody could be disowned. We may deafen each other screaming, but we won't shoot each other. From the outside, it appears that we're a cold family because we don't talk about feelings, but it's quite the opposite. We do communicate and we know each other well. We know every emotion. As a result, our family is strong.

I want my mother to be proud of me and I think she is. When I was very small, she made it obvious that she was proud of my intellectual achievements. But otherwise she didn't act like she was proud of me or say it directly to me. I'm an entertainer – I write films. I've just written the movie of Stonewall for the BBC. I write my own shows and I act and sing. I've been doing a musical for the BBC, which I wrote and choreographed. We did a performance of it on stage, which my mother came to. People were saying to her, 'You must be so proud of your son.' She said, 'Oh yes, I am.' I was shocked to hear it because she seldom says it to me. I'd like her to be more gushy, to say how wonderful and beautiful I am all the time. But in my family, everyone does their own business and we don't ask anybody else's approval.

Mother's partners

Until my mother had a long-term, stable relationship, I was the second parent in my family, being the oldest and a take-charge type of person. Together with my mother, I helped bring up my brother and sister. When I was seventeen, my mother started living with a woman who was the same age as me. I felt relieved, because my mother was very unhappy unless she was in a proper relationship. Also, I wanted to get out and do things. I didn't want to be at home with responsibility for my brother and sister.

She [my mother's girlfriend] took on the role of mother with my brother and sister and brought them up. They grew up with a sense of having two mothers. They didn't call her mummy, but definitely looked on her as their mother. She was more domestic than my mother, which they really liked.

The relationship lasted a good twelve years. When they broke up, my brother and sister were in their twenties. My mother was worried about telling them it was over, in case they took it badly, which they did. They are very family orientated and wanted the family to stay together. It was like any divorce situation where children don't want their parents to break up and move on. They wanted to continue to have a relationship with her but she drifted off and led her own life. It upsets them to think about it even now, because she was a mother to them.

She didn't bring me up, because she was the same age as me. I saw her as a member of my family, but more like a sister than a mother. I moved out at the age of seventeen, so I never lived with them for any length of time. I was less sentimental than my brother and sister, though it still was very sad. We all loved her very much.

Before she met this woman, my mother had a sadness that we didn't understand and that she couldn't discuss. When real love came into her life, the sadness disappeared, the sun shone for her. She was complete and happy. My whole family was happier because our mother was happier. Each successive long-term relationship was a good thing, and the one with Sue was fantastic. It goes to prove that a happy parent is the best parent. And that's partly why my brother and sister were so unhappy when the relationship broke up.

Being gay

I don't have a particular moment in my life when I realised I was gay. But I understood I was gay before I recognised that my mother was and possibly before she even realised she was. I was very young, maybe six or seven. At that age, girls and boys of my own age seemed equally attractive to me.

As you get older, other children tell you you're gay, by the way you talk or the way you behave. They tease you, insult you or just make observations about your behaviour. I got a bit of teasing when I was very young and as I grew older, I got tons of it. But I was never pushed outside of my group of friends. All my friends were tough street kids, the kind who run around causing trouble. But all of them accepted me because I was very creative, had lots of ideas and I led a lot of activities. So my friends excused me for not being as masculine as you're supposed to be. I had a vigorous personality and that got me by. Certainly there were other kids in the neighbourhood who gave me lots of trouble for being gay. Starting when I was ten or eleven, I was bullied often.

When you're young, you instinctively don't like the idea of being labelled. I still don't like labels. They're very limiting. I hated the idea of being what people said I was. If someone said to me, 'You're queer,' most of the time I would say, 'Oh, so what if I am.' But actually inside I'd be thinking, 'I don't want to prove them right. How boring to be just what they say I am.' To this day I hate having to live up to a stereotype. Or even having to think about it. Why should I have to think about other people's image of me?

We all use these labels – I'm as bad as everyone else. But it's a scary thing to take on the label, especially at seventeen when you know that the world hates gay people. Even when somebody very sympathetic says to you, 'Are you gay? It's not a problem for me,' I couldn't bring myself to say yes. It seemed too big a thing to say about yourself, even to yourself. I wasn't one of those people who looked in the mirror and said, 'You are gay!'

Coming out to Mother

People often say to me that it must be so cool to have a gay mother, that she would be much more understanding. But in the end your mother is your mother, and you don't want her to know too much about you. You spend your whole childhood with her watching you, and you want to do things that she can't see. You just don't want to talk to your mother about sex when you're sixteen.

She didn't disapprove of me being gay. But telling her wasn't particularly easy. I was seventeen and she brought it up just as I was leaving home. She said to me, and not in a very nice way, 'You're gay, aren't you?' I knew that she wasn't going to throw me out of the house, murder me or drag me off to be exorcised. She'd have been mad to do that, as she was gay herself. But it still felt awkward, because she was uncomfortable talking to me about personal things.

Now she'd be terrific about it. It's nice having a mother you can share things with. She always says to me, 'Are you coming to Gay Pride this year? I'll meet you by this tent. We'll do this. We'll do that.'

Being different

As a gay person, you learn that there's only one thing wrong with being gay, and that's that some straight people don't like it. The only possible drawback to having a lesbian mother is other people's behaviour towards us but in our case, it never was a problem. It sounds like a cliché, but it's more important to be loved by your parents than who or what they are. And to be taught common sense by your parents is more important than to be taught to behave in an acceptable way.

There are only disadvantages if you care what other people think. Children are affected by what people say, it can't be denied, but it's impossible to go through your childhood and not have anybody say anything bad about you or your parents. Kids will always find something. My family was completely different from the others families we knew in many ways. There was only one black family where we lived, which made us very different. Although we had no money and were working class, I was well spoken and literate because my mother had taught me to read early. That made me stand out from the other kids. As I grew older, I came to realise that I had an unconventional family, but we didn't worry about what other people said about us.

That my mother was a lesbian didn't make us different in the eyes of other people. It wasn't something that we displayed to other families. My brother had more to lose by introducing his friends to his mother, as he's not gay, but he used to bring all his friends home. If any of my friends asked me if my mother was a lesbian, I would say yes. I never lost any friends because of it, though I don't know what they said amongst themselves. I had a boyfriend when I was fourteen and fifteen who used to stay over. My mother didn't know that he was my boyfriend. He knew that she was gay, because we could hear them making love in her room. But he seemed fine about it.

Her being lesbian didn't affect me and it affected me even less as a teenager. I did want a more conventional mother, I have to be honest. I wanted a mother who would pick me up from school and make sandwiches and be domestic. My mother wasn't domestic. But I didn't particularly want my mother to look like other mothers. I liked my mother standing out, especially with her big wigs, which I always liked.

In the black community

My mother had lots of black friends, but I didn't. We didn't live in a black community. There was one other black family where we lived in Bermondsey and we immediately made friends with them. But otherwise all my friends were white, and we didn't have to deal with the black community accepting my mother's or my sexuality. Now I live in an area with lots of black people. It's always been the case that if you're gay and black, other black people who aren't gay react very badly to you. In fact, it's increasingly the case. I get more abuse now from black people than I did ten years ago.

It's because gay people are hiding themselves less, so of course if you're out, you are more of a target. Basically black people are not on top in this society. So the way you get a sense of being on top is by pushing someone else down. You can't fight white society, so you choose other targets and gay people are easy to assert your aggression against. Working-class people tend to be more vociferously homophobic because they're on the bottom rung of society and black people are even lower. Minorities always turn against one another. Obviously it's a foolish waste of energy and time for black people to turn against other black people who are gay or against white people who are gay. For people to turn against anybody because of who they are is mind-bogglingly pointless. But people do it. This is the world we live in.

We live in a society where you have to watch yourself all the time. My family has had trouble from white people putting fireworks through the letterbox because we lived in a National Front area. As a black person, you expect to be treated badly. You learn that very early. And as a gay person you learn that as well. Luckily my mother and I haven't had any abuse because of being gay.

Mother's influence

One thing people often say is that if you've got gay parents, you will be gay yourself. I suppose that can be said of me, but it's not true of my brother and sister. I don't really think it affected us at all. Not everything we do is due to her influence. You do rebel against your parents and when parents hide things from their children, you want to do them even more. There are many things I want to do now which are things my mother didn't want me to do.

In some ways, you become your parents, but I wouldn't say that I model my romantic relationships on my mother's relationships. With my friends, I recreate the relationships within my family, not my mother's relationships particularly. But I don't do that with my romantic interests at all. My mother's relationships used to be very volatile with lots of screaming and arguing, and I don't do that.

Family announcements

After the relationship broke up, my mother became involved with K, who got pregnant by artificial insemination. When the baby was three years old, my mother suddenly announced it over Christmas dinner. She said, 'Well, I'm definitely with K and we've had a baby. We had him by artificial insemination. I consider him to be your brother.' It was a new way for her to do things, quite a middle-class way really. My brother and sister looked as if they couldn't understand what on earth she was thinking of. And then they exploded. They were so angry with her and were determined not to accept this child or this other relationship. They felt that our mother had gone off and had another family and excluded them. It was a big mess. My sister muttered, 'That little boy's not my brother.' And I said, 'Well, let's keep an open mind. And let's be civilised.' I was told that we're not the Waltons and that being civilised has no place in our family. It's not as traumatic as it sounds, because screaming and shouting is bread and water in my family. There's never a whisper when someone can shout. There's never a tip-toe when someone can stomp.

In my family, everyone accepts everything eventually. Now of course my brother and sister love the new family. They see that our mother is happy and that their little boy is lovely. He's a year older than my brother's little boy. My mother, her partner and the two little boys go away together at least twice a year and they're good friends. My mother is the other strong parental figure in his life. They don't live together, though they certainly see themselves as a family. He definitely knows who his mother is, as opposed to having two mothers. It will be better for him, because he's being brought up to be talked to. He'll expect everything to be explained to him. He'll find it very odd if they just do things without explaining them to him, because he's come to expect that; that's the currency he's going to be dealing with.

Others like us

What was missing for my mother and for us was a sense that there was a community of people like us. It would have helped us to feel normal. One of my mother's girlfriends had children and they lived with us for about two years. So we knew that there were other lesbians with children. But still we could never turn on the TV and see somebody with parents like ours. It is easier for kids like Ian growing up now. There is a range of visible gay people and gay families. I want to make some films which show families where there are gay parents. When you're asking for equal acknowledgement, it's not just for gay people themselves but for all the people around them, their families, children, parents and friends. If you don't acknowledge gay people, you're denying a lot of other people as well.

Three mothers – Alice's story

Alice was fifteen when she gave this interview in 1995. At the time, she was attending an inner-city secondary school in London. She has three lesbian mothers – Jane, Ruth and Francesca – none of whom is her birth mother. Jane and Ruth are a lesbian couple she lives with in one house. In the other half of the week she stays with Francesca, whose girlfriend does not live with her.

My biological mother, Sarah, got pregnant by accident when she was on holiday in Australia. When she came home, she realised that she didn't want to be heterosexual anymore. She lived in a communal household in Bristol and all the women living there agreed to help with my birth and to bring me up in the household. Over the years the numbers of women in the household dwindled away and we moved into our own house.

Eventually I ended up living with my aunt Jane, who is Sarah's sister, with Jane's girlfriend Ruth and with Francesca, who was a friend of Sarah's. When Jane, Ruth and Francesca moved to London, I moved with them. Sarah stayed in Bristol. At first I saw Sarah on weekends. But the situation became more difficult and she came up to see me less and less often.

One day when I was four [this was in 1984], Sarah came and took me away. She said, 'You're coming to live with me in Bristol. And you're not going to see Jane and Francesca and Ruth again.' I wasn't very happy. Three weeks later, strange people wearing wigs burst into the flat and carried me out. At first I was scared because I didn't know who they were. They'd followed us to the flat in a blue van, burst in and snatched me back to London. The only person who didn't have a wig on was Ruth, because she was driving. I said to her, 'Ruth, who are all these funny people?' She said, 'My dance group.' They started taking their wigs off and then I recognised them. I don't think they thought they could get me back any other way.

Legal battle

We had to go to court, because it became a legal battle for custody. Jane and Sarah had a really big row about it. Sarah got cross with the rest of the family who took Jane's side because they thought Sarah was unable to look after me properly at that time. I don't know the full story. In the end the court decided that I should stay living in London with Jane and Ruth. The fact that they were a lesbian couple was only brought up at the last minute. At one point they thought that I might be taken into care because the court was freaked about me living with a lesbian couple. I was five at the time. It went on for about a year. Jane got legal custody of me and has had ever since.

I'm a ward of the court, which means I have to write to the court for permission every time I leave the country, and they have to know everything I do. It makes my life really complicated. We're going back to court to try and get the wardship abolished, which would give me more freedom. What I want is for Jane, Ruth and Francesca to get a joint residence order. It would be a precedent-setting case, because not only is it women sharing the wardship, it would be three women. What we really want is to get recognition for all three being my parents, and there is no history of anything like that. So whatever we get, a precedent will be set. That's why we feel it's so important to do it. All of us agree.

My family is great! I love it. My parents are particularly easy to talk to about nearly anything. I get on brilliantly with all of them. We hardly ever row. They each have their little irritating points and I'm sure I have mine, but on the whole, the four of us get on fantastically. I'm quite good about not playing one against the other. I have quite a lot of opportunity, but I don't take advantage.

The fact that we live in two separate houses is a plus. As soon as I get sick of one, it's time to go to the other house. That's how it's been since I was six, so I'm used to it. I don't find it at all disruptive. The only problem I have is that I'm always leaving my tapes at the other house and that annoys me. Apart from that, I have my stuff at both houses and my own room in each house. Both of the houses are equally mine.

I have complaints, but not about my parents being lesbians. The only thing that really irritates me is when they get together and talk about me, when they start going, 'Alice never does do her homework at my house. She always spend hours on the phone,' or 'Alice goes to bed really early at my house. Alice is always tidy at my house.' And then they come back to me and say, 'Francesca says that you're always going to bed early at her house.' I have to come up with good excuses. I try and keep them apart. But it's nice to have family get-togethers and catch up on things. We do that very rarely, usually when I've been with one set of them and not seen the others for a while.

They all get on really well, and trust each other, which helps. Francesca never knew whether Jane would honour Francesca's role as parent through the years, because they've got no kind of personal relationship to each other. With Jane and Ruth, it's easier because they're a couple.

School

My school's lovely. I'm trying to work out if my English teacher is a dyke. She must be, she can't be straight. My parents have decided that my tutor will be my foster mum if anything happens to them. And she's agreed. They say that her cats would be quite happy with me. It's all very jokey. There are a lot of very right-wing people at the school. It's next to an estate which is full of BNP supporters. You have to be careful who you talk to. But considering the violent area the school's in, we have very few fights. There's a girl in my class whose father is in the BNP. She lives on the estate, is in a gang, and has got an eighteen-year-old boyfriend. She's as working class as they get. She's absolutely great. I explained about lesbians to her, and she goes, 'Well you know, my dad would kick me out of the house, and kick me down the street, if he found out I was a lesbian. But you're an all right person. I don't care.' Some of the other kids are horrible.

I'm not scared of being battered. If anybody ever tried anything, they would not get away with it. The school is very good actually in dealing with things, if they know about them. They'd suspend the people involved and if it was very serious they'd think about exclusion. There hasn't actually been any gay bashing. There was a threat to beat up one boy because he got off with another boy. He was scared. He told his tutor and they dealt with it really seriously. They phoned his parents and sent him home [to protect him]. He didn't come to school for a few days. I spent a whole day with him, outside of lessons. But he has to be careful, really. He's quite camp and I feel protective of him.

Bad reactions

I'd say the down side of having lesbian parents is other people's attitudes towards lesbians. I've had some bad reactions at secondary school. I get people judging me on my parents, saying, 'Your parents are gay, so you must be as well.' And I say to them, 'So what if I am? I can do what I want.' All my friends know. My class knows. All my teachers know. My form tutor's really supportive about it. In my Religious Education class, they didn't know anything about lesbian mothers until about three months ago, when I said, 'You're speaking complete garbage because you've never met any lesbian mothers. And actually why shouldn't lesbians be mothers? I have three who are my mothers.'

I like people who just come up and say, 'So what's it like? Is it a bit odd?' One kid at school said to me, 'But your mum's a lesbian.' And I said, 'yes' and he never spoke to me again. I can't say I was too upset! There's a lot of kids at my school that use the word gay as an insult. I feel sorry for them that they're so ignorant about it. I don't get cross when people say anything homophobic. I just laugh at them.

When I see those talk shows about lesbian mothers, I sit there and laugh at them. I can't believe the people who go on them have ever met a lesbian. I feel very strongly about gay rights. It makes me furious when anybody says anything against gays. I'm trying to set a legal precedent so that other lesbian families can establish themselves legally as families. And I always go to Gay Pride every year with my parents. I had a big banner last year that said 'Gays make great parents'. I carried it the whole way. It was very heavy. I handed out leaflets for gay action.

Boyfriends and girlfriends

Jane's a bit unreasonable about boyfriends. She keeps thinking I should be careful. She's the over-protective one of the three. Jane says, 'No, you can't the spend the night with a boy. You might get pregnant. And you never know about date rape. Have you ever met him?' Pathetic. But Francesca goes, 'Oh yeah, it's fine as long as you're happy.' When I tell them about someone I fancy, all my parents are incredibly curious. They say, 'Oh no, not her!' or 'She's great.' Francesca tries to fix me up with people who are rich. She always says I should go out with so-and-so because she's got lots of money. My mums don't say, 'Yes, it's all right if you go out with a friend of the same sex.' I know I'm allowed to – they don't even care what sex my friends are. Either one is absolutely fine with them. They're perfectly happy, as long as they think the person is nice. I'm interested in boys or girls, depending on my current mood. My mothers don't like my taste in girls, actually.

I have a BIG, BIG family. I don't lose people from my family when they move out of the house. And I count close friends as family too. I have three mothers – Ruth, Jane and Francesca. And I've got all their extended families – their brothers, sisters, parents, and children. I started with three mothers, but I've got four now that I've met up with my biological mother, Sarah, again. I didn't see Sarah for nearly ten years. We're very good friends now and get on really well. I just met my dad for the first time, so I'm kind of gathering all my family back.

They're all really nice about counting me as family. Francesca's mum is the most straight and conservative out of all the immediate family I have. But she definitely counts me as her granddaughter, which I feel really happy about.

I've claimed Francesca's girlfriend as well. She's not a mother. She's like a partner. But she's definitely family. She'd hate me to think that she was another mother. She's not into all this family business. She's her own person.

'That's your dad'

I met my dad in passing about two weeks ago in Bristol. He knew that I was his daughter. He and his new partner had arranged a birthday party for my mum, and I was invited, not knowing that he was going to be there. Francesca suddenly came up to me and goes, 'Oh, that's your dad.' I was shocked. He was actually too scared to say anything to me and I was too scared to say anything to him. So I just went, 'Hello. Bye.' I wanted to see him but now that I've seen him, that's enough. I don't need to collect any more family. I'm satisfied with my three immediate families.

One advantage of living with lesbians is that, in general, women are not that violent towards each other. We're safe. A disadvantage is that I'm actually quite scared of some men. I don't feel shy, but I don't feel very safe. I'm not scared of boys or people my own age, but I'm not sure I trust grown men.

I see myself as different and it's kind of because my mothers are lesbian. My friends all have straight parents, but they think my family is fine. I don't feel uncomfortable about it. It does give you a bit of a different outlook.

Speaking out – Callum's story

I interviewed Callum when he was fifteen. He had lived in London all his life with his two mothers, Annie and Stella, and his brother Liam. Stella gave birth to Liam in 1979, and six months later, Annie gave birth to Callum, who was conceived by self-insemination using an anonymous donor. The two women separated when Callum was four and the boys lived in both households. Callum has learning difficulties and cerebral palsy – he is very interested in the rights of disabled people and other groups. This interview was carried out in 1995.

When I was born, Stella and Annie were living together. Since they split up, one part of the week Liam and I have lived with Stella and the other part of the week with Annie. They both now have relationships with other women.

Kate is Annie's partner and she has three children – the youngest is an eighteen-year-old daughter, Jess. This is how me and Jess became brother and sister. On August 15th, 1991, we were having a barbecue. Jess came up to me and asked if I wanted to be her brother. I said yes and so we adopted each other. I really think she's a good sister. Jess used to live in the house with us, but now she's at university. That's a long way away. I miss her. We don't see each other very much.

Self-insemination

Self-insemination is something that a woman can do to get pregnant without having sex. I feel fine about having been conceived in that way.

Nobody asked anything about a dad when I was at primary school. It never seemed strange to me. It's what I've always known. It is very ordinary to have two mums and I feel fine about it. I know lots of other children who have got lesbian mothers and no dads. Some are my good friends. And that also made it very easy. I find it fine not having a dad. Some of my friends asked if I had a dad, and I said, 'No.'

At school

I've been to three schools. When I was eleven, I went to a school for people with physical disabilities. I was there for three years. I was so unhappy there. Those three years were the worst time of my life, for lots of reasons. We had this woman helper who was horrible to me. She knew my mother was a lesbian. She made fun of me, saying things like, 'Ooh, you're wearing those clothes.' About lesbians, she would say, 'Actually, they are disgusting.' I just hated her. I did complain about her to the headmistress, but nothing was done. The headmistress was very nice, but she never dealt with anything. A cookery teacher was horrible to me and I hated her too. I still hate her. She forced me to put Cape apples in a fruit salad [during the boycott of South African produce]. I stand by Nelson Mandela. She said, 'Don't bring your politics in here.' She also forced me to cook meat sausages, even though I'm a vegetarian. Some teachers have said things like, 'You can't have two mums.'

There was another teacher who said, 'Everybody has a father.' I said, 'I don't have a father.' He kept saying, 'But everybody has a father.' I just kept saying, 'No, I don't have a father.' I was twelve then and was at the first special school that I went to.

When I was in the first year, I was forced to do a sponsored silence for Telethon by one of my teachers. The problem for me is that Telethon portrays disabled people in a horrible way, showing us as poor pathetic victims all the time. So I was upset about that. Lots of my friends have been involved in organising actions against Telethon, such as blocking the roads. I supported them. My teacher said, 'You've got to do the sponsored silence for Telethon.' I refused and she said, 'Oh no, you can't do this. Oh no.' I wrote 'I want rights now' in my drawing book and I got told off for it. When they gave me the sponsorship form, I tore it up and threw it in the bin. When she asked, 'Where is your sponsorship form?' I said, 'What happens if you didn't get any sponsors?' 'Is that what you're telling me?' she says. She's not disabled and has no right to say that to me. I left that school.

[Now I'm in another special school where] I'm the only person with my kind of physical and learning disabilities in my class. It's a lot better than my other special school and I have felt supported there. I'm much happier. I'm just starting to study art, science, maths, English, social studies, Craft Design and Technology. I might not take the GCSE exams, because they're quite hard.

The teachers are really nice. I haven't talked to them about having lesbian mothers, though Annie told the head teacher when we went for the interview and my teacher knows. There are some lesbians working in the school and that makes a difference. I've been bullied in this school and the staff are very supportive. The school's very good in that way. At my old school, I never ever got any support for anything at all. So I feel a thousand times better being at this school, because I know that I can go and tell someone and they'll go and talk to the bully.

Telling friends

When I was thirteen, I told my friends at school that I had two mothers. They found it very hard to believe that. One girl felt like having a go at me.

... She made a point of telling another friend of mine that Annie is a lesbian, and she made it hard for me to have a friendship with her.

At my new school, I've made the decision to tell my friends about having lesbian mothers. Most of my friends know now. Just a few don't know. The first friend I told was fine. The next person I told said that she will keep it secret and I think she has. Her parents don't know. Another close friend of mine said, 'You shouldn't tell anybody because they'll go and blab to everyone.' And then I told a friend who was fine about it because her mum works with lesbians. Several other friends have been fine about it too. One asked, 'Do you mind having them?' I said, 'No.' I'm glad I told my friends. I feel better with the friends that I've told.

Disability rights

I've been involved in lots of disability rights protests. I was on TV protesting against *Children in Need* when I was in the second year. In September 1994, Annie and I went on a march. I saw a news item on TV about a protest against inaccessible transport where people were chaining themselves to buses. It said that there was going to be another action the next day. And it said where it was going to be. So I came rushing down the stairs saying, 'Yes, yes, yes! Could we go, *please*?' Annie and I went to the meeting point at Central Hall Westminster. I brought a pair of handcuffs so I could chain myself to something, though we definitely did not want to get arrested.

We went up to the Mall, walking and singing and waving. We were shouting, 'We want disability rights now!' We started weaving in and out of traffic looking for accessible transport, but we didn't find any. Then we turned around and saw a line of policemen and white vans. They started arresting absolutely everybody. They didn't give us a warning [as they had promised to do]. They were lifting up all the wheelchairs and putting them in the vans. They said to us, 'Right, now. Get on the pavement, you two.' And Annie said, 'That's our warning. Come on. Let's do as he says.' And we got up on the pavement. And this policeman said, 'All right, officer, arrest these people.' I said, 'But you haven't even given us a warning.' I was crying. He apologised for arresting us. He said, 'I'm sorry about this, but...' as if he was apologising for breaking a cup. He charged us with 'behaviour likely to cause a breach of the peace'. They told us to get into the van, so we did. I was in tears and was very upset because I didn't think we'd get arrested.

The policewoman who was driving the van asked us, 'What are you being arrested for? Was it behaviour likely to cause a breach of the peace?' I stopped crying and said, 'No. We're being arrested for fighting for our rights.' And then I burst into tears again.

They took us to Charing Cross police station and booked us. They looked in Annie's bags and found my video camera and handcuffs. They took the handcuffs away as evidence, and then they locked us up in a cell together and locked other people in different cells. We were there for about two and a half hours. They were nice to us once we were in the police station. They did bring us sandwiches and tea. I was scared at first, but then I was bored.

The confidence to be myself – Amanda's story

I interviewed Amanda in 1995 when she was 24. Her mother and father separated when she was one and her father had little to do with her as a child. She grew up in London (as an only child) with her mother, who was open about being a lesbian.

Everything was fine in my life until I was ten. Although my mum and dad had separated when I was one, I was too young to know about that. My mum apparently told me that she was a lesbian when I was four. They were just words and I didn't understand what they meant. All my life, my mum's lesbianism has been normal to me.

I felt I was a special child. I had lots of mummies and people who loved me. I had loads of friends and loved playing and being with people. I was secure and confident, happy and bubbly, artistic and creative. Although I got on with a lot of people, I've always been very independent and even a bit of a loner.

From TV to court
When I was ten, Mum had been active in the women's movement for years and had been fighting hard for what she believed. She was one of the few

lesbian mothers who were out at that time. This was 1980, and the subject of lesbian mothers was very hush-hush.

Mum was invited to appear on a BBC programme called *Gay Life* to talk about being a lesbian mother. She asked me if I wanted to go with her and of course I did. Ask any kid if they want to go on TV and they'll say yes. My participation in the programme was to swing on a swing and be Mum's daughter. I remember her sitting on a green corduroy cushion talking to the interviewer.

The TV programme changed my life. Three days later, my father started a custody case to take me away from my mum. He'd found out she was a lesbian by watching the programme. Mum had never hidden it, but she had avoided the subject with him. My world went to pieces. It was the first time I'd seen my mum out of control, in real pain. She was so frightened.

Mum did her best to keep some stability in our lives while this was going on and to protect me so I wasn't connected to the real craziness of it all. She never made me fear my dad or try to alienate me from him. She tried to explain the danger to me because she knew it was possible that he would come and take me. Mum also warned the headmistress of my school that my dad might try something.

And he did. He arrived at my school out of the blue. It was like a dream to me: I thought he'd come just to see me; I wanted to go out with him and have an ice cream. But we were put in the library and he wasn't allowed to take me. The headmistress phoned my mother to say that my dad had just arrived and was trying to take me out of school. She phoned the police, but found that she could only keep me in the building for an hour and then she would have to let him take me. They couldn't stop him legally.

I couldn't understand why they would think my dad was doing anything wrong. I didn't realise he was trying to take me away from my mum. There was no way I would have considered going with my dad: I loved my mum, I wanted to stay with her and I would have fought to be with her. Obviously I was very afraid. I didn't understand what was happening. Eventually the police got there. I stayed at school and he went off. He gave me 50p and that was the last time I saw him until I was about twelve.

It was very frightening to see my mum so distraught. The day Dad filed suit for custody, I came home from school and found Mum hyperventilating and crying. She had a look of desperation and crushed me in her arms. She was devastated. I had never seen her like that before. Mum is so well controlled and balanced. She has always taken responsibility for herself and introduced that to me at an early age. But at that point, I felt I had to protect her. I didn't see her as weak, but as human.

My mum was so determined not to let my dad get me that she took me to America, intending to live there if she had to. But my dad dropped the court case about three weeks after we got there. He must have realised that he didn't really want me to live with him. His motivations were not very clear and it was never that likely that he would succeed. He had had no real involvement with me for the first ten years of my life and had never paid any child maintenance. That was Mum's choice too, because she wanted to be independent and didn't want his money. My father's second wife certainly didn't want me. She was hostile to me throughout my childhood.

I flew back from the States on my own and stayed with Nan, my mum's mother, for about two weeks. The stress of the court case had exhausted Mum so much that she needed a break and she stayed on in the States. My nan loves me very much but she was naïve and said some painful things to me, threatening to call me a lesbian if I mentioned Mum's lesbianism. Hearing that as a ten-year-old child from my nan was really scary. I thought she was saying there was something wrong with my mum. It alienated me from her. I went through seven years' struggle with her on that, but it doesn't matter anymore now. I'm much stronger and I'm no longer affected by Nan's opinions about Mum's sexuality. I never did stop loving her.

At school

The TV programme had a major effect on my school life. I left school on Friday evening a secure and happy child. When I went back to school on the Monday, I'd lost all my friends. I was picked on. I imagine that my friends' parents were scared by the TV programme. I don't think the kids knew what a lesbian was. In heterosexual society, it was scary to admit that there were gay people in this world and to believe that it's OK to be gay.

Some of the teachers were supportive. But some didn't know how to deal with it. My form teacher was fantastic and acted like a friend. I was very emotional with her. She helped iron it out with my class and they very slowly adapted. But it never was the same as it had been when they didn't know about Mum's lesbianism.

I grew up overnight because of the custody case and people's reaction to the TV programme. It was like a whoosh from my guts – it was that physical. I changed from feeling safe and happy to feeling scared, from nothing being wrong in my life to suddenly being alienated for something that I didn't understand. The world that had been mine until I was ten suddenly wasn't there anymore.

After the custody case, I became frightened of being rejected. I didn't want to tell my friends. My best friend at secondary school didn't know about Mum's lesbianism for three years because I was so scared I would lose my first long-term friend. I was not ashamed of Mum's lesbianism; it was purely about my fear of being rejected. I'm very alert to rejection, even as an adult. Losing everything, Mum's happiness and my happiness, had such an impact.

For about three years after the custody case, we had a rule that my mum and her lover didn't hold hands, or make any display of their relationship when we went out or were near my friends. I loved her lover at the time. We were all very close, a great family. But I needed boundaries and rules to protect me when I started secondary school. My mum supported that. I was never angry with my mum, just frightened of reactions after her sexuality came out into the open.

Dad – the wish and the reality

Since I was one and until I was ten, I'd probably only seen my dad about six times, as far as I can recall. My dad has always been the deepest, most painful issue for me.

I saw my dad when he tried to take custody of me when I was ten and then I didn't want to see him for a couple of years. When I was twelve, I went to my mum and said that I'd like to see my dad. It was a nervous day for both of us. But she didn't deny me. She got in touch with him. She was nervous about what shit he would feed me about what she was. She couldn't afford to have too many situations where people could play with my child mind to alienate me from her. Children are vulnerable.

My dad and I went for a walk in the woods. Neither of us said much. He held my hand and we walked and talked, but about nothing deep or heavy. He'd bought me an expensive gold chain, which terrified me. He let me open the box and he took it out and put it on me. It was as if he were buying me. I have never liked that kind of thing anyway. Give me a skateboard and I'd be fine. He was scared that because my mother was a lesbian, she would corrupt my life and I would become a lesbian. I knew he was thinking, 'My girl's going to be a little girl. She's going to be feminine.' Little did he know that I thought he probably would have corrupted my life a lot more than she ever could have. I cried when I had to leave him.

I haven't got a clue why I asked to see him. He has always been a mystery to me. I have moments when I don't want to deal with him or even to know him. But then there are moments when the daughter in me comes out and says, 'I've got a dad.' And I get this immediate pang to meet him. I grieve over him. I wish my dad could give me a big cuddle and sit me on his knee. But that desire doesn't last because it is only fantasy. It's about my image of a father. I never had him as a father. I don't know who he is really.

Now I see him maybe once a year. When I am with him, he's suppressed. He's threatened by me because I'm very open. I'm not swayed by other people's opinions and I'm not naïve and innocent. If my mother had stayed married to him, we would have had such a limited life, with far fewer choices.

A strong mother

There was a unity my mum and I had when I was ten, a bond between us. The custody case enhanced our relationship. We became friends. There was just her and me. She's a strong and dominant woman and she fights for what she wants in her life. Seeing my mum like that was partly what got me through. I fight strongly in my own right now, because I know what she had to go through just to be herself.

For many years I felt empowered by her strength. To me, she was like a goddess. I had her on a pedestal. To this day, I've never rebelled, though I've had my difficulties with her. We've talked about this, because there probably should have been some sort of rebellion. There was a lot inside me that needed to be expressed.

Our relationship is based on talking. Even from the age of three, Mum would ask me something and I'd say, 'Why?' and she'd tell me. Whenever Mum and I had problems we needed to deal with, we talked them over.

I've always listened to her. She taught me about being female in this society, about loving your body in a positive way but being aware of the need to protect yourself from abuse by men. She was very good at introducing periods and going through the bra syndrome with me.

Mum was a well-known feminist, fighting for women's rights. She was always open about her sexuality. I was involved in her political activities and went on marches and demonstrations. I was like a little child star because I was one of the very few children well known in those circles. Because of Mum's lesbianism and feminism, I've had lots of women around who loved me, who put their arms around me, and who talked to me. I was surrounded by adult conversations. Many of Mum's friends took an interest in my upbringing. Jade would take me out to fly kites, another would take me out for a boat ride. I had lots of love and support. As a result, I love people and I'm very talkative.

Mum's lesbianism and her strength of character have given me many choices in my life and so much freedom. It has been tough for us both but my life has been spectacular. I didn't see that my friends at school had that kind of support. My mum brought me up so that I can take care of myself and so I'm confident enough to be myself. She made me aware of racism and other important issues at a very young age. I learned to believe in myself. I'm a separate person from my mum. I stand as myself now.

Other mothers

Mum had had relationships with men until she met Jade, when I was three. Mum said that it took me a couple of days to get used to Jade. One night after I'd just met her, she came to my room to put me to bed. I must have been thinking, 'You're not going to put me to bed. My mum's going to put me to bed.' So I bit her foot. She was howling and jumping about and my mum was shouting, 'What is going on?' But from that point on, I bonded with Jade. She was loving, so I took to her very easily. Since then, Jade has been my surrogate mother. At a very young age I was dependent on her. I loved her very much and still do. Jade and I are very close.

Mum and Jade had a relationship for two years. When they separated, Mum let Jade be part of my life. It would have had a major impact on me if somebody of Jade's significance in my life had disappeared at that age. They both went their separate ways. When I was eleven, Jade separated from a long-term lover, and came to live with us for six months because she was so distraught from the relationship ending. Mum then sold her house and Mum and Jade bought a house together as friends. They have always remained close friends. My mum and Jade lived together for six years in south London and they were the best, most secure years of my life.

I didn't accept two of Mum's lovers. One woman had two children, and I'd never had to share Mum. I never got close to the other one, but luckily it was a short relationship.

When my mum got into a relationship with Sally, I was a teenager and knew what was what. I understood that it was a sexual relationship. Sally was a big kid, and she was great with kids. We did things together all the time. She was into the music I liked. She accepted me, which made me accept her. I loved her so much. So there was Mum, Sally, Jade, and then Jade's lover Jackie – we all became a close unit. There were four women who became my family.

But my world fell apart again when I was sixteen. Mum and Sally separated because Sally wanted to have another relationship. That was the second time I saw my mum in pain and out of control. And then three weeks later, Jade separated from Jackie. Suddenly I lost two major figures in my life. That was all very peculiar. One minute, the relationships were fine and the next minute they were over. And they both went out of my life completely. Plus neither Jade nor Mum would talk about the separations, for whatever reasons. I was really isolated. I'd invested a lot in them. That was probably the one time when I really felt bad about all the shit that I had gone through in my life. Eventually, Jackie and I started seeing each other again. We're really close now. But I don't see Sally very often.

I was seventeen when Mum got together with Chris. We have a beautiful relationship, but it's taken many years to get to the point where I can say that. Mum had never lived with a lover, so I'd never had to deal with that before. I think that the relationship with Chris is the only one of Mum's relationships I've really had to challenge. I've had to accept that I've got to share my mum because Mum really loves Chris. I've never seen that woman love someone the way she loves Chris. And that is saying something. Seeing Mum so happy with Chris has reinforced my respect for her. At first, I resented Chris, because I still loved Sally and I couldn't love both of them. And I didn't like Chris. She is calm, reserved, stern, a lot older in maturity and attitude than Sally, who was very bouncy and young. Chris is political and active intellectually, while I'm artistic and carefree. I saw my fun mum gradually start changing on me. I think Chris had a lot of difficulties accepting me. It's hard to take on board somebody else's kid, especially a teenage kid. I tend to be overpowering sometimes. But Chris and I are family now.

Relationships with men

There weren't many men around during my childhood and I feel fine about that. There were the odd few that I saw with some continuity, but nothing like the colossal number of wonderful women friends that Mum had.

At the age of fourteen, I had my first boyfriend. Not having much awareness of men, I went for someone I wouldn't go near now – the typical down-the-pub-with-his-pint kind of bloke. I lost my virginity on my fifteenth birthday. I was emotionally pressurised into it, although I made the decision. I remember crying and crying afterwards. I felt dirty, unappreciated and unloved. But I stayed with him for four years, engaged in a massive power struggle. At a young age, I knew about my rights and what I wanted for my life. I wasn't suddenly going to tie myself down to a bloke and have kids at the age of sixteen. I wasn't a raging feminist, but I was aware and outspoken. By the age of sixteen, I was also open about Mum's sexuality.

My mum was great about both these relationships. She let me do what I needed to do, which is why I got out unscathed, never having had a kid or been married. I think she was very concerned about both men because all they ever tried to do was suppress me and put me in a pretty little box where they could own me. She felt that they fed off of me and that I was lucky to get out with my strength and my independence intact. As a teenager, I didn't see that. I thought that I was in love. I wasn't, of course.

It's been a hard battle with men and me. I've been in stereotypical male-dominated relationships. I had to go through that because i hadn't had much experience of different kinds of men. Now, at the age of 24, I know it's OK to look for what I want in the person. One of the meaningful things I've learned from Mum's relationships with Chris, Sally and Jade is to respect your own space and to be aware of other people's needs, too. I see how Mum and Chris give each other a tremendous amount of support.

They are inseparable individuals in a very bonded relationship. But they respect their individuality. They can agree to disagree. I want a man who can hold me, who can talk to me, and who can have intellectual conversations. It's important to have the option of individual bedrooms and to have your space and independence noted and appreciated. I don't think I would have got that growing up in the heterosexual world. My values are all down to my mum's choices.

I doubt very much I'll ever get married. Marriage represents absolute pain. All I've ever seen is break-ups. Most of the marriages in my family have broken up, and all of my friends at school have single parents. Marriage seems to ruin the commitment. My mum always emphasised her mistake of getting married and having a child so young. She was really scared that I would do the same as she did. She's never regretted having me, and she's fought very hard. But it took a lot away from her life. I see that.

Tough times – Emily's story

At the time of the interview in 1995, Emily was twenty-one, the oldest of four sisters. Her parents separated when she was eleven. A year later, her mother came out as lesbian and has been living with her partner, Natalie, for the last ten years. Emily went to boarding schools and didn't have the experience of living with a lesbian mother. She herself is a lesbian, in a committed relationship with a woman.

Mum came out to me and my sister Kerri when I was twelve. We were sitting in the car and Mum said, 'Do you know what a lesbian is?' We didn't have much of an idea at all. Mum then said, 'Well, I'm a lesbian.' Kerri and I just said, 'Oh right, fine.' Mum went on to say that we shouldn't talk to school friends and people in the village about it. She was trying to protect us, but I didn't understand the social significance and stigmatisation attached to being a lesbian.

We were living in a small village. My dad was teaching at a posh boarding school in the village. All the members of staff lived in the village and their kids went to the school. Everyone knew each other. Dad was the favourite schoolteacher and a surrogate father for many of the kids at the school. He was seen as a jolly and helpful man.

We had a different view of him within the family. He had had a couple of mental breakdowns and was abusive towards Mum, which no one in the school or village knew about. Mum tried to leave him three times. Each time he pushed himself to the edge of a nervous breakdown and she went back to him. When I was eleven, Mum finally left for good. Dad was seen as the victim by people in the school.

My sisters and I were left with my dad but six weeks later, Dad had a nervous breakdown and disappeared for several weeks to a mental hospital. My two youngest sisters went to live with my aunt. Mum collected Kerri, and I stayed on at Dad's school as a boarder. We were spread out round the country and it was very confusing, because we were unsure of each other's whereabouts.

I went through a short but intense phase of hating Mum. As far as I was concerned, she was the cause of my family falling apart. I felt very alone – I didn't have a home anymore, didn't know where my parents were, didn't know where my sisters were, didn't have any friends left. This phase of anger with Mum passed and I got very angry with Dad.

This was the context in which I naïvely told some staff at the school that Mum was a lesbian. It was a big mistake and turned into a major village scandal. I ended up leaving the school because of the homophobia that emerged, though there were other reasons as well. I came north to live with Mum for a year.

The five-year custody case

Dad initiated a custody case after he got out of mental hospital. He wanted us back and thought he was in a position to care for us. He didn't believe he'd ever been mentally ill. He claimed he'd just been reacting to my mother, that she'd pushed him over the edge.

The case turned into one of suspected abuse. Mum was scared of what Dad might do to us, based on her experience of his abusive behaviour towards her. He'd never abused me, but I've always been worried about his relationship with one of my sisters. Mum told the social workers how worried she was about us and when I was about thirteen, we were put on the at-risk register.

Up until the last year of the case, it had felt like the authorities were on our side – on the side of Mum and us four sisters. Even though they weren't coming up with revolutionary results, they were supportive. While they were investigating the allegations of abuse made against Dad, they were concerned about our safety and hadn't been interested in what Mum was.

When I was nearly sixteen, a court welfare officer came along and interviewed all four of us sisters, as well as Mum. She then said she'd better go and interview our father. Mum tried to dissuade her, saying, 'He's three hundred miles away. As soon as you meet him, you'll be charmed. You'll take his side, and you won't believe a word the kids told you.' As far as I was concerned the authorities were meant to be representing my view in court, which had nothing to do with what my dad thought. I knew he thought I'd been brainwashed by Mum and that I was in danger from her. But I was in a lot more danger when I was around Dad. He is emotionally unstable and a big emotional manipulator, a real guilt-tripper.

The court welfare officer went off to talk to Dad and came back with a report which predictably said the major issue was the risk to our safety from Mum being a lesbian. She used words that my father had already repeatedly said to me – that I'd been brainwashed by Mum and that my sisters were at risk of being influenced by both of us. She wrote that I was idolising my mother and that I was gay because Mum was and that if I were taken out of Mum's care, I would no longer be lesbian. I became sceptical about authorities and people who claim to help.

There were a lot of controversial issues involved in that court case – suspected abuse, lesbianism, Dad's mental health. Mum says that her sexuality was a minor issue, which is probably a more accurate analysis than my memory. But the way lesbianism was dealt with had a major effect on my acceptance of my sexuality. That is why I remember it as a big deal in the custody case. After hearing the welfare officer's report, I started feeling that my sexuality was subversive, that I was different because of my sexuality.

The custody case went on for four years. In the end, Mum got sole custody when I was nearly seventeen. Dad got access rights. She never contested his right to see us.

My own sexuality
I was about nine when I started thinking that I was attracted to women. My first affair was with a woman at Dad's school in the village. I'd gone

back from the north and was a boarder for two terms, because I was on the at-risk register and wasn't allowed to live with Dad. The whole school knew about my affair. It was a huge scandal. The custody case was going on and the headmaster felt he had to protect Dad, so I was asked to leave. I was indignant at the time but looking back, it was actually the right decision for me.

I left that school and went to a boarding school in the north with my sister Kerri. I was not out at school. I was terrified of anyone guessing my sexuality and covered up as much as I could. Evidently I was successful, because none of them guessed at the time. One of the typical sixth-form conversations the girls used to have was what if one of us was a lesbian. I used to think it was directed at me, but I realise now that it wasn't. I was so worried about discovery that I made sure one girlfriend called herself by a different name every time she rang. I was also extremely heterosexually promiscuous. That was the way I coped at the time. I don't judge myself about it. I'd much rather have been brave enough to come out but I couldn't have done at the time.

Since I left school, I've been determined to be out. My old school friends have all been great about it. Most of them were upset that I'd deceived them.

Now I'm in a long-term committed relationship. Jay's the first person I've made plans with. We have a level of security that you get when you know you're going to be together for a lot longer. I've never felt that kind of permanency before.

On the edge

I've been to places in my head where I felt like I was on the edge. When I left school I went through a hard patch. I was very lonely, made suicide attempts, ended up on different medications and had to go and see a shrink at the hospital. I used to self-mutilate. I got addicted to cutting myself up. It lasted for four years when I was about fifteen till about nineteen. I'd never do it again, though I still think about it. It was a coping mechanism. I have an addictive personality. Most of my addictions have been self-destructive, but that's the nature of addiction. A lot of my life I've had it really hard and sometimes the only way to deal with it is to express it in unconventional ways.

Most of it was to do with different forms of abuse that I've experienced. I wouldn't say that any of it was to do with my mum being a lesbian. But some of it was to do with internalised homophobia. I was really angry that my sexuality had caused so many problems socially. I couldn't do anything about being a dyke and I couldn't change my situation. I couldn't make people listen. I didn't have any other outlet for that anger. I'd had one experience of homophobia and there was no way it was ever going to happen again. The only way that I could ever get rid of any of those feelings was to take it out on myself. It's something that you only understand if you've actually done it. There's a feeling of relief and a sense of letting something go when you cut yourself. It's masochistic but it's really relieving, it feels good and it's effective.

The reason I stopped cutting myself is that I woke up and realised it wasn't helping me at all. My girlfriend at the time was incredibly unsympathetic. It was a very short, relatively insignificant relationship, but her reaction made me wonder why I was doing it. In addition, I got a job where I had to wear a short-sleeved uniform. People used to see the scars and I was mortified. That motivated me to stop.

Lesbian daughter – lesbian mother

I'm a dyke. I define myself as a dyke. If Mum were forced to classify herself, she would say she is a lesbian or that she is gay. But given the choice, she would prefer not to label herself. That's a cop-out to me, but I can't judge her for it. I'd rather that she call herself lesbian because it's important for me to have that identity. Mum's not into categories. She believes that everyone is fundamentally bisexual. I think there is no clear-cut divide. Sexuality should be on a continuum, rather than put into distinct categories, but I'd still rather she called herself a lesbian. It doesn't matter so much anymore and when it did really matter to me, she did call herself a lesbian.

Because of the way lesbianism was dealt with in the custody case, I needed to prove to myself that my sexuality was my own, that it wasn't to do with Mum. In the welfare officer's report, Mum was accused of influencing me. I was told that it was just a phase, that it wasn't my decision. It's been important for me to realise that I was attracted to women before I even knew about Mum. As early as age nine, I was on a primary school wildlife trip and I wrote a love-note to one of the female residential teachers there. That's a bit of evidence that I'm not a lesbian just because Mum is.

I know a lot of people with lesbian mothers and I've done research on it for my women's studies course. You can't generalise about what effect it has on kids, but I've never found any evidence that it influences the sexuality of the children. It really helped me accept my sexuality. It's made a big difference. I am happy with my sexuality and I feel really calm. I don't feel I've got anything to prove anymore.

Having a lesbian mother has made it easier because there's an acceptable role model for me. Mum has always been my ally. She is like me and she understands me. Her life experience is similar to mine. For quite a while, she was the only out lesbian that I knew. She's been a good mother, has done brave things and deserves to be happy. She says she is happy. I have felt really close to her. In the last three years, Mum and I have been away for two weekends together and had a really good time. Both times we went out and searched for the lesbian bars in the area and went dyke-spotting.

Whenever my friends, most of whom are dykes, find out I've got a lesbian mother, they always think I'm really lucky, which I am. But there are down sides to it when you're a lesbian yourself. It doesn't mean that she has no problems with my sexuality. She said recently that a lot of satisfaction in her life has come from having kids. She believes that having children in a straight relationship is an easier experience, and that it's very difficult to have them in a lesbian relationship. She's lived for a decade as a heterosexual family and a decade as a lesbian family. In the heterosexual family, she was not as happy personally, but it was better for raising children.

The differences

Mum admitted to being more critical of my girlfriends than she is of Kerri's boyfriends. Because Kerri is straight and Mum is lesbian, Mum feels she's got to prove to Kerri that she's not anti-men or hostile to her and her boyfriends. It's important to Mum that Kerri feels able to talk to Mum about her relationships. Because I'm a lesbian, she can be very critical of my partners in the same way she would be, if she were straight, with Kerri. It's a weird kind of logic. At first I thought, 'Oh great, cheers Mum. Thank you!' But it was good to hear her spell it out. I don't like it and I wish that she wouldn't do it, but it makes sense and at least she is honest with me.

I appreciate that. That's the most that she can give me. She's trying to protect me when she criticises my girlfriends. I know that she'd support me and help me as much as she could, if needed. Still it would be nice to hear her say how great it is being a lesbian.

Mum and I have such different lifestyles and such different political views now. Mum's become a lot more liberal. I've got to respect it, but I don't like it and it's put a bit of a wedge between us. Mum used to be what I would call radical. She was very politically active, especially in the years before she came out, when I was about ten or eleven. I admired her for that and I wanted to copy her. She was a role model for me then. I took on that political aspect and got into all sorts of left-wing and human rights groups.

Mum has spent eight years working her way up the social services ladder. She's become a career woman, a professional. I've watched her lose a lot of compassion and political awareness that she used to have. She was never on the scene, which I can understand because I hate it myself, but she used to be out and proud. She doesn't smile as much as she used to. She doesn't have as much fun. She doesn't go on Gay Pride. One day I want to get her there. That would be an uplifting experience for me, and I think for her as well. She won't go while she's working, I know that.

She has made mistakes and often says that she wants me to be angry with her. She worries about my lack of anger and thinks that I should be expressing some. There were times when she wanted to protect me, but didn't. I think she blames herself a lot.

Mum and I have grown apart, but my relationship with her hasn't fallen apart. There's no big event that's made it deteriorate. I used to rely on her and be really close to her. But when I was addicted to self-mutilation, I felt like I could not turn to her. I then lost the only support that I'd ever had. It's through no fault of hers or mine really, it's just the way it happened. Her partner moved in and they built a home together at the same time as I went away to a new boarding school. I felt really excluded from that. However much they tried, spending only three months of the year there just didn't make me feel part of it.

A married couple

Mum met Natalie about a year after she left my dad. They've been together for nearly ten years now. I started getting to know Natalie the year I lived with them when I was twelve, but I've never lived with them since. They're madly in love and are good for each other. They make each other happy. They're a family. It is difficult for me to feel comfortable in something I've never felt a part of.

Natalie was a straight feminist. Mum's the only woman she's ever been out with. It was love at first sight and about two years later they moved in together. Natalie never expected to be going out with a woman or to have a family. I've really appreciated her generosity and commitment to Mum and the sacrifices she has made.

However, my relationship with Natalie has not been good. We have big communication problems, which has put Mum in a difficult position. I'm not blaming anyone. It's just circumstances – the fact that I wasn't there and Natalie was. Natalie thinks that I was jealous because she took my place in Mum's life. That is a pile of crap, because I wasn't there anyway. I was close to Mum but I didn't have the experience of living with her that Natalie's had. My version of it is that I went through an angry rebellious phase, during which I was suspended from school several times, ran away from school and used to cut myself. I would come home with huge scars on my arms. Every time I did it, it hurt Mum, though that wasn't my objective in doing it. Natalie was the one who was there dealing with Mum's tears and anger. She's protective of Mum and it seemed to Natalie that I was doing it on purpose. Natalie's been making more of an effort to get to know me now that I'm no longer hurting Mum. Equally, I've had more time for her as I've matured and become less self-engrossed.

I respect Mum and Natalie's relationship and their commitment to each other. But they've turned into a closeted couple. They want as few people to know as possible. I can understand it, but I don't like it. I know lesbian couples who've been together for many years and who lead a lifestyle which I would aspire to much more than I do Mum's and Natalie's.

It was too late for Natalie to take on a parenting role with me, but she has with my two youngest sisters. She is their parent, financially and emotionally. Ali has lived with Natalie since she was six. Ali thinks they're a pain in the arse most of the time! I envy Ali having grown up in a stable, woman-orientated household. That is totally alien to me. I've moved around so much as a kid.

It would have made a huge difference if I'd lived with Mum when I was a teenager, but my philosophy of life is that I don't wish anything had been any different because I like who I am now and I like where I am – take away any part of my life and I wouldn't be here. There's no point wishing for a different life.

Part VI

The Outside World

The world can be a tough place for lesbian families. Two issues are highlighted in this part of the book – dealing with homophobia in schools and gaining legal recognition of the co-parent's role. The stories in the last of these chapters show how families have coped with difficult circumstances.

In the Classroom 277   Legal Recognition 283   Facing Challenges 291

15

IN THE CLASSROOM

Our children often encounter homophobia at school, from both teachers and other pupils, ranging from invisibility in the curriculum through to bullying and violence. But it doesn't have to be that way, as this chapter explores.

The untold story

Homophobia at school is as much a problem for children with lesbian mothers as it is for lesbian and gay young people. Yet our children's stories are rarely heard. In all the campaign literature calling for the repeal of Section 28, there has been no acknowledgement of the damaging effect of homophobia on our children and how crucial it is that schools should make themselves safe and nurturing for our children.

When my daughter was at primary school, we were living in Hackney, a London borough well known for its high concentration of lesbians. I sent her to the local state school, chosen because of its commitment to diversity. Not only were some of the teachers out as lesbians but there were a fair number of other children with lesbian mothers. One lesbian mother became a parent governor and helped write the school's sex education policy.

At the age of seven, my daughter felt supported enough by the school to speak at an assembly about families. This is her account:

"I told everyone that I have three mummies and a daddy. I also have a part-time mummy who I live with some of the time. My daddy lives with his boyfriend and I like them both a lot.

"After I told everyone about my family, lots of children raised their hands to ask me questions. Ahmed wanted to know how many cars our family has. I was going to count them but my teacher said that the assembly was about families, not about cars. Someone else asked which mummy had sexed with my daddy to make me. I said that they didn't sex, that my daddy put the sperm in a jar. Rahul asked, 'Shouldn't some of those people be married to each other?' I said, 'No, they don't have to. They can do what they want.'"

In the playground, she encountered the usual name-calling against lesbians and gays but, surrounded by supportive teachers, classmates and community, she had the confidence to challenge the more ignorant children. One day she told me how silly the boys in her class were – they had told her that a lesbian is half girl and half boy, the halves being the right and the left sides of the body. My daughter gave them the correct information.

She started secondary school when we moved to Bristol and was shocked to discover how prejudiced the majority of the children were against any kind of difference. School was no longer a safe and supportive place where she could be accepted as she was. The pervasive homophobic name-calling was no longer just silly, but threatening and abusive. She sensibly protected herself by keeping quiet about her home life and seeking out a few safe friends to hang out with. She noticed how silent the school staff were on the subject of homosexuality and homophobic bullying and became alienated from school. How could she respect anything they taught her when what they taught contradicted her own lived experience?

"My science teacher told us that at puberty, the hormones in our bodies make us attracted to people of the opposite sex. That is just bollocks," she told me.

Fear and bullying

My daughter's experience is not unusual, as I discovered when I became involved with the Bristol-based Lesbians and Children Network. Some of the mothers formed an action group to put pressure on our schools. I spoke to Fiona, mother of a twelve-year-old daughter and a ten-year-old son, who is a founder member of the action group.

The first step the group took was to consult the mothers in the Network and find out what their children were saying about their day-to-day experiences at school. The findings were disturbing. "Some families have had to cope with direct physical abuse, and most have had to deal with direct or indirect verbal abuse. Many lesbian parents choose not to come out to schools, for fear that this will affect their children and, similarly, most children in these families do not feel safe to disclose their parents' sexuality at school," says Fiona.

"We've told the school. Nothing gets done," said one mother, who had been to the head to complain about homophobic bullying. Several lesbian mothers in the Network had approached their children's schools, expecting the staff to clamp down in the same way they would with any other type of bullying. But they were all disappointed. Despite assurances that "something would be done", there was no follow-up and no explanation as to what action had been taken.

In one incident that occurred after school, several children with lesbian mothers witnessed a vicious attack on a gay student. They expected the head to condemn the attack in assembly the next day as he had done about other beatings. But it was never mentioned. "It must have sent a message to pupils that beating up somebody because they are gay is not as serious as bullying of other kinds," said Fiona.

Bullying does not have to be physical to hurt. The most common term of verbal abuse in both primary and secondary schools is "gay", "queer" or "lezzie". Younger children use these words without even knowing what they mean, bandying them about to show their disapproval or fear of any kind of difference. "If you miss a goal, you're gay," reported one child to his mother while others heard "gay" used to put down children who were good at French, had the wrong fillings in their sandwiches, or sat with their legs crossed!

A lesbian teacher in the Network said, "I taught boys whose every second sentence seemed to involve queer this, queer that, in a really nasty, hateful way. Often they didn't understand the word and it was just used of something that wasn't right. 'It's queer, Miss.' 'Do you mean it isn't working?' I would ask. 'Yes, Miss.'"

An end to name-calling?

But children with lesbian mothers know exactly what gay, queer and lesbian mean. They understand all too well that these are terms of abuse and refer to their mothers. Understandably, they find this confusing and threatening. To protect themselves, they mostly keep quiet about their mothers' sexuality.

Mothers in the Lesbians and Children Network felt it was the responsibility of the teachers to put a stop to this constant homophobic name-calling and to inform children of all ages what the words lesbian and gay really mean. The Bristol Local Education Authority (LEA) endorses this. In its guidance to Section 28, sent to all governors of Bristol LEA schools, the Council said that Section 28 "does not prevent discussion of homosexuality in the classroom", that teachers "need to be aware that there are young people who are being brought up in lesbian and gay households", that "young people should feel their home circumstances are valued and they should not be led to feel that they are in some way set apart from their peers." But mothers in the Network could not see that this guidance was put into practice.

Invisibility

There are few, if any, obvious signs of recognition of the existence of lesbian or gay parents in the schools and fewer positive images of diversity of family types. Fiona points out that "Schools' silence on alternative families, and reinforcement of one heterosexual model as the norm, lends no support to our children, who consequently suffer from feelings of inferiority and confusion, and fear of being 'discovered'." A mother in the Network claimed, "They are denying my children equal access to education, as they cannot express themselves freely."

One theme that mothers raised was that homophobic bullying and lesbian/gay invisibility in schools affects all children, not just those with lesbian mothers or those who are gay or lesbian themselves. Fiona summarises their view: "Fear of being ostracised for being different is common to all children, and it's unhealthy for all. So, the failure of schools to speak out against this form of oppression is bad for every pupil in every school, not just the children of lesbian and gay parents."

The Network's action group presented a report to the Chair of the Education Committee of Bristol City Council with concrete suggestions for what school governors, heads, teachers, the Council and parents can be doing. The report and an interview with a member of the action group were included in the teaching pack and video prepared by the LEA and sent to every school in the authority.

You can read how other people have dealt with these issues in some of the stories in Chapter 17.

16

LEGAL RECOGNITION

It is possible for lesbian co-parents to have their role recognised in law by applying for a joint residence order. This chapter examines the pros and cons of this and of other means of acquiring legal rights.

Parental responsibility

A lesbian co-parent may have been involved in the planning and the insemination, supported her partner through pregnancy and childbirth, bought a home together and taken on financial responsibility, done the bulk of the childcare and made a commitment to care for and love this child forever. Legally, that does not make her a parent.

The parenting relationships that lesbian co-parents and step-parents form with children are not automatically recognised in law, but lesbian couples have been taking advantage of a little-known provision in the Children Act 1989 to ensure legal recognition of their parenthood, by applying for a joint residence order.

In law, a parent is the person with "parental responsibility". This is a legal concept defined in the Children Act as "all the rights, duties, powers, responsibilities and authority which by law a parent has in relation to the child and his property." Only the birth mother and the father, if he is married to her, automatically have parental responsibility. Unmarried fathers, i.e. known donors, can acquire it (see Chapter 2, "You and the Donor").

Residence orders

Under the Children Act, people other than the birth parents can apply for a joint residence order if they live with the child all or part of the time. This order in effect gives them a limited version of parental responsibility to share with the birth mother and anyone else who already has it.

A co-parent or step-parent (from now on, I'll refer to anyone who is not the birth mother as the co-parent) can apply for a residence order if she has lived with the child for three years or if she has the written consent of the birth mother and anyone else who has parental responsibility.

If the birth mother does not consent, the co-parent can apply for leave of the court to apply. She can apply for a joint or a sole residence order. ("Residence" is the term now used for custody.)

The benefits

Given the co-parent's legal invisibility, this section of the Children Act is an exciting step forward in recognition of non-biological parenting. When a lesbian couple are living together and raising children together, it is natural to want to have some legal acknowledgement of the co-parent's position. Parental responsibility via a court order gives her status with doctors, schools, officials of all kinds and society in general. She is entitled to be involved in major decisions regarding the child. It could also be important for the child to grow up with parents of equal legal status and potentially equal power in the family. But as long as they are co-parenting amicably, possession of the residence order has little practical effect on their day-to-day life. Its real importance is as a symbol of legal recognition and as a safeguard for the co-parent if they separate.

The limitations

Exciting as this is, it is still not as good as it should be. The legal rights of a co-parent are not the same as those of the birth mother. Applications for residence orders can be expensive, time-consuming and involved.

You can do it yourself, which is cheaper than engaging a lawyer. But Gill Butler, a solicitor who specialises in lesbian mother legal cases, recommends paying a lawyer. She says, "In the mid 1990s, so many applications were going through on the nod that I started encouraging women to do it themselves to save on the lawyers' fees. But then I heard about a few cases that had gone badly wrong because they didn't have legal representation. The risk is that you'll come across a judge who doesn't understand the issues."

Legal Aid is hard to get. Since April 2000, same-sex couples have their income aggregated, which means that most people, other than those on a very low income, will not be eligible.

Even if you get the residence order, anyone else with parental responsibility can contest the order and take it back to court, where it can be lost. If a donor acquires parental responsibility, he has equal rights to the birth mother and greater rights than anyone else who has acquired it via a residence order.

In Gill Butler's experience, even donors *without* parental responsibility are often asked to get involved when a co-parent applies for a residence order: "Courts now require that donors are served with notice of the application. If you are going to make an application, then you should get a letter from the donor confirming that he does not wish to be heard on the application and ideally that he supports the making of a joint residence order."

Other limitations include:

- A residence order only lasts as long as it is in force – usually until the child is 16 but it can be extended to 18.
- A co-parent cannot change the child's last name or agree to the child being adopted.
- A joint residence order does not give the child the right to inherit from the co-parent's estate.
- A residence order does not commit the co-parent to

financial responsibility for the children, so the birth mother cannot pursue her or him for abdicating this responsibility.

Are applications successful?

There have been many successful applications for joint residence orders by lesbian couples. For example:

- In June 1994, an order for joint residence was made in the High Court in Manchester to a lesbian co-parent whose partner had conceived a son by self-insemination. The judge, Mr Justice Douglas-Brown, decided that the boy's welfare was paramount and that it was in his interests that an order be made.

- In a subsequent case, a lesbian couple was granted a joint residence order in a London court for their two children. Each has a daughter conceived by self-insemination and the donors are not involved in their upbringing.

- In 1997, a precedent was set in a Birmingham court case by a High Court Family Division judge. The lesbian couple had applied to a magistrates' court for a joint residence order for their daughter conceived by donor insemination clinic. The couple had been referred to the higher court where the judge established that uncontested applications for residence orders can be successfully dealt with in a magistrates' court. In their case, there is no known donor and no possibility of an unmarried father appearing to contest the co-parent's application.

Gill Butler says, "In London, where I practise, it's not a unique experience any more for a court to hear these cases. They are quite happy to be making these orders. It's a pleasant surprise to them to be asked to involve people as parents. They're used to dealing with adults who are in dispute and who often seem to have no idea of how to take responsibility for their child. Most of the cases go through on the nod. But you still get judges who need convincing that there is a reason to make an order. If there is a problem, it tends to be that under the

Children Act, the court is unwilling to make an order unless there is a good reason to make one."

Splitting up

Advice from Gill Butler: "As a lawyer, I have to bear in mind that everything is not always going to be wonderful between the partners. I take the approach that this co-parenting arrangement might break down. There is no reason to expect that their relationship is not going to last, but if it does break down, the birth mother might take one position and the co-parent might take another. The job of a lawyer is to point out to people things that they hadn't thought about. I'm not pitting them against each other. I'm advising them about the reality and about what the law would do. Inevitably when there is a situation of conflict, if they both go to law, their interests diverge.

"From the co-parent's point of view, I can't think of any reason not to have a joint residence order. There's everything to be gained and nothing to be lost. It doesn't carry any financial commitment, so she can't lose.

"But from the birth mother's point of view, she's giving up control. She's got an obligation to consult with the other woman, whose relationship to the child has to be recognised. So the birth mother has to be satisfied that it's worth the risk. Without a residence order, she could use the argument that this woman was just a friend, that she wasn't really a parent, and make life so difficult that the co-parent gives up. She could move to another city if she wanted to. I see it all the time. Everyone is capable of rewriting history. But if you've got a residence order, it's very hard to do that because what you agreed to is written down in black and white.

"Going to court should be a last resort – particularly for lesbian parents, because their issues are not necessarily going to be understood. There are other ways of dealing with conflict. If you do go to court, you may not be financially eligible for legal aid, so you will spend a very considerable sum of money. The average fully contested case costs £15–20,000 in London [in the north of England, the costs are in the region of £2,000 to £5,000, year 2000]. But it's not just the money. Your life will not be your own: someone else will be making a decision about your child, and neither of you are going to be happy about the outcome. It's all done with other people sitting there hearing it, reading all about you. That's scary. Also, the children know their parents have gone to court and that they are being fought over. I wouldn't recommend it, not at all."

If the couple do not have a joint residence order before they separate, the co-parent may apply to court for a residence order or for a *contact order*. The latter gives the child the right to visit her, but does not give parental responsibility.

The co-parent can apply for a residence order if she has been living with the child for at least three years. Anyone else who has gained parental responsibility, such as the donor or a married father, will be notified by the court and can object to her application.

Ideally there should be a neutral conciliation service within the lesbian community to sort out these conflicts without having to resort to the courts.

When a birth mother dies

If the birth mother dies, the co-parent can potentially acquire parental responsibility (if she doesn't already have it) as follows:

i. If the mother has appointed her to be the child's guardian
(Sections 5 and 6 of the Children Act.) To do this, the birth mother writes a simple statement appointing the guardian, dates it and signs it in front of two witnesses. (She does not need to go to a solicitor.) Or she can appoint the guardian in her will, or make a formal deed. See "Guardianship" below for the limitations.

ii. By applying for a residence order
Especially if the co-parent has been living with the child and no one is contesting her application, she will have a good chance of getting it. According to the welfare checklist, the court would rather not change a child's circumstances unless it is absolutely necessary.

iii. By applying for an adoption order
Seek legal advice to find out if this is appropriate in your case.

Joint residence order

If the co-parent had a joint residence order with the birth mother, then the child will continue to live with the co-parent, who will continue to have parental responsibility (but see "Competing claims" below).

If the co-parent does not have a joint residence order when the birth mother dies and the birth mother has failed to appoint a guardian, then it will be open to the co-parent to apply to court either to be appointed the child's guardian or for a residence order (which would, as stated above, grant her parental responsibility).

Guardianship

If the birth mother has appointed a guardian, this will not take effect if there is anyone else alive with parental responsibility. For instance, the child's birth father could have parental responsibility because he was married to the mother when the child was born (even if later divorced) or because he had acquired it under Section 4 of the Children Act. Then the birth mother's appointment of the co-parent as guardian will not automatically take effect until the father's death.

The exception to this is when the birth mother had a residence order for the child when she died. Then her appointment of a guardian for the child *will* take effect on her death, even if the father is alive. The co-parent will then hold parental responsibility for the child jointly with whoever else holds it.

Competing claims

If the birth mother has appointed the co-parent as guardian, but the appointment does not take effect because there is someone else who holds parental responsibility, then it will be open to the co-parent to apply to court for a residence order. In this case, the court will decide between the co-parent and the other people who hold parental responsibility for the child (generally the child's father).

Even where the co-parent's position has been protected, either because her appointment as guardian has taken effect or because she held a joint residence order with the birth mother, there is always the possibility that the father may object to the child continuing to live with the co-parent. He can apply for a residence order.

It is also possible that grandparents and others may step in at this stage and apply for a residence order if they want the child to live with them.

The court will look at what is in the child's best interests in deciding between competing claims. If the child has lived with the co-parent for all or most of their life, then this will be an important factor which the court will have to take into account.

Informal arrangements

If the co-parent does not have parental responsibility through guardianship or a residence order, she can continue to look after the child informally. But she doesn't have any legal standing. She is considered to be a private foster carer and should really notify the local authority, as it has the duty to supervise private fostering arrangements and the power to disqualify or prohibit a person from privately fostering a child.

If disqualified, you can appeal to a magistrates' court but the court does not have to go through the welfare checklist. People have been disqualified because they have a history of very minor offences. It is a criminal offence, punishable by up to six months in prison, to foster privately if you have been prohibited. Because of this, it is a good idea for the birth mother to appoint the co-parent as guardian or for the co-parent to apply for a residence order when the mother dies.

The co-parent's estate

The co-parent should also make a will to make financial provision for the child in case she dies. Otherwise, even with a residence order, the child does not have any right of inheritance to her estate.

17

FACING CHALLENGES

The problems with schools and the legal system discussed in the last two chapters are just part of a picture of discrimination against lesbian families. But we often find ways to challenge prejudice, as shown by the stories in this chapter.

Parenting in tough circumstances

As lesbian mothers, we and our children are up against prejudice in many forms, from denial of our very existence to physical and verbal assault. We are a stigmatised group and this can lead to us feeling isolated and marginalised, struggling with self-esteem.

But in these challenging circumstances, we are each doing the best we can. We are courageous and inventive in our own ways. Some of us confront prejudice head-on and publicly, arguing with bigots on TV chat shows. Others display just as much bravery by coming out to a neighbour or a parent. And sometimes, the boldest and wisest action is to keep quiet and let your child deal with the situation in their own way.

We make contact with other lesbian mothers for informal support. We organise support groups for ourselves and our children. We are not victims, but active participants in our society.

The eight stories in this chapter focus on different aspects of our struggles with the outside world. Caroline and Lynn had to take out a court injunction to stop a *News of the World* front page headline, but could not avoid expulsion from the Girl Guides. Jess talks about being out at her son's school, in their small English village, and in the Church; while Frances has an unusual strategy for dealing with homophobic bullies in the neighbourhood.

Audre is struggling to fit all the different pieces of her life together, in her son's school and in her neighbourhood. Susan writes about life in her village, bullying at the children's school, getting outed at a Mother and Toddler group, the lack of support for lesbian mothers, and the effect of the failure to repeal Section 28.

Pat is struggling to come to terms with her sexuality and with rejection by her parents, siblings, neighbours, ex-husband and children; while Myra is not accepted by her parents or by her ex-mother-in-law, and her daughters fear coming out at school.

Finally, Justine writes about being out with her parents, friends and the group that supported her after the stillbirth of her first son (described earlier in the book).

Expelled from the Brownies – Caroline and Lynn's story

Caroline and Lynn were both married when they met at their children's school and fell in love. They divorced their husbands and moved in together, along with three of Lynn's four daughters and both Caroline's sons. They have been living together as a family for the last six years. They gave this interview in 2001.

Lynn: When I was married, I had been active in the Brownies for about three years. I took a meeting of Brownies every Monday and to church once a month on a Sunday. I had taken many tests and exams to be able to lead packs, to take a large number of children away and to do first aid. I'd done my pack holiday licence. I did all the accounts. We'd won awards. I was training up with the Guides so I was preparing to take over the complete Guide unit. I would go away maybe two or three times a year with the Brownies or the Guides. I was the Tawny Owl.

While Caroline and I were just getting together and had not yet left our husbands, I took thirty Brownies away on a week camping trip. Caroline came as my assistant. A few weeks after we got back, the phone rang and a man said, 'Oh hello, is that Lynn?' I said yes and he gave a name which I assumed was one of my husband's colleagues. We had a short conversation and then he said, 'Is it true that you're a lesbian?' I said, 'I beg your pardon' and slammed the phone down on him.

Caroline: He rang again and I answered this time, asking him to clarify who he was. He said, 'I am so and so from the *News of the World*. I hear you've taken a pack holiday of Brownies.' Straight away I could see his angle. I said, 'I'm not prepared to discuss this with you,' and put the phone down. My boys were with a teenage babysitter. I immediately phoned her and she had also had a call from him. She had told the journalist that she was the babysitter, [at which point he] called her a fucking liar. A family friend had had a phone call from the same journalist asking where my husband was. The Brown Owl of the pack had been contacted by him as well as the District Commissioner of the Brownies. He even approached our children's school. I phoned the *News of the World* and told them not to have any further contact with us or I would seek legal advice. The headline that was going to be run the next Sunday was 'Lesbian Lovers Take Brownie Pack Holiday'.

Lynn: The next day we went straight to a solicitor. He told us not to leave our houses for fear of being photographed.

Caroline: Our solicitor was excellent. There was no homophobia from him. He pulled out all the stops. We got an injunction to stop the paper publishing the story, until the children reach eighteen.

Lynn: I was thrown out of the Brownies right away. I was asked to leave by the County Commissioner and by the District Commissioner. They felt that the parents of the Brownies would think me unsuitable to look after their children. It was all very hush-hush and under the carpet. Goodness gracious, you can't possibly be allowed near any of these girls now. I felt really hurt. I didn't appeal. The sad thing is that only this year, they disbanded the Brownie group after forty years because there was nobody to run it.

Caroline: We had only just declared our feelings for each other and then this happened a few weeks later. It was extremely stressful. Looking back on it now, we must have felt so strongly for each other that it helped us get through it. If we had had any doubts whatsoever, we couldn't have tolerated it. We were very fragile at the time. As well as all this business with the *News of the World* and our relationship being so very new, we were both going through divorce.

All this hostility made our bonds absolutely invincible. In the beginning, we had a stone clad wall which nobody and nothing could get through. We became insular for about a year. With hindsight that was probably not the best thing. We did lose friends; we closed ourselves off. So much had already hit us that we didn't want anymore.

Lynn: Eventually, we felt ready to meet some people and make new friends. Just as we started to come out of this phase and to come into life and to people, Caroline became very unwell. After many months, it was diagnosed as Grave's disease and was a result of all the stress. She was unwell for the next nine months and has only been fit and well for the last two years.

Village church – Jess's story

Jess had two sons, Richard and Stewart, when she was married to John. Although she recognised there was something different about her sexuality when she was fifteen, she didn't come out as a lesbian until she was forty. At that time, her sons were ten and thirteen. She has been living as a single parent in a small English country village for the last seven years. She gave this interview in 2001.

My oldest son, Stewart, says that it was very difficult for him growing up with a lesbian mother. He went to a big comprehensive in the next village. My youngest son, Richard, did not want to be out as having a lesbian mother. He had already been the subject of homophobic bullying directed at him when he was ten. He had enough to cope with, without having to deal with 'your mum's a dyke'. He went on to a small comprehensive in the city, a different school than the one Stewart went to. One of his friends from that school, a mixed-race boy, used to make the most appalling anti-gay jokes. In the end, I couldn't stand it anymore so I said to my son that I was going to tell this boy I'm gay. I told him [the friend] that it hurt me and that I didn't want to hear those jokes. There was an odd sort of moment when I could see him thinking, 'can I eat her food?' He was staying the night and the next day when I was taking them home, he started telling me his experiences of racist jokes and how bad they make him feel. We've been good mates ever since.

I've lived in the village for eight years. I'd been a scout leader and active in various political things and with the local church. People know who I am. The reality of village life is that people do notice you. It's not anonymous, like city life. If you split up from your husband, people notice. If you start going out with someone and they frequently come to your house, people notice and comment. Once my ex-husband came to see me to sort out things about the kids. We were in the pub. The following morning, I was at the post office when someone came up to me and said, 'I see you and your husband are back together.' That's what village life is about.

My experience has been that very few people in the village are homophobic. When I told one or two people, I saw a look of disgust flit across their face, but you can get that anywhere. A few people said nothing and thought their own thoughts and eventually got to the point where they could talk to me and be quite affirming. People could see I was happier.

I want my sons and their friends to realise that being a lesbian mother is part of normal life. It's about going to work, picking up the kids from school, going to the supermarket, much more humdrum than anything on telly. Once I was driving my sons and two of their friends somewhere. There was a woman standing at the bus stop who knew that I'd left my husband and that I was going out with a woman. She stared at me as we drove past in the car and then looked the other way. Two of my son's friends cried out, 'Oh, that's so-and-so. Let's go and duff her up because she hurt you.' I did tell them that violence is not the answer to everything. But it was affirming for me that they liked me and wanted to sort things out for me. So it's not all gloom and doom.

We never stop coming out. The most useful thing I've learned is to let people get used to you first, to come out obliquely and slowly. You don't say, 'Hi, I'm Jess and I'm a lesbian.' What are they going to do with that? You say, 'My partner Gillian and I went for a walk in the New Forest.' Then they're OK.

I've also discovered that people are not as interested as you think. We all think we're the centre of the universe, but we're not. Even in the village where people gossip, it's a nine days' wonder and then they move on to the next thing. Not all gossip is hostile, some is just nosy. These days because of soaps, people are much more aware of lesbians and gay men. It's within the normal range more than it ever used to be. It has a curiosity value but they're not necessarily being negative.

I've learned not to give up on the possibility of change. When I was forty and just started coming out, I was very afraid of my mother's reaction. She refused to meet my girlfriend and somehow never managed to mention it again. But recently I dropped in on her with the woman I hope is going to be my serious partner and she was very pleased to meet her and was welcoming to both of us. She said to me, 'You look so well. Gillian is obviously good for you.' It took my mum five years to work this through, but at least she's got there.

I was brought up as a Catholic, but left over the issue of women priests. It's funny what you can accept – I didn't leave over contraception or over sexuality. It was when the Vatican said women can never be priests that I started looking around for other churches. I decided to join the Church of England because I liked the church in our village. It has a very lovely woman priest.

I hadn't realised that you could be a lesbian and a Christian until I met a woman at a party who was a member of the Lesbian and Gay Christian Movement. This was a revelation. It took a great weight off me. Slowly, over time I've become much clearer about it. I've thought about this very deeply and I've prayed about it. In my soul, in my heart, I believe that this is how God made me. Being a lesbian has given me gifts, strengths that I would not otherwise have had.

Unlike some people, I've found the Church to be affirming. Before I came out, I spoke to a monk at an abbey who said, 'You have to accept yourself as you are. That is the great challenge of life. That is what God wants you to do.' It was important for me to find people who are in authority in the Church, people who listen, who think new thoughts.

I decided that I wanted to be accepted as I am before I signed up and gave them my money. I wouldn't want to go to the altar rail to accept communion under false pretences. I didn't want that feeling of 'if you really knew who I was, you wouldn't want to give me this.' So I came out to the priest and she was wonderful, very celebratory. One of the first things she told me was that she'd been asked to officiate at a celebration mass for her uncle and his male partner who were going to celebrate 25 years together of their partnership. That was her way of saying it's not just OK to be gay, it's part of you. This is how God made you. That helped me to move on.

Five years later, I have an active role in that church. I'm one of a small group of people that makes things happen. No one has suggested that I be healed. I have not personally had those experiences, though I know people have. I'm not out to everybody at church because it's a classic English country village. There are a lot of people who haven't even started to think in a positive way about sexuality. The priest's advice was to come out slowly as people have got to know me. When we've had away days, I've talked about the importance of it being an inclusive church. With other people, I've said, 'as a lesbian Christian, this is how I feel.' So I'm reasonably out.

Our diocese is linked with the Church of Uganda. Two years ago, there was a worldwide synod, a great gathering of bishops at Lambeth. There was a lot of discussion about homosexuality, which became the focus of angry arguments that were reported in the press. The priest in my village church rang me up to say she felt for me because she knew I'd be hurt by what they were saying. She wasn't just paying lip service. The Ugandan bishops in particular and some of the other African bishops were extremely homophobic. I wrote a careful letter to each of the Ugandan bishops whom I have met, explaining why I'm a lesbian, why I'm out and why it's important that we be out. I said it was the secrecy that led to problems. I sent a copy to the co-ordinator of the committee in our diocese, saying I feel I have to do this and if the committee wants me to resign, I will resign. The co-ordinator rang me up and said, 'Writing the letter is fine, if this is how you feel. You have a lot to give and we want you to stay.' I've met all the people on the committee several times since then and everybody has been just the same towards me. There wasn't the slight hesitation that you get with some people after you've come out. I'm still a key member. The Ugandan bishops never replied to my letter.

I feel that was good enough from the Church, given how ambivalent the Church of England is about sexuality. They have a 'don't ask, don't tell' approach. There are some in the Church who believe that it's one thing to *be* gay but to *act* gay is ungodly. I have to accept that a lot of people feel that way. But my experience with the Church has been affirming and positive.

Trick or treat – Frances's story

Frances and her partner live in a large provincial city with Frances's twelve-year-old daughter and eight-year-old son. She wrote this in 2001.

Even before we moved into our road, we were known by a couple of the neighbourhood bullies. At school, one of them had told my son, then six, that if we moved anywhere near their house they would kill our cat. A 'campaign' of intermittent trouble has ensued over the last three years that we have lived here. Physically, it has never amounted to very much. It seems to stem from the fact that we are different: a family with two women; a car that is a different shape from all the others in the street; adults who will play games with their children rather than send them to play outside unaccompanied.

Both of the children have been called names and been threatened with the usual – rather bizarre – things that bullies dream up. This treatment is also meted out to other children in the neighbourhood and even, we've since found, to some of the older adults who live nearby. Our approach has largely been to ignore any taunts and jeers that come from the bullies when they have the courage that comes from being in a gang. When we first moved here, we tried to communicate with the bullies themselves. I felt that this might turn out to be a successful long-term strategy. I don't think it worked at all, in fact I think that my interest in them, and willingness to talk about their perspective, was perceived as weakness and further, as evidence of how different I was. Since then, when our children or their friends have been picked on, we have gone and sorted it out with the main bully's mother, who at least has a little control over his behaviour. Her response is usually to burst into tears.

This 'zero tolerance' of his bullying has worked, we feel, since he will never directly pick on our family because he knows there will be an outcome. This hasn't stopped the indirect 'nuisance causing' that happens once in a while, but apart from a couple of incidents, the bullying problem has seldom troubled us. In fact, the main bully and his cronies are probably pretty inept and insignificant as bullies go. I have often thought that if children have to come up against bullies at some point in their lives, then my two children might as well learn some coping strategies with this bunch, whilst we're around, than with another nastier bunch some other time.

My son, though, will always remember the night that the bullies called round. It was Halloween, and my son, who never likes the idea of trick-or-treaters, had just filled up his large water pistol. It's the kind that has a reservoir the size of a thermos flask, and a pump action that pressurises the spray. If you have trouble with aphids on plants, get yourself one. He was standing in the kitchen, miming what he would do if a bad trick-or-treater called and, at just that moment, the doorbell rang. I walked down the narrow hall to open the door to the two bullies, heavily masked but recognisable due to the familiar slouch. 'Trick or treat,' they said. I paused and said, 'Well, I'll have to ask my son, I think'. Stepping into the hallway, he jubilantly shouted 'Trick!' simultaneously spraying them both in the face with his high-power, jet-thrust mega-squirter. Their shock left them speechless for a few seconds. Then one said, 'Oh, fair enough.' I admit to feeling a fine sense of revenge as they slunk away dripping to the sound of our laughter. We paid for this in eggy windows, but it was a moment of real empowerment for my son.

In the minority – Audre's story

Audre is a lesbian of mixed Nigerian–English parentage who is co-parenting her eight-year-old son Tyler with his father. Audre's girlfriend recently moved in with her and Tyler, and they are gradually evolving new family relationships. They live in a racially diverse inner-city area in the south of England. This interview was done in 2001.

A few months ago, I took Tyler out of the primary school he was in and moved him to a school which is far less socially and racially diverse. Tyler has mild dyspraxic symptoms and has a slight delay developmentally. With advice having been sought, we tried to provide an environment that would be less demanding academically or at least where lots of motor skills for writing etc. were required. I don't know if the new school is the right environment for him. We have to see whether or not it is where he will thrive. It is so difficult because there are so few choices available.

We're expected to join in with the school community, but we don't fit neatly into that. It's about being a minority. Tyler is aware of his identity. He's mixed-parentage – I'm mixed-parentage Nigerian and his father's English and Irish. Previously he was in an inner-city school where white children were very much in the minority, and now he's surrounded by children who are white and very much in the majority. There is a higher percentage of two-parent [heterosexual] families and so the environment is quite different. I'm never quite sure how accepting people are of difference and different family set-ups because again and again, that isn't made clear. The assumption is so often that families are man, woman, two children etc. The acceptance of difference is never forthcoming. I find that I repeatedly have to search out the safe areas in amongst the silence. I remember going to an employer once and seeing big bold posters on the wall saying 'This is a safe zone. We accept no homophobia, racism...' I can remember thinking how incredible that felt and that just by stating those points, it was a way of stating that those issues impact on all our lives.

Standing in the playground waiting to pick Tyler up, it brings me back to my childhood, when I was the only black person in the playground. The physical feeling of being the only one gives me difficulties, even now at age 38. What must it be like for him? He saw a photo of my class at school when I was a child, and his first comment was, 'There's only you and one other black girl there!' That was a complete shock to him. That's not been his world, and now I feel that I am returning to that world in some way. I surround myself with people that I feel more comfortable with where possible and I can no longer bend to be what people would sometimes rather I be. We have a wide range of people in our lives.

We do have contact with my adoptive parents, although the relationship between us is quite strained. I do visit with Tyler because they are some of his grandparents. I would ideally like the situation to be different for him, with better contact, but it isn't like that after all these years. I keep the contact quite brief in that if there is a difficult atmosphere I would prefer Tyler not to be in it. I think when he is older he can work out the bits that work for him with them and start a fresh relationship. They speak little of my being a lesbian and I don't have a strong sense of how they feel. They don't ever bring it up.

Keeping secrets – Susan's story

Susan and Tracey are a lesbian step-family with four children – Tom, age thirteen; Louise, eleven; Samuel, five and Ruth, fifteen months. They live in separate households in a small village in the north of England and have been together for four years. Interview done in 2001.

When my kids were in primary school, in a nice trendy inner-city school, they were effectively outed. People realised that their mum was a lesbian, and they had the experience of being asked for several days running, 'Is your mum a lesbian? Is your mum a lesbian?' Tom was denying it, saying 'No, no, no,' but Louise turned round and said, 'Yes, she is'. So that was awkward, because there was no family consensus on these issues. Then some serious harassment started up. We went up to the school and talked to them, and they were brilliant about it. They took it on, and they talked to the children who were harassing my son in a homophobic way. They stopped being harassed. I was quite impressed.

Nevertheless, it meant that when we moved to the rural community where we live now, neither of my children wanted to be out at all. For my family that's the biggest effect of homophobia. It's the secrecy that we live with that I find depressing and upsetting at the moment. My kids aren't out to their school-friends, and they're not out to the school, and we've got no reason to suspect that the friends or the school would be supportive if we were out. Tracey and I had the baby together, which hasn't been acknowledged to their friends or to the school. It's complicated for my children. In her first week in Year 7, Louise had to write about her family, and she had to sit there and struggle to tell the truth but only tell half the truth. My children have to do that day in and day out. They have to think about what they're saying. They have to make excuses. They have to tell lies, all to cover up the fact that me and Tracey are lovers and have been for years. We're not in an abusive relationship, or a violent relationship – we're quite nice to each other and to each other's kids. We've got quite a lot to be proud of about our family. I think that it's very, very sad that in the year 2000 they have to keep this huge secret, and it affects our family in the things we can and can't do, the places we can and can't go.

The kids themselves didn't want to be out. I do consider it appropriate to give children that choice, but several years down the line, I would say it's a very complicated position to be in. Especially with the amount of children we've got and their age range, and how difficult it is not to trip up. Tracey and I did a rough count the other day and worked out that there's probably between twenty and thirty people in this village who know that we are lesbians. We've coined this phrase 'spilling out' to describe coming out by accident. I managed to spill out to the person who was selling me rabbit food. It was either that or act like I was lying about being Samuel's step-mother. She said, 'Have you got any children starting at the new school?' and I pointed to Samuel. Then she said, 'Oh, isn't he the one who's got a mother who's pregnant?' I couldn't say, 'Oh yeah, I forgot, he's not mine!', so I had to say, 'Actually, his mother is my partner.'

Having a family and being in a relationship makes it more difficult. I think it's easier for single lesbian mothers to maintain a level of secrecy. It's not really possible for us. I take Ruth to a Mother and Toddler Group, and stupidly I never thought about whether I would be out or not. Within the first ten minutes on our first day there, one of the mothers asked me, 'How was your labour? Do you breast-feed?' At which point I had to decide whether to lie and pretend I'm super-mum and got my figure back really quickly, or say that my partner gave birth to her. That is what I have done, so I am out now. I checked whether any of them had kids old enough to go to secondary school, and whether it was going to affect Tom and Louise, and no, it was all all right. But some of the mothers had children at the primary school where Samuel goes, so I've effectively outed Tracey. Tracey's had people suddenly turning unfriendly to her. The woman in the bank refused to serve her and closed the till in her face – this was a woman who used to be friendly to her and is a mother at Samuel's school.

Other people are over-friendly, and I am sad enough to be grateful to people who are over-friendly. It does hurt if one minute they're friendly and the next minute they're not. That's part of the problem of being a lesbian; you don't quite know if they don't like you or whether it's because you're a lesbian. Having said that, when it was Ruth's first birthday, the mothers at the Mother and Toddler Group gave her a card addressed to Ruth with my last name. They all sang Happy Birthday to her. The small pockets of acceptance that we do find in our rural community mean a lot to us. When people are accepting, we appreciate it.

We haven't had any harassment in our neighbourhood. In general it's been quite positive and relaxing. Most of our neighbours in this street know about our family set-up. They've been quite favourable. If I were to generalise, I'd say beware of straight middle-class women who don't get on well with their husbands. Avoid them. There are various Christians that I worry about. I don't go to the nearest Mother and Toddler Group because it is based at the church.

The secondary school my children go to doesn't deal with the issue. When I first went round to see the school, I did say vaguely, 'What support could you offer a child whose mother is a lesbian?' They said, 'Well, we've got a school counsellor who comes in once a week.' So that was a disappointing response. In the current political climate while Section 28 has not yet been repealed, I feel that all the schools in the country have the ideal excuse not to deal with the issue at all. I did come out to Tom's tutor, and shortly after that they had a science lesson and they talked about the fact that gay people could have children. The teacher asked everyone in the class to put their hands up if they thought it was wrong for gay people to have children. Only one person put her hand up – the Christian in the class. That was quite interesting, and they have been quite inclusive in that way. It's very difficult with this situation of not being out. It's hard to access any support for your children. When I came out to Tom's tutor, that was against Tom's wishes. I intended to respect his wishes, but there was something about her that I felt it would be OK to come out, and it was worthwhile. But in general I would respect their wishes.

Tom's experience at school at the moment is that all bullying is around sexuality. They get called gay all the time. Tom is a nice, sensitive boy who gets on well with girls, does art and plays the piano, so he gets called gay for those things. He knows what it means. That's what hurts, that gay is used as a term of insult, and that it's about his mum and Tracey and quite a few of his friends' mums. He has found it intimidating and difficult, but now he's in a stronger position and we joke about it. His recent stance is to call people homophobes in a loud aggressive way. Most of the kids don't quite realise what he's doing and take it as a term of insult anyway. Because he's managed not to be out about me, it's not directly personal. Yet Tom and Louise both do take it personally. Louise has got very upset when her best friend and close friends of hers have used gay as a term of insult. We talked about different ways of approaching this. She worked out a strategy which I'm really proud of her for thinking of – she says to her friends that she doesn't like it when they use the term gay as an insult because her mum has got lesbian friends. That opened things up a bit because then one friend said that her step-mum used to be bisexual. So we have been able to take things a step forward even with the cloak of secrecy that we live under at the moment.

Because we're not out, we haven't had direct homophobic bullying, but we live in fear because we could easily be outed. Enough people know enough about us in this village for that to be a likely thing to happen. We've had to prepare ourselves for that, and we've talked about what we'll do and how we'll approach that if it happens. That's quite a difficult way to live, for all of us.

I've been shocked by the lack of support for lesbian mothers. There was a lesbian mothers' group in the city I used to live in that chose to fold within months of me joining it, and that was quite depressing. I thought I could either start up my own lesbian mothers' group or I could cope without. The trouble with being a lesbian mother is you're often quite stressed out anyway. Me and Tracey have got four kids and three jobs. It would have been nice to have had some support.

Since I've become a lesbian mother, I've never felt that I've had anywhere I could go to for support, apart from what I've created myself. I've had quite a lot of negative experiences of trying to access support, where people have then been homophobic. For example, phoning the Samaritans, and them basically saying, 'Well what do you expect? It's bound to be difficult.' I don't trust those mainstream services. They look on being a lesbian as the problem, and won't offer any support for other things. There's nothing in this area apart from what my girlfriend and my mate have started up between us. But it's difficult that there's nothing else.

I cried and felt quite depressed when the Section 28 debate went on again. We were turning on the news every night. My kids couldn't understand why it wasn't straightforward for the Labour Government to repeal Section 28. We all feel totally flabbergasted by it. Now they've become aware of the level of prejudice against them, my son's angry about it. I was beginning to wish that they'd never tried to repeal it. My stomach churns with anger sometimes, about all the lies that are said about us. I work with a lot of families, mainly with heterosexual parents, and I know full well the shit that goes on in those families, and I know full well the positives that a lot of lesbian mothers are giving to their children. To hear Baroness Young saying, 'The trouble with lesbian and gay people is they're not active in their local community, they've got nothing to give,' makes me want to throw up. So many lesbians I know are always there on the front line – in any debate on racism, Ireland, the disability movement, the lesbians are always there fighting their corner. And now I turn round and think who's there fighting our corner? I know of no straight organisations who've got involved with supporting lesbian and gay rights.

What makes a good family isn't to do with the family make-up. I disagree very strongly with the whole tone of the Government's Supporting Families document. It says that the best families are ones where the parents are married, where both people are biologically related to the child. From my own experience and from watching a lot of other families struggle with a biological parent, I don't agree with that.

I teach parenting courses and communication skills to parents. There's a cloak of silence among lesbian mothers about the difficulties being a lesbian – we want to act like it's all jolly. Being a lesbian mother's quite a compromised position to be in for yourself and your kids. I relish it when lesbian mothers do feel that it's OK to say how hard it is on the edges of society. Three years ago, I started to do a lesbian mothers' group and that was very supportive for everyone who came. In lesbian-only groups, you get the chance to talk about homophobia and the effect of it on your family. We can talk about how it's going and how we're dealing with it, and how difficult it is. These discussions sustain me and cheer me up.

Never at ease – Pat's story

Pat was married and had four children before she found herself attracted to women. She now lives with her partner and her two youngest children. She wrote this in 2001.

I never really considered myself to be gay. I never had any feelings towards women at all. I was brought up to believe that these feelings were wrong and, to put it in my mother's words and those of my separated husband, 'perverted' and 'disgusting'. So I was really horrified when seven years ago, I realised I felt attracted to one of my son's teachers. I put it out of my mind until I started work and felt very attracted to a woman I worked with. It was then that I had to do some soul-searching. I left my husband two years ago, after having a relationship with my best friend for nearly three years. We now live together with my two youngest children, who are eight and eleven years. My two eldest, who are fourteen and sixteen years, live with their dad.

Being in a lesbian relationship is the best I could have wished for. It is brilliant and I could not see myself being in any other relationship than a lesbian one. Having said that, I do not feel at ease with being a lesbian. I struggle each day to come to terms with my sexuality. I cannot get to grips with the fact that something that feels so good to me can make me feel disgusted with myself, ashamed, dirty and even, at times, unclean. Most people I know think that it is perverted to be gay and at times, I feel that way too. Over the years, the only way my feelings have changed is that I no longer feel so depressed about being attracted to women. I used to wish the attraction to women would disappear but now I just have to accept that it won't.

I was brought up by a devout Christian mother and so I have found it harder to accept my sexuality because of that. I was brought up to believe that same-sex relationships were not acceptable and that I would be punished by God if I embarked on this sort of relationship. I thank God that my parents are not alive because I know for sure that they would have had nothing more to do with me. My religion has not affected my feelings towards other lesbians, only towards myself. I do not consider myself to be Christian anymore.

I have had no contact with my brother and very little with my sister. My sister's first statement when I told her that I was attracted to women and was going to leave my husband for a woman was, 'The thought of kissing a woman makes me feel sick.' She could not understand my attraction towards women. Also, her husband was homophobic. In fact, I would say that all of my family are homophobic, probably including myself.

My neighbours may suspect and do sometimes make comments about the situation, that is, me sharing a house with another woman, but we have kept our relationship a secret.

Some of my friends have kept their distance when I told them and have not wanted to know me anymore. I know that a couple of them were influenced by their husbands, who felt that I was a threat to their relationship (that I might even convert them to lesbianism!). One 'friend' told me that gay people made them feel sick and [they] could not bear to be in the same room as me. I do have one friend, though, who has been brilliant and has been there for me regardless of my sexuality, even to the point of encouraging me to set up home with my partner. I had one friend with whom I worked (well, I thought she was a friend) who every time I got close to someone at work, she would purposely warn them to watch out for me because I fancied women.

When I first spoke to my ex-husband about my sexuality, it was not to tell him that I was a lesbian, but to tell him that I had found myself attracted to another woman and that I was frightened of these feelings. It took five years before I actually came to the conclusion that I was lesbian. My husband was angry and upset that he had wasted fifteen years of his life with me. He felt that, like most lesbians, I had only used him to have children.

I was really scared of telling my children that I am attracted to women. They know that I love my partner, but then they know that I love many people, so they would not find that unusual. I am scared that they will reject me and no longer love me. You see, adults have been so cruel when they find out that you are a lesbian. Everything seems to hurt so much. How can I risk telling my kids? I love and care about them so much that my life would not be worth living if they rejected me.

My three eldest children now know of the situation but my youngest daughter, who is eight, has not been told, because she would go and shout it from the rooftops. I told my two eldest daughters that I was gay before I left my husband and they were upset and shocked. They could not really believe it, but the second one, who is fourteen, has now told me that she does not mind me being a lesbian. She does not want me to tell the neighbours or anybody who may be a parent of her friends. She is afraid of being bullied at school and made fun of by her closest friends. My son, who is eleven, was told four months ago. I was really worried that he would reject me, but he has been brilliant, although he does not want to tell his friends. That may be because I have told him that many people do not accept lesbianism and that he could be bullied for having a gay parent. In fact, he seems to be the child who is most at ease with me being gay. My eldest daughter is now sixteen. Since I left my husband, she has become a devout Christian and has nothing to say on the subject, although I know that she has been brainwashed into believing that my lifestyle is wrong.

I am not very open at all about being a lesbian mother, unless I come across someone who is lesbian themselves. I find it easier to be open about being a lesbian mother when emailing complete strangers whom I will never meet. I found that the Lesbian and Gay Switchboard offered minimal support. The Lesbians and Children Network in my area has been some support and would probably be more support if I attended meetings and mixed with other lesbian mothers to build new friendships. I'm trying to find a lesbian counsellor. More lesbian counselling services are needed.

Protecting ourselves – Myra's story

Myra left James, her husband of seven years, when Nicole was four and Chantelle six years old. She gave this interview in 2001.

I told my mum I was a lesbian for the second time when I left my husband. The first time was when I was twenty. My dad didn't know for two years after I left James. My mum kept saying to me, 'Don't tell your dad. He'll have a heart attack.' Eventually I thought to myself, 'Why am I listening to this woman?' She was trying to scare me into not being honest. Eventually I did tell him. He said, 'I don't mind what you do – it's the children. You're putting your children at risk by doing this – they'll be bullied.' Then he told me a long story about how he was bullied at school because he had a stammer. He told me about the horrors of bullying and how that was going to happen to my children.

My mum and dad haven't told anybody else I'm a lesbian. My brother and his wife know and have made me guardian to their baby. I said something about being a lesbian and they said, 'Well, obviously we've accepted that, haven't we?' I thought, 'Oh, that's big of you.' They don't want to talk about it. They're very patronising. My mother has lesbian friends. She tells me that they're just like ordinary people, as if they shouldn't be. She used to say that only ugly women were lesbians, because they can't get a man. She doesn't say that anymore. She hasn't told her sisters, and my dad doesn't talk about it at all.

I don't want my parents around as much because they don't accept me for who I am. With my mother, I can't talk about the things I want to talk about and a lot of my life is censored. When my mum was looking after the children last year when I was in hospital, she told them my lesbianism is just a phase I'm going through. ...

Once the children asked if Granny had had a talk with me. I didn't know what they were talking about. They said that my mum had told them she was going to have a talk with me and then I wouldn't be a lesbian anymore. They were hoping that she would. I don't want that attitude and prejudice around my children. It's very undermining and hurtful.

I called my mother-in-law a month after I left my husband and told her we'd split up. My husband hadn't told her. She said very snidely, 'What did you do? Run off with the babysitter?' – which ironically I would have done, if she had been around. I said, 'No. Do you want our new address so you can keep in contact with the children?' She didn't so I said 'OK, then' and put the phone down. I've seen her once since in the last five years, and she visited me in hospital, which was surprising.

I thought we had an independent friendship, but she didn't want to know me once I had left her son. I used to give her lots of listening time when she found out that her other son was gay. She would cry on the phone to me about how he'd never be a father and how nice it would be if he got married. She gave me a sapphire and diamond ring as thanks for all the support I'd given her. It made me think we had a genuine relationship. She doesn't know I'm a lesbian. My children know her views about lesbianism, because she's told them how disgusting it is that a daughter of a friend of hers had a child by self-insemination. The children see her when they're with their father but basically, they don't want her putting me down through her prejudice.

Chantelle has been scared about what other people would think about me being lesbian. She wasn't scared at primary school because there were other children with lesbian mothers there, plus there was a gay teacher. It was a very positive experience. They were very accepting of me. The gay teacher made a family display and as the centrepiece included pictures of families with same-sex parents. It was the only family display I'd seen like it. I felt very affirmed. He used to tell me about homophobic complaints from fundamentalist Christians. Since he left, there haven't been any overt efforts to make different sexualities accepted. Each year I tell the class teacher that I'm a lesbian and if there's any prejudice, I want the teacher to tell me. I want my children to be treated fairly. If there's any homophobic bullying, I want to know about it. I want it dealt with in the same way that racism is dealt with. I'm very clear about that. They're fine about it. I don't know how it's actually dealt with, but I get my point across.

Chantelle was really scared at one time that she was going to get bullied because I was a lesbian. I told the deputy head at her secondary school that I was a lesbian, because I wanted to make sure that she wasn't harassed. Chantelle told me that she had asked a girl at school what she would do if her mum was a lesbian. The girl had replied, 'That's disgusting. My mum would never be anything like that!' Chantelle persisted saying, 'Yes, but what if she was?' The girl said, 'Why? Is your mum a lesbian?' Chantelle said, 'No, no, but I wouldn't mind if she was. It's up to her anyway.' I thought that was fine. She's growing up with a more aware mind and she's protecting herself, which she needs to do. Another example is when her close friends wanted to protect Chantelle, so they made out that they knew this cool lesbian called Candy who had loads of money, a massive house and a big car. Which counts for lots at her school.

Nicole has got a friend with lesbian parents but they've stopped calling themselves lesbians and that's confused her. She doesn't know what they are. She used to confide in this friend. She felt solidarity with this friend and would go round to her house. She said to this friend, 'I'm so pleased that your mums are lesbians, because my mum's a lesbian, too.' But they stopped calling themselves lesbians. It's difficult for Nicole.

When Chantelle brings friends around, she wants me to take lesbian pictures off the wall so that it's not obvious. I don't do it. I'll take pictures of naked women off the wall as these girls are only twelve, but I wouldn't take a picture off [just because it's] of lesbians. I don't have anything that blatant anyway – mostly symbols, and pictures of my family and friends. I don't really go around with any straight women except for one whose son is one of Nicole's best friends. I don't have many straight people come in my house. I worried that one couple wouldn't come back, and they didn't, but I didn't ask why. That's always what I think when something goes wrong in a relationship with a straight person – I wonder if it's because I'm a lesbian.

Building bridges – Justine's story

Justine is a lesbian mother who has had two sons with Simon, a gay man who agreed to donate sperm and co-parent with her. Her first son, Connor, died at birth and she has been active in SANDS (the Stillbirth and Neonatal Death Society). Their second son, Declan, is three years old. She gave this interview in 2001.

Both of our families are aware of our situation. I was so nervous about coming out, but my mum and dad have dealt with it. I had reason to be nervous, but I've found that as we've all got older, we've been able to build a lot of bridges. I came out to my parents when I was pregnant with Connor. Our plan was that we would introduce Simon as a friend from the same part of the country. Once he had met them and they'd seen what a nice chap he was, I'd tell them that he's the father of their grandson. That is more or less what happened. Telling them I was a lesbian was part of that process; I felt I could not hit them with too much information in one sentence. I was asked, indirectly, if we would be getting married and I said no. My dad wanted to know what would happen if he found another woman. I am paraphrasing here, but my response was that I thought that would be very unlikely. He eventually suggested that could only be the case if he were gay. I was so relieved I said yes, that Simon was gay and that I was a lesbian. I told my parents I was a lesbian and that I was pregnant by self-insemination. It was a lot for them to take in, and we did not talk about it again that weekend. But I was completely bowled over by their response. I am so proud of my dad especially; we had a very long and frank phone conversation a couple of weeks later.

I'm out at work and I'm out with my friends. I have heard people talk complete rubbish about gay parents, especially when they're discussing what they've read in the tabloid newspapers. I don't know if I'm unusual, but all of my friends are really cool with it. But they wouldn't be my friends if they weren't. I know it's not always the case, but I believe that you often get the reactions you expect. When I come out to people, I never say, 'Hello, I'm Justine and I'm a lesbian.' I always act like my sexuality is not going to be a problem for them. Usually I get to know them and then as early as possible, I engineer a situation where it can be addressed more directly. I don't live in a closet.

As far as I know, I am the only lesbian mother on the SANDS register. Although I've been quite open with the national office, I hadn't come out to everyone in my local group. It has been such an important part of my support since Connor's death that I chickened out about coming out more overtly. Also my sexuality wasn't why I went along; I went because my baby had died. I've never called Simon my partner; I've always called him Declan's dad. It just never came up, but it got to the point where it felt deceitful. I didn't want to make a big thing of coming out, because then people might get really wound up. It's been a bizarre situation because we meet in the same building as the local lesbian and gay helpline, of which I am a member.

However, I recently made a decision to come out more overtly. Shortly after this, someone in our group was separating from their partner and someone new asked me about what happened with Simon and me. I said we had never been a couple in that sense, that we were lesbian and gay parents. It was fine, and has been fine. When I said I had been worried about coming out to the group, some of my older friends said they had known for ages. They have been to my home, and I never de-dyke the house when people come around, so I guess they worked it out for themselves. All that angst for nothing.

Resources

This section lists organisations and publications of interest to lesbian families and those who work with them

PinkParents UK

A UK-wide organisation of lesbian, gay and bisexual parents, parents-to-be and their children.

Contact
Address: Box 55, Green Leaf Bookshop, 82 Colston St, Bristol BS1 5BB
Phone: 0117 904 4500
Email: enquiries@pinkparents.uk.com
Website: www.pinkparents.org.uk

Aims
To offer support and information
To build a strong and supportive community
To raise awareness and confront prejudice

Enquiry service
We answer enquiries by phone, email and letter on all aspects of LGB parenting, including referrals to local lesbian mother support groups.

Membership
Membership is welcome from anyone who agrees with our aims. When you join, you will get a quarterly magazine, free guidebook to LGB parenting, discounts on PinkParents products and services, access to contacts, information, resources and advice on all aspects of LGB parenting, access to member-only web-based services.

Publications
We know how hard it is to find anything written about LGB parenting

that isn't American, so we are distributing a wide range of leaflets and articles. Have a look at our publications order form.

Helpline
Phone 0117 377 5794 Thursday 7 to 10pm.
The aim is to provide informed advice and reliable information by supportive LGB parents and parents-to-be to anyone who wants to talk on the phone about lesbian, gay and bisexual parenting issues. It is not a counselling service.

Workshops
We run "Challenging Conceptions" workshops for lesbians and gay men considering parenthood. These are women-only, mixed and men-only. We're setting up "Parenting Support" Workshops for parents to talk about the impact of homophobia on family life and how LGB parents can support their children to deal with prejudice.

Lesbian parenting

Organisation

Rights of Women (ROW)
52-54 Featherstone Street, London EC1Y 8RT
Phone: 0207 251 6577
Fax: 0207 608 0928
Email: info@row.org.uk
Free confidential telephone legal advice to women on all issues of family law, including lesbian parenting, domestic violence and sexual violence.

Publications

Benkov, L, *Reinventing The Family – The Emerging Story of Lesbian and Gay Parents*, Crown Publishers, NY, 1994

Clunis, DM & Green, GD, *The Lesbian Parenting Book – A Guide to Creating Families and Raising Children*, Seal Press, Seattle, 1995

Corley, R, *The Final Closet – Gay Parents' Guide for Coming Out to Children*, Editech Press, Miami, 1990

Dunne, G (Ed), *Living "Difference" – Lesbian Perspectives on Work and Family Life*, Harrington Park Press/Haworth Press, London/NY, 1998

Golombok, S, *Parenting – What Really Counts?*, Routledge, London, 2000

Griffin, K & Mulholland, L (Eds.), *Lesbian Motherhood in Europe*, Cassell, London, 1997

Harne, L & Rights of Women, *Valued Families – The Lesbian Mother's Legal Handbook*, The Women's Press, London, 1997

Martin, A, *The Guide to Lesbian and Gay Parenting*, Pandora, London, 1994

Pies, Cheri, *Considering Parenthood*, Spinsters, San Francisco, 1988

Pollack, S & Vaughn, J (Eds.), *Politics of The Heart – A Lesbian Parenting Anthology*, Firebrand Books, Ithaca, 1987

Rafkin, L, *Different Mothers – Sons and Daughters of Lesbians Talk About Their Lives*, Cleis Press, San Francisco, 1990

Saira, K, "Lesbian Couples and Single Women: Discrimination and UK Licensed Fertility Clinics", Dissertation, School of Law, Manchester Metropolitan University, 2000

Tasker, F & Golombok, S, *Growing Up in a Lesbian Family – Effects On Child Development*, Guilford Press, NY/London, 1997

Wells, J, *Lesbians Raising Sons – An Anthology*, Alyson Books, LA, 1997

Wells, J, *Home Fronts – Controversies in Nontraditional Parenting*, Alyson Books, LA, 2000

Weston, K, *Families We Choose – Lesbians, Gay, Kinship*, Columbia University Press, NY, 1991

Parenting and relationships

Organisations (mainstream)

Parentline Plus
520 Highgate Studios,
53-79 Highgate Road, Kentish Town, London NW5 1TL
Parentline: 08088 002222, open Mon-Fri 9.00am to 9.00pm, Sat 9.30am-5.00pm, Sun 10.00am-3.00pm
Website: www.parentlineplus.org.uk
National helpline run by parents from all walks of life. Don't have all the answers, but want to help. All helpline workers are volunteers and have been trained within Parentline's equal opportunities policy. This means they have an understanding of how prejudice and discrimination can affect family life and add to the strain of parenting.

National Family Mediation
9 Tavistock Place, London WC1H 9SN
Phone 0207 383 5993
Fax 0207 383 5994
Association of sixty local services which offer help to couples, married or unmarried, in process of separation. Mediators help couples to make joint decisions, focusing on arrangements for children.

Relate
Local Relate offices listed in phone book and on website.
Phone: 01788 573241 – national centre
Website: www.relate.org.uk
Counselling and mediation service for people having difficulties in their adult relationships. No family therapy. Will help whether or not you are married and whatever your age, race, personal beliefs, sexual orientation or personal background.

Step-families

Publications

Baptiste, DA, "The Gay and Lesbian Stepparent Family", in Bozett, FW (Ed.), *Gay and Lesbian Parents*, Praeger, London, 1987

Hayman, S, *Relate Guide to Second Families*, Vermillion, 1997 (No mention of lesbian and gay step-families, but contains useful advice)

Kahn, T, *Learning to Step Together – Building and Strengthening Stepfamilies – A Handbook for Step-parents and Parents*, National Stepfamily Association, London, 1995

Wright, J, *Lesbian Step Families – An Ethnography of Love*, The Haworth Press, New York/London, 1998

Adoption and fostering

Organisations

British Agencies for Adoption and Fostering (BAAF)
Skyline House, 200 Union St, London SE1 0LX
Phone: 0207 593 2000
Advice and information to members of the public, to social workers and other professionals on adoption, fostering and childcare issues.

Department of Health Adoption Website
http://www.doh.gov.uk/adoption
Intended for anyone with an interest in adoption, it provides detailed information on government adoption policy and the adoption process. It signposts the reader to associated information and links to the websites of adoption organisations and other government departments.

Lesbian and Gay Foster and Adoptive Parents Network (LAGFAPN)
C/O Stonewall, 46-48, Grosvenor Gardens, London SW1 OEB
Phone: 0207 881 9440
Email: LAGFAPN@aol.com
LAGFAPN is a group for individual lesbians and gay men who are interested in and involved with the fostering and adoption of children and young people. It provides support, puts people in touch, distributes information to members, outside agencies and the general public, while maintaining confidentiality. It also campaigns to obtain wider acceptance and support of fostering and adoption by lesbians and gay men.

National Foster Care Association (NFCA)
Leonard House, 507 Marshalsea Road, London SE1 1EP
Phone: 0207 828 6266
An association of foster carers and others which encourages high standards in foster care.

Northern Support Group, Lesbian & Gay Foster & Adoptive Parents' Network (LAGFAPN)
PO Box 2078, Sheffield, S2 4YQ
Email: shicks1@uclan.ac.uk
Covers Greater Manchester, Lancashire, Yorkshire and surrounding areas. The group meets every other month to offer mutual support to any lesbians and gay men involved or interested in fostering or adopting children. (Creche provided.) Also involved in some campaigning and training work.

Publications

"Adoption and Fostering for Lesbians and Gay Men Reference List", available from PinkParents UK

Hicks, S & McDermott J (Eds.), *Lesbian and Gay Fostering and Adoption – Extraordinary Yet Ordinary*, Jessica Kingsley Publishers, London and Philadelphia, 1999

Getting pregnant

Self-insemination kit

Kit contains 10 ml syringe, extending tube, fertility awareness charts, self-insemination leaflets (advice for donors and advice for women). Available from PinkParents UK (see p315) for £5.

Organisations

Donor Conception Network
PO Box 265, Sheffield S3 7YX
Phone: 0208 245 4369
Network of parents with children conceived with donated sperm or eggs and those contemplating or undergoing treatment (DI, IVF). Aims to provide support and to increase public awareness and acceptance of family creation through donated gametes. Members include single women and lesbian couples. Newsletter, meetings and local groups for parents and children.

HFEA, The Human Fertilisation and Embryology Authority
Paxton House, 30 Artillery Lane, London E1 7LS.
Phone: 0207 377 5077
Website http://www.hfea.gov.uk.
Has list of all the clinics licensed for donor insemination and other assisted conception techniques in the UK. It produces a free booklet, "The Patients' Guide to DI and IVF Clinics", with information about each of the clinics – address, services, success rates.

Women's Health
52 Featherstone St, London EC1Y 8RT
Helpline: 0207 251 6580
Minicom: 020 7490 5489
Email: womenshealth@pop3.poptel.org.uk
Website: www.womenshealthlondon.org.uk
Enquiry service, library, publications, consultancy on all aspects of women's health.

Publications

Glenville, M, *Natural Solutions to Infertility – How to Increase Your Chances of Conceiving and Preventing Miscarriage*, Lifestyles Healthcare, Danegate, Eridge Green, Tunbridge, TN3 9JA (2000)

Pepper R, *The Ultimate Guide to Pregnancy for Lesbians – Tips and Techniques from Conception through Birth*, Cleis Press, San Francisco, 1999

Resources for and by children of lesbians

Publications

Booklist for children and teenagers, featuring lesbian and gay parents and role models available from PinkParents, 2000

Hauschild, M and Rosier, P, *Get Used to It! Children of Gay and Lesbian Parents*, Canterbury University Press, Christchurch, New Zealand, 1999 (Personal accounts with photos)

Howey, N and Samuels, E, (Eds.), *Out of the Ordinary – Essays on Growing Up with Gay, Lesbian and Transgender Parents*, St Martin's Press, New York, 2000 (Personal accounts)

Film

Spadola, M, *Our House*, Independent Television Service, USA, 1999 (A very real documentary about kids of gay and lesbian parents – available for loan from PinkParents UK)

Resources for teachers

"Beyond a Phase – A Practical Guide to Challenging Homophobia in Schools", Health Promotion Service Avon, Henshaw House, Lodge Road, Kingswood, Bristol BS15 1LF, 1999 (Video and teaching pack)

Biddle G and Forrest S, "Talking about Homosexuality in the Secondary School", AVERT AIDS Education and Research Trust, West Sussex, UK, 2000

Bristol City Council, "Section 28 – A Guide for All Staff and Governors of Bristol LEA Schools", Bristol, 1999

Casper, V & Schultz, SB, "Gay Parents/Straight Schools – Building Communication and Trust", Teachers College Press, Columbia University, New York and London, 1999

Douglas, N; Warwick, I; Kemp, S and Whitty, G, "Playing it Safe: Responses of Secondary School Teachers to Lesbian, Gay and Bisexual Pupils, Bullying, HIV and AIDS Education and Section 28", Institute of Education, University of London, 1997

Joint Action against Homophobic Bullying, Intercom, PO Box 285, Exeter, Devon EX1 2YZ (Guidelines for schools)

Mason A & Palmer A, "Queer Bashing: A National Survey of Hate Crimes Against Lesbians and Gay Men", Stonewall, London, 1996

Mole S, "Colours of the Rainbow – Exploring Issues of Sexuality and Difference – A Resource for Teachers, Governors, Parents and Carers", Camden & Islington NHS Trust Health Promotion Service, London, 1995 (Guidance, lesson plans and photocopiable materials for the health and PSE curriculum)

Robinson, G & Maines, B, "Safe to Tell – Producing an Effective Anti-bullying Policy in Schools", Lucky Duck Publishing, 3 Thorndale Mews, Clifton, Bristol BS8 2HX, October 2000 (Video and training pack commissioned by Bristol City Council, based on the no-blame approach. Price £30, plus £5.25 VAT)

USA Organisations

Alternative Family
Website: www.altfammag.com
Online directory of national, state and local LGBT parenting groups
in the United States.

Children of Lesbians and Gays Everywhere (COLAGE)
3543 18th St, Suite 17, San Francisco, CA 94110
Phone: (415) 861-5437
Fax: (415) 255-8345
Email: info@colage.org
Website: www.colage.org

Family Pride Coalition (formerly GLPCI)
P.O. Box 34337, San Diego, CA 92163
Phone: (619) 296-0199
Fax: (619) 296-0699
Email Pride@FamilyPride.org
Website www.familypride.org
Dedicated to the advocacy and support of LGBT parenting groups
throughout the country. Sponsors an annual conference.

Gay Fathers Support Network
Providence, RI
Phone: (401) 431-2953
Email: TJFronczak@aol.com
Website: www.gayfather.org

Kinnections for Families
c/o True Colors Sexual Minority Youth and Family Services of CT
P.O. Box 1855, Manchester CT 06045-1855
Phone/Fax: (860) 649-7376 or toll-free 1-888-565-5551
Website: www.ourtruecolors.org
Provides support, education and advocacy that promotes the

development of LGBT people into full and productive members of society. Works to create positive change in healthcare, education, religious organisations, etc.

Love Makes A Family
c/o Family Diversity Projects, Inc.
P.O. Box 1209, Amherst, MA 01004-1209
Contact: Peggy Gillespie & Gigi Kaeser
Phone: (413) 256-0502, 9.00am-5:00 pm EST
Fax: (413) 253-3977
Email: famphoto@aol.com
Website: www.lovemakesafamily.org
Distributes the "Love Makes A Family" photo-text exhibit of GLBT families to colleges, schools, libraries, churches, conferences, etc. Also created and distributed three other photo-text exhibits showing the diversity in all different kinds of families.

Momazons
P.O. Box 82069, Columbus, OH 43202
Phone: (614) 267-0193
E-mail: momazons@aol.com
Website: www.momazons.org
A national organisation for lesbian mothers and those who want children. Facilitates connections between mothers seeking information and support. Bimonthly newsletter, directory of supportive resources.

National Center for Lesbian Rights
870 Market Street, Suite: 570, San Francisco, CA 94102
Phone: (415) 392-6257
Fax: (415) 392-8442
Email: nclrsf@aol.com
Website: www.nclrights.org
Free legal information and referrals, partnership protection documents and videos, publications on family issues – including adoption, custody, foster parenting, reproductive technologies and litigation strategies. Annual membership $35.

National Institute for GLBT Education
3932 Broadway, Box 45600, Kansas City, MO 64171
Phone: (816) 960-7200
Fax: (816) 960-7297
Email: info@thenationalinstitute.org
Website: www.thenationalinstitute.org
Comprehensive educational programs to assist individuals, families, communities of faith, corporations and professionals facing GLBT issues.

Parents, Families And Friends of Lesbians and Gays (PFLAG)
1726 "M" Street NW, Suite: 400, Washington, DC 20036
Phone: (202) 467-8180
Fax: (202) 467-8194
Email: info@pflag.org
Website: www.pflag.org

Proud Parenting
Website: www.proudparenting.com
National magazine for LGBT parents and their children.

Straight Spouse Network
8215 Terrace Drive, El Cerrito, CA 94530-3058
Phone: (510) 525-0200
Email: info@ssnetwk.org
Website: www.ssnetwk.org

Index

adoption, 125-41
adoption order, 289
advertising, *see* donors
age and fertility
    in men, 49, 81
    in women, 4, 6, 98-101, 110
AIDS, *see* HIV
Alan's story, 37-40
Alice's story, 247-52
Amanda's story, 256-64
Amy's story, 92-94
Andrea's story, 113-15
Angela's story, 180-84
anonymous donor, 12-13, 21-22,
    23-27, 84, 184, 203, 227, 252
antibiotics, 25
anxiety, 104
Audre's story, 188-90, 299-301

basal body temperature, 68-69
Benkov, Laura, 224
bereavement, 103
Bernadette's story, 195-96
birth, 70-71
birth certificate, 16, 20
bisexual identity, 161
black and mixed-race families,
    91-92, 137-41, 188-90,
    195-96, 234, 239, 245-46,
    299-301
black donor, 91
black identity, 189, 300
blighted ovum, 111
blood groups, 51-52
boys, 178-80, 183-84, 231

Bronwen's story, 36, 77-78
Brownies, 292-94
bullying, v, 243, 250, 253, 254,
    258, 278-81, 298-99, 301, 303,
    310
Butler, Gill, 18, 156

Callum's story, 252-56
Caroline and Lynn's story, 163-66,
    207-12, 292-94
Casey's story, 109-113
Cathy's story, 190-94
cervix, 66, 67-68
Children Act, 15, 16, 283, 284
children of lesbians, 217-25, 227-72
Child Support Act/Agency, 17-18, 20,
    200
Church/Christianity, 296-98, 303,
    306, 308, 310
clinics, 6, 13, 18, 83-96, 98, 99, 110
    lesbian-friendly, 85
    refusal to treat lesbians, 86-87
Clomid, 89, 99, 111
coming out, 296, 311-12
    to children, 28-29, 158, 160,
        167-72, 197, 227, 307-8
    to mother, 243-44
conception, 97
contact, 39
contact order, 288
co-parenting (*see also* step-parenting),
    184-88, 189, 207-12, 283-90
    with donor, 41-44
    with ex-husband, 157, 200, 207-8
couple relationship, 186

custody, 284
   disputes, 155, 156, 235-36, 248,
      257-58, 265-66
cystic fibrosis, 52

'daddy' donor, 16-17, 41-44
death
   of child, 115-21
   of mother, 288-90
   of donor, 31
decision to get pregnant, 3-5
disability, 252-56
discrimination, 85, 125-27
diversity, vi
divorce, 156, 157, 165, 207, 235, 294
donating sperm, 81
donors, 74, 182
   advertising for, 32, 41, 76
   advice for, 79-81
   agreements with, 33-34
   relationship with, 12-17
   screening, 47-57, 80
   search for, 9, 31-32, 83
Dunne, Gill, vii

egg donation, 99
Emily's story, 264-72
Eunice's story, 76-77
ex-husbands, 156, 157, 307

family, definition of, vi, 190, 251, 262
family, extended, 300-301, 306-7,
      308-9, 311
fathers, 259-60
   role of, 178-79, 231-32
fertility, 6, 39, 61-71
   problems (see also age), 87-88,
      97-106
   male, 48-49, 80-81, 101

financial responsibility, 19, 20
fostering, 143-150
Frances's story, 298-99
freeing order, 134
friends, 233, 244-45, 254-55, 258,
      307, 312

gay donors, 23, 27, 41-44,
gay son, 239-47
genetic conditions, 52-53
Golombok, Susan, 156
government, vi, 18, 44, 126, 305
guardianship, 288, 289

heterosexual relationship, leaving,
      155-166, 167, 199
HIV and AIDS, 28, 30, 47, 49-51, 83
home birth, 71, 115
homophobia, v, 16, 155, 168, 169,
      178, 195, 245, 252, 265, 277,
      297, 301, 305, 307
   internalised, 306-7
   strategies for dealing with, v, 172,
      218-25, 250-51, 291
Human Fertilisation and Embryology
   Act, 13
Human Fertilisation and Embryology
   Authority (HFEA), 85
hysterosalpingogram, 89, 90, 110

identity of father/donor, 14, 23, 84,
      232, 252
income support, 18
infertility, 101
inheritance, 20
insemination, see self-insemination
intermediaries, 13, 26
invisibility, 280-81
intra-uterine insemination (IUI), 88, 90

in vitro fertilisation (IVF), 88, 90, 99

Janet and Teri's story, 145-50
jealousy, 104
Jean's story, 184-88
Jess's story, 159-61, 197-98, 294-98
Jude's story, 70-71
Justine's story, 41-42, 115-21, 311-12

Kat's story, 44-45
Kim's story, 108-9
known donor, 33, 77, 178

labour, 71, 118
legal position of donor, 20
legal recognition, 283-90
lesbian daughter, 268
Liberty, 86-87
luteinising hormone (LH), 68, 95

maintenance, 17
male role models, 130, 178-79, 183-84
Marian's story, 137-41
Mark's story, 23-27
marriage, *see* heterosexual relationship
media exposure, vi-viii, 21, 229-30, 238, 256-59, 293
mediation, 157, 166
medicalisation of conception, 88
miscarriage, 107, 109, 111-12
mixed parentage/mixed race, *see* black
mother–daughter relationship, 185, 237, 260, 269-70
mucus, fertile, 61, 62, 64, 65-67
Myra's story, 161-63, 199-203, 308-311

not getting pregnant, *see* problems

overseas adoption, 136-141

ovulation, 61
  kits, 68

parental responsibility, 15, 16, 17, 43, 283, 284
Parent Network, iv
Pat's story, 306-308
PinkParents, iv, 24-27, 315
polycystic ovaries, 89
positive images, 280
pregnancy
  planning, 1-7
  signs of, 70
  testing, 70
  workshops, 1-2
prejudice, 172, 218, 224, 225, 291
preoccupation, 104
private foster carer, 290
problems getting pregnant, 97-106, 108-109, 113-115

Rachel's story, 233-38
racism, 195-96, 246
relationships
  with partner's children, 184-86, 197-98, 201, 205, 208-12, 271
  with men, 263-64
residence orders, 16, 126, 156, 249, 284-90
rhesus factor, 51-52
Rikki's story, 239-247
rural/village life, 176, 178, 180, 182, 228, 264, 294-96, 301, 304

school, 194, 228, 238, 250, 253-55, 258, 277-81, 294-95, 300, 301, 303, 310
screening, *see* donors
secrecy, 221, 301, 307

Section 28 (Local Government Act), 303, 305
self-esteem, 168, 189
self-insemination, 5, 7, 13, 21-22, 27, 70, 98, 203, 227, 233
  groups, 22, 48, 76, 106, 108, 110, 113, 204
  technique, 73-81
  unsuccessful, 97-106
  workshops, iv, 109
semen analysis, 48
sex with a man, 5, 44-45
sexuality of children of lesbians, 199, 218, 232, 237, 246, 251, 266-67, 268
sexually transmitted diseases, 47, 49-51, 83
Sheila's story, 21-22, 203-6
sickle cell anaemia, 52
Simon's story, 42-44
single mothers, 180, 182-184, 188, 201, 203-6, 228, 231, 294
speculum, 67
sperm, 73-73
  frozen, 83, 87, 98
sperm count, 25, 48, 74
splitting up (see also heterosexual
relationships; divorce), 180-81, 242, 261, 262, 265, 287-88
step-parenting (see also co-parenting), 159, 173-80, 190-94, 195, 261-63, 271
stillbirth, 115-21
straight donor, 36, 37-40
stress, 106
support/support group, 106, 110, 187-88, 201, 204, 224-25, 232- 33, 247, 304, 305, 308, 312
Susan's story, 157-59, 176-80, 301-5

Tara's story, 27-31
Tay Sachs, 52
teachers, see school
teasing (see also bullying), 228, 243, 278
teenagers, 190-94, 196
telling children, see coming out
thalassaemia, 52
Theresa's story, 94-96
Tim's story, 227-233
traceable donor, 14-15, 27-31

ultrasound, 89
'uncle' donor, 15-16, 32-36, 37-40
unknown donor, see anonymous

village life, see rural

waiting to get pregnant, 103
White Paper on Adoption, 126-27, 128
wills, 288, 290